The Race Bomb

Other books by Paul R. Ehrlich

ECOSCIENCE:
Population, Resources, Environment
(with Anne H. Ehrlich)

THE END OF AFFLUENCE:
A Blueprint for Your Future
(with Anne H. Ehrlich)

HOW TO BE A SURVIVOR:
A Plan to Save Spaceship Earth
(with Richard L. Harriman)

THE POPULATION BOMB

THE
RACE BOMB

Skin Color, Prejudice, and Intelligence

PAUL R. EHRLICH

S. SHIRLEY FELDMAN

Quadrangle/The New York Times Book Co.

Third printing, July 1977

Copyright © 1977 by Paul R. Ehrlich. All rights reserved, including the right to reproduce this book or portions thereof in any form. For information, address: Quadrangle/The New York Times Book Co., Inc., Three Park Avenue, New York, N.Y. 10016. Manufactured in the United States of America. Published simultaneously in Canada by Fitzhenry & Whiteside, Ltd., Toronto.

Library of Congress Cataloging in Publication Data

Ehrlich, Paul R
  The race bomb.

  Bibliography: p.
  Includes index.
    1. Intellect. 2. Intelligence tests. 3. Racism.
I. Feldman, Shirley, joint author. II. Title.
BF432.A1E38   155.8'2   76–52821
ISBN 0–8129–0681–0

BOOK DESIGN: VINCENT TORRE

For our parents,

who tried to keep us free

of prejudice

CONTENTS

PREFACE

In our years of teaching about the question of whether race is related to intelligence, we have become convinced that it is one of the most complex and difficult issues at the science-society interface. On few topics is the public more generally misinformed, in part because of prejudice and in part because a small segment of the scientific community has disseminated a wholly erroneous answer to the question—but one that is well suited to presentation in brief newspaper and magazine articles and in two-minute television news stories.

That answer—that Blacks are innately stupid—is readily accepted by those Whites who are weary of seemingly endless (and unsuccessful) attempts at school integration and of efforts to provide equal opportunity to Blacks in housing and jobs. And it is a reassuring answer for those Whites who need to boost their egos by believing that they were born into a naturally superior group. That answer reinforces the racist attitudes of various government officials involved in everything from administering welfare programs to designing foreign policy. What, after all, is the point of improving the diets of Black schoolchildren if they are already handicapped with poorly wired brains? Why give genuine support to the aspirations of Rhodesian Blacks if, to quote a White Rhodesian, "the Blacks have only been out of the trees a short time and haven't had time to get smart."*

The damage that such nonsense does in an increasingly interdependent and dangerous world is incalculable. The "race bomb" must be defused if humanity is to cooperate in solving pressing problems. Centuries-old myths of racial inferiority and superiority must not be allowed to poison human relations further. This book, we hope, will be a contribution to extirpating these myths once and for all. We have attempted to deal with the complexities of the race-intelligence issue in lay terms but without oversimplification (and with thorough documentation of all important points). The book progresses logically through the maze of facts, nonsense, and red herrings related to race

* Salisbury hotel owner to P. R. Ehrlich and M. E. Soulé, July 1966.

and intelligence, so that when you are finished, not only will you see why the "innate stupidity" notion is false, you will also be able to explain to others why it is false.

In the first chapter, the importance of the race-intelligence controversy is detailed, and some of the history of scientific racism is discussed.

The second chapter demonstrates that *biologically* there are no such entities as human races, and that the race-intelligence question really reduces to one of skin color and intelligence (a question of no more scientific interest, than, say, the relationship between height or eye color and intelligence).

Chapter 3 shows that although there are no biologically defined races of *Homo sapiens*, there are *socially* defined races. These races are defined differently in different cultures—and minority races so defined are often subjected to severe prejudice. In short, races have a social reality that is seen by the ignorant as a biological reality and associated with a variety of prejudices about inferiority and superiority. The responses of both laypersons and scientists to this socially created reality are discussed in this chapter.

In Chapter 4, we turn directly to the question of intelligence—how it is defined and tested. Intelligence, it turns out, can be defined rigorously only as the scores achieved on certain kinds of tests (IQ tests). These tests have inherent limitations, but do have some usefulness in predicting school performance and some things related to it.

Chapter 5 asks the question, Is the ability to do well on IQ tests primarily innate? The answer is unambiguous: there is no reason to believe that it is genetically fixed.

Chapter 6 is, in a sense, the meat of the book. It discusses different average scores of Blacks and Whites (and other groups) on IQ tests and asks the question, Is there any evidence that these differences are caused by genetic differences? Again the answer is no. Furthermore, we show that the answer would be no *even if the answer to the question asked in Chapter 5 were yes!* Various ways in which the environment influences an individual's IQ are then discussed, and it is demonstrated that there is ample reason to believe that cultural differences can explain observed Black-White differences in average IQ.

In the first six chapters, the whole race-IQ debate is revealed as a scientifically useless discussion. Since there are no biological races to begin with, the question of the inferiority or superiority of a race is meaningless. IQ itself is a measure of limited significance; there is no sign that ability to do well on IQ tests is largely inherited, and if it were largely inherited, this would tell us *nothing* about the cause of group differences. Furthermore, group differences in average IQ (regardless of how the groups are defined) are readily explained by the different environments to which members of different groups are exposed. The question of whether group differences are to any degree the result of genetic differences is both scientifically trivial and practically unanswerable. The persistence of the question is traceable primarily to a misunderstanding of genetics by a small group of scientists.

In spite of all this, the question, Are Blacks innately stupid? *does* persist. In the final chapter, we return to the importance of the race-IQ issue and ask, among other questions, the following one: *If* there really were races, *if* IQ really were a supremely important human characteristic that was determined almost entirely by the genes, and *if* genetic differences between races gave them different average IQs, would that racial difference be important?

Since the implications of the race-IQ question are so broad, it was inevitable that, in writing this book, we would periodically have to leave our own areas of expertise in genetics, taxonomy, and psychology. Over the years numerous colleagues have helped to educate us on various aspects of the controversy, and several have been of direct assistance with this manuscript. Richard W. Holm (Department of Biology, Stanford University), Carol Jacklin (Department of Psychology, Stanford University), Richard C. Lewontin (Department of Biology, Harvard University), Donald Lunde (Department of Psychiatry, Stanford University), John Meyer (Department of Sociology, Stanford University), and Jon Roughgarden (Department of Biology, Stanford University) have all read the entire manuscript or portions of it. Their critical comments have been invaluable. We are especially indebted to D. L. Bilderback of the Department of History, Fresno State College, who has been deeply involved in this project from the beginning. In addition to very detailed criticisms of the entire manuscript, he has supplied bits of prose that we have shamelessly inserted at various points. Similarly, the efforts of Marc Feldman and Anne Ehrlich are scattered throughout the text without specific acknowledgment. The book has benefited immensely from their expertise in mathematical genetics and the sociology of birth control, respectively, and also from their extensive editorial efforts.

Jane Lawson Bavelas and Patricia Hallenbeck also applied their fine editorial skill to the manuscript, providing an extremely helpful series of corrections, queries, and suggestions. Darryl Wheye and Suzanne Taylor cheerfully struggled with the typing of the manuscript and provided excellent feedback on points that were unclear, sections that were boring, and so on. And finally Peggy Craig and Claire Shoens of the Stanford biology library were extraordinarily helpful in running down obscure sources and generally providing the kind of assistance that could serve as a model for all technical libraries. All of these people have our deep gratitude.

Human life is full of tragedy, defined in the Greek sense as the opposition of two rights. The opposition of the moral belief in the equality of men to the scientific fact of hereditary inequality may be the source of such tragedy.

—H. J. Eysenck

Of all the vulgar modes of escaping from the consideration of the effect of social and moral influences upon the human mind, the most vulgar is that of attributing the diversities of conduct and character to inherent natural differences.

—John Stuart Mill

The Race Bomb

1

Race and Your Future

The week of the Los Angeles riots was also the week when
Malaysia broke apart because brown men could not control their
dark suspicions of yellow men, and when black and brown men
resumed their efforts to slug it out in southern Sudan. All the
evidence is that there is potential trouble wherever people of
different colours rub shoulders uneasily together.
                                    —*The Economist* (London), 1965

Look at the backs of your hands. They may explain a great
deal about your past and tell you a great deal about your future—
not by their size or shape or by the number of wrinkles or size of the
veins, but by their color. Are they a pale pink? A light brown? A blue-
black? William Shockley, a famous scientist, has claimed that people
are "color-coded"[1] so that one can divine much of a person's worth by
classifying him or her according to skin tone. He believes that people
with dark skins are inherently not as smart as those with light skins.

The correctness of that premise is examined in detail in this book.
Correct or not, it is a subject of overriding importance to you, because
vast numbers of people assume it to be correct and act as if human
beings were "color-coded" for intellectual qualities. In the process, they
help to push civilization toward the brink of catastrophe. For few things
stand more squarely in the path of extracting mankind from its present
predicament than the complex of problems commonly associated with
skin color and lumped under the heading of "race."

Consider attitudes in the United States today as the grip of a
population-resource-environment crisis gradually tightens. Many people with pink skins already consider the population problem to be one

3

generated by too many dark-skinned people: "Too many nigger-babies from welfare mothers in the ghettos." Many dark-skinned people think that the ecological crisis is purely and simply a gambit of the pink-skinned to distract attention from the manifold problems of the dark-skinned: "Those honky racists care about cleaning up Lake Erie and the ecology of trout; they don't give a damn about cleaning up the black ghetto and the ecology of roaches and rats." How will those people, both dark- and light-skinned, behave as the crunch worsens?

As the age of affluence ends, massive readjustments in society are starting to take place, adjustments that bungling politicians are ensuring will not occur through rational planning.[2] Unemployment is high and will probably continue to be high—and the burden of unemployment is falling and probably will continue to fall unequally on people of different skin colors. For instance, a major source of racial tension in the mid-1970s in the United States has been the conflict between the last-hired–first-fired policy of unions and the preponderance of non-White employees in the last-hired category. Racial problems are not, of course, restricted to the United States. Around the world, fear of being outreproduced by peoples of other colors, tribes, nations, or ethnic groups is, for example, an important barrier to achieving population control. And without population control, all causes are lost causes.[3]

The problems of race relations were difficult enough in an era when it seemed that the pie was ever expanding and that sooner or later there would be abundance for everyone. Now that this vision of abundance is fading fast, the probabilities of racial conflict may well be increasing, for, as psychologist Gordon Allport has put it, "Downward mobility, periods of unemployment and depression, and general economic dissatisfaction are all positively correlated with prejudice."[4] Watts in 1965, Boston in 1974, and Soweto in 1976 may have been harbingers of much worse to come.

The Role of Skin Color

There is, then, no doubt that the color of your skin is not a trivial matter today, and it could become more important tomorrow. This prediction flows easily from the history of skin color in human affairs.

No personal physical feature, except sex, has had such an impact on the fates of individuals and entire groups. The reasons for the social importance of color are not entirely clear; it is a superficial characteristic not usually well related to other characteristics that vary from person to person. Perhaps human beings attach such importance to it because they are basically "sight animals"—in comparison with many other mammals, our senses of smell and hearing are weak indeed. But whatever the reasons for it, one cannot deny the paramount role of color. Sociologist Edward Shils put it nicely when he said, "It attracts the mind; it is the focus of passionate sentiments and beliefs."[5]

Since the rise of the West, the major color differentiation in the world has been between "White" and "non-White." It is this dichotomy or the related one of White and Black that holds the attention of most Americans. And yet this rather crude division does not do justice to the refined use to which humanity has put skin color. In Spanish colonies, for example, legal rights were assigned by skin tone, with explicit distinctions made for each degree of whiteness (needless to say, the whiter one's skin, the greater were one's rights).[6] Among Filipinos today, there is an obsession with color: "It appears in almost every aspect of everyday family life, in dating and mating, in the raising of children, and at every point of contact between people of varying groups and kinds in the population."[7]

Perhaps the most elaborate system for sociopolitical categorizing by skin color, however, is the one that has evolved in South Africa. There, rights are assigned purely and simply by color in a system designed to maintain White supremacy.

A superficial analysis of the functions played by skin color in the world today might lead to the conclusion that White supremacy is behind all of the attention paid to color. That even relatively dark-skinned peoples look down on darker-skinned peoples, as happens, for example, in India and Latin America, could be explained by emulation of the dominant European. Until the recent rise of Black pride in the United States, there was a color hierarchy in the American Negro population, with the darkest on the bottom, the lightest on top, and a steady flow out of the latter group into the "White" category. Such "passing" was so common and so feared by Whites in the 1920s that hotels and nightclubs in Chicago hired Blacks as "spotters" to expose their fellows attempting to gain entrance; the theory being that "one coon can recognize another."[8] In spite of such ludicrous activities, many millions of "White" Americans today have ancestors who would have been classified as "Negroes."

Although white Europeans have certainly developed the use of prejudice against dark skins to a fine art, there is reason to suspect that it has deeper roots in humanity. The Japanese, for instance, had strongly developed prejudices favoring "whiteness" long before they made contact with the West. In the eighth century, Japanese women used powder to whiten their cheeks, and Japanese literature of a millennium ago is replete with the praises of whiteness as an essential component of feminine pulchritude.[9] Interestingly enough, the white skin so admired by the Japanese is not the white skin of the "Caucasian." Consider, for instance, this quote from a modern Japanese:

This may be completely unscientific but I feel when I look at the skin of a Japanese woman I see the whiteness of her skin, when I observe Caucasian skin, what I see is the whiteness of the fat underneath the skin, not the whiteness of the skin itself.[10]

In many different cultures, dark colors, especially black, are negative symbols—connoting ill fortune, impurity, bad weather, death, and so on. The roots of this symbolism are obscure. It has been suggested that they may be found in the day-night dichotomy, in the loneliness and fear experienced in the dark, especially by children. Or it could have developed in the course of cleanliness training, where darkness is associated with dirt.[11] Neither explanation seems entirely satisfactory. For example, night is for many comforting and relaxing; and against black skin, dirt may appear light.

Cultural attitudes toward colors and skin colors probably have complex origins, origins that may never be fully understood. But it is beyond dispute that *Homo sapiens* is a species with a high degree of sensitivity to skin color. And that this sensitivity is often transformed into social action is also beyond dispute. Consider for a moment the correlation of skin color with income and educational opportunity in the United States. In 1974, some 12.4 percent of White families had incomes over $25,000, while only 4.0 percent of non-Whites were similarly blessed. At the lower end of the scale, the situation was reversed. Only 11.1 percent of White families had incomes below $5,000, while 29.6 percent of non-Whites faced this extreme of poverty. Similarly, in that year, 14.0 percent of White persons 25 years old or older had completed four years of college; but only 5.5 percent of Blacks had. Just 3.5 percent of Whites had less than four years of schooling; for

Blacks, the figure was 12.9 percent.[12] Although during the 1960s redistribution of income in the United States tended to favor Blacks and poor Whites, in the first five years of the 1970s that trend reversed and the gap once again widened.[13]

These statistics represent just one set of handicaps that the darker-skinned citizens of the United States must suffer. How can such inequities (to say nothing of the myriad indignities of exclusion and outright insult) persist in a society that ostensibly believes all are created equal? The impact of prejudice on our Black citizens is, for many, unbearable. Unlike our other minorities, Blacks have been cut off from their cultural roots and subjected to unrelenting and methodical discrimination sporadically reinforced with violence. And the result of this, for some, is a personal distress, a tendency toward psychological crippling that constitutes both a further penalty for having dark skin and a further handicap to escaping the consequences of that pigmentation.[14] It is no wonder that mentally ill Blacks often suffer the delusion that they are really White—that their skin is dirty, dyed, or painted, or that they have eaten something that has caused their skin to darken![15] It is sad that even some otherwise mentally healthy Blacks think that black is both an undesirable and an unattractive skin color.[16]

In the past few decades, the view has grown in the liberal community that the prejudicial attitudes and actions of many Whites were purely the result of ignorance and that antidiscrimination laws and education were slowly improving things (the latter notion being supported by statistical trends).[17] Scientific investigations had not substantiated prejudices about the supremacy of some races over others. All that remained was to provide equal opportunity, and the inequities between groups would disappear. There would be proportionately as many rich and brilliant Blacks as Whites, as many educated and successful Native Americans as Japanese Americans. And Blacks would no longer commit a disproportionate number of crimes nor make up a disproportionate number of the victims of crimes.

Scientific Racism

In the last decade, however, a few scientists have returned to the assumptions popular in the nineteenth and early twentieth centuries that differences in skin color are representative of much more fundamental divisions of humanity. They support the "color-coding" hypothesis and maintain, for example, that people with dark skin are, on the average, likely to carry genes that will limit their intellectual development to a level below that of the average light-skinned person. They present, in essence, a scientific version of the redneck's conclusion, "Niggers is dumb."

Scientific racism is not new. It has been a feature of biological science as long as that discipline has existed. This is not surprising since scientists, being only human, have often incorporated their cultural biases into their work (as we, perforce, must in this book).[18]

The great Swedish biologist Linnaeus incorporated his own racial views into the first "scientific" classification of races (as will be seen in the next chapter), and the early German champion of Darwinism, zoologist Ernst Haeckel, seated Blacks on a limb of the evolutionary tree below the chimp and the gorilla. Haeckel put forth a theory that remained in vogue in biology for more than half a century. His theory was that each individual, in the course of its development, in a sense relived its evolutionary history—that "ontogeny recapitulates phylogeny." Under the theory of recapitulation, each of us, for instance, was supposed to go through a fish and an amphibian stage as an embryo. Racists easily exploited the recapitulation theory. In 1890, D. G. Brinton wrote:

The adult who retains the more numerous fetal, [or] infantile . . . traits is unquestionably inferior to him whose development has progressed beyond them. Measured by these criteria, the European or white race stands at the head of the list, the African or negro at its foot.[19]

Guess what race Brinton belonged to?

In the twentieth century, the theory of recapitulation was gradually discarded by biologists. In the area of human evolution, a quite contrary view developed—one that is current today. In that view, many of the most "human" characteristics of our species are those found in juvenile primates (and often in juvenile mammals in general). These traits include a brain large in proportion to body weight, a short jaw, a

2
Gorilla.

1 Schimpanse

3 Orang.

Neger.

Figure 1-1. A racist interpretation of evolution from the 1874 edition of
Ernst Haeckel's *Anthropogenie*.

relative lack of hair, a hand with five movable digits (as opposed to, say, fused digits as in a horse's hoof), and so on. This reversal of what is viewed as "primitive" did not, of course, phase the racists. In 1926, L. Bolk wrote:

On the basis of my theory, I am obviously a believer in the inequality of races. . . . In his fetal development the negro passes through a stage that has already become the final stage for the white man. If retardation continues in the negro, what is still a transitional state may for this race also become a final one. It is possible for all other races to reach the zenith of development now occupied by the white race.[20]

Would you like to guess Bolk's skin color?

Coming to identical conclusions on the basis of opposite sets of data or theories, as Brinton and Bolk do, is far from unknown in science as a whole—facts can be cited selectively, and theories come and go. Historically, however, it is difficult to find a more persistent record of scientific bias than the now two-century-long crusade of various White Western scientists to justify a view of the natural supremacy of their own kind.

This crusade flowered in the early 1960s with the publication of the "George Report"[21] and Carleton Coon's book *Origin of Races*.[22] Both of these works claimed that Blacks belonged to a different subspecies of mankind from Whites, a subspecies that became "sapient" much later than the White subspecies. The George Report was frankly against integration and in favor of protecting the White race from contamination by the Negro. Its author, Wesley Critz George, professor emeritus of histology and embryology, noted that

One swallow does not make a summer, and a few intelligent Negroes do not make a race. . . . To be sure, we should value every man according to his merit—within his own race. It does not follow that virtue would be served by admitting every man or woman that we value, regardless of his race, into those areas of Caucasian social life where mates are chosen. If we open those doors to select Negroes of high merit, we also open them in the end to millions of inferior individuals. If we allow ourselves to be deceived by that Trojan horse, we may expect a fate similar to that of ancient Troy that accepted the original trick and in consequence was overrun and destroyed.[23]

The "evidence" in the George Report is a pathetic mishmash of ancient quotes, nonsense, half-truths and misinterpretations, unworthy of systematic refutation and unworthy of being cited as "science" (as racists are wont to do). As a single example, an experiment of the famous embryologist Victor Twitty, in which skin from one species of salamander grafted to another species of salamander was rejected, was cited as if it were pertinent to the question of human racial differences[24]—much to Twitty's amazement. One need only recall the frequent failure of organ transplants between close relatives to see how preposterous that notion is.

The book by Carleton Coon, a well-known anthropologist, was, on the other hand, considerably more sophisticated and was refuted in detail by anthropologists and evolutionary biologists.[25] We will return to it briefly in Chapter 3.

In contrast to earlier scientists who simply seemed dedicated to proving the natural superiority of Whites, those most recently claiming inborn intellectual inferiority for Blacks see themselves merely as scientists reporting a lamentable fact. Indeed, they feel they are providing needed information for finding ways of improving the lot of those cursed with dark skin and the dull minds that they believe are associated with it. For example, electrical engineer William Shockley, a Nobel Laureate, has stated:

I intend my actions in raising these questions [about race and IQ] to have the effect of a visitor to a sick friend who strongly urges a diagnosis that seeks to expose all significant ailments. If study shows that ghetto birthrates are actually lowering average Negro intelligence, objectively facing this fact might lead to finding ways to prevent a form of genetic enslavement that could provoke extremes of racism. I feel that no one should be more concerned with this possibility than Negro intellectuals.[26]

Shockley, a member of the National Academy of Sciences, has long been after that group to sponsor research on the genetics of racial differences in intelligence.

While Shockley has been the most vocal proponent of the notion that inferior IQ-test performance by Blacks probably stems in large part from bad genes, much of the weight of professional support for this view is supplied by the writings of psychologist Arthur Jensen.[27] Therefore, we will refer to this general notion as the Jensen hypothesis.

Quite naturally, an enormous furor has been raised over the Jensen hypothesis. The debate has all too often been characterized on both sides by a profound lack of knowledge of the pertinent science— knowledge that is essential to understanding why the hypothesis is hopelessly flawed. The issues involved are, unfortunately, rather complex. They involve these questions, which will be dealt with in the chapters that follow:

1. What are human races?
2. What is intelligence?
3. How are race and intelligence related?
4. What difference does it make?

These are questions that, like it or not, are important to your future, regardless of what color you saw when you stared at the back of your hand. If the color was black, you probably have already been mightily concerned by them. If you saw white, you may not have been concerned—but if you weren't, you surely should be. In the United States, crucial problems of unemployment, escalating crime rates, deteriorating school systems, and the decay of cities are intimately connected with questions of skin color and will continue to be. The chances of keeping American society from coming unglued depend to no small degree on overcoming irrational attitudes toward the colors of our fellow human beings. Is our only future alternative a return to Watts-type riots or more repression?

Around the world, most people don't see white when they look at their hands, and the actions taken by nonwhite hands are going to be crucial to everyone's future. Slavery and colonialism are things of the past. And while Whites still hold much of the power in the international arena, the non-Whites far outnumber them. And the tables are gradually being turned. Men with dusky skins control most of the world's petroleum, and many of its other resources. The hands on the nuclear trigger are no longer all lily-white. Indeed, at the rate that nuclear-power technology is being exported by the United States and European nations, an impressive array of different colors will be represented among fingers on doomsday buttons. To whatever degree color differences continue to generate dislike and friction among groups and nations, the future of humanity will be further jeopardized.

Questions of race and intelligence are thus of considerably more than academic interest—they are of vital concern to us all. Creating a world that accepts diversity will be difficult enough if *Homo sapiens* is not carrying a burden of racial mythology. With such a burden, the task will be well nigh impossible. Learning the truth might just save our hides.

2

What Are Races, Really?

If the bodies of, say, a Negro and a European were both flayed, so that skin and hair were removed and the face obliterated, it would be impossible to tell for certain which was which. "Racial" differences, it has been said, are only skin deep.
—S. H. Barnett, *The Human Species*, 1971

Few ISSUES in the world today seem so pervasive, so intertwined and interrelated with other human problems, as those described under the broad heading of "race." "Racial" problems create strife within countries as diverse as the United States, the Soviet Union, Brazil, India, Malaysia, Nigeria, and the Sudan. And "White racism" has been claimed to underlie such international phenomena as colonialism, neocolonialism, slavery, and recently the cavalier disregard for Vietnamese lives displayed by the armed forces of the United States.

Problems of race can be dealt with conveniently on two levels. The first is biological, where one considers the known facts of human "racial" variation. The second is social—involving the complex superstructure of human behavior that has evolved in response to that variation.

Species and Races of People and Other Animals

Different kinds of organisms are called different species by biologists. Dogs are one species, coyotes another, and wolves a third. All people living today belong to the species *Homo sapiens*; some fossil

13

people are considered to have been different enough from us to be placed in a different species—such as *Homo erectus*, the Java and Peking "men." By convention, groups (populations) of contemporary organisms that are able to breed freely with one another are considered to be the same kind and are thus part of the same species.[1] Since different breeds of dog can be successfully crossed with each other, all dogs are placed in a single species *Canis familiaris*. Similarly, there is no evidence of biological (as opposed to social) barriers to interbreeding among groups of people, and there is abundant evidence of successful interbreeding. That is why all living people are classified as *Homo sapiens*.

The individuals belonging to the same animal species are never identical. If the species is bisexual, there are, of course, sexual differences between males and females. No two members of the same sex are identical either—there is *individual variation*. And, typically, populations classified in the same species but from different areas differ in many characteristics. That is, there is *geographic variation*.

Geographic variation has been one of the most widely studied phenomena in biology, and many patterns of variation have been explained. For instance, individuals of a species of yellow "sulphur" butterfly living in the Arctic have a dark gray coloring on the underside not found on individuals living in the temperate zone. The dark wing surface, when exposed to the sun, permits the butterfly to warm more rapidly and thus to be active during brief periods of sunshine.

In 1758, the Swedish biologist Linnaeus established the modern science of animal taxonomy with the publication of his classic work *Systema Naturae*. It was he who began giving all kinds of animals two-part Latin names, the system that is followed to this day. Thus, *Homo sapiens* is made up of the generic name *Homo*, indicating the group (genus) to which the species *Homo sapiens* belongs, and *sapiens* designating a particular member of the genus *Homo*. Similarly, the dog *Canis familiaris* is a species of the genus *Canis* along with, among others, the wolf species *Canis lupis* and the coyote species *Canis latrans*. Every species is classified into a genus, and genera are grouped into families. Thus, both *Homo* and *Australopithecus* (a genus of fossil people) are grouped into the family Hominidae, while *Canis* and *Vulpes* (a genus of foxes) are in the family Canidae.[2] In the Linnaean system, families are grouped into orders, orders into classes, classes into phyla, and phyla into kingdoms (animal or plant) in a hierarchical arrangement. As in any hierarchy (Figure 2-1), each

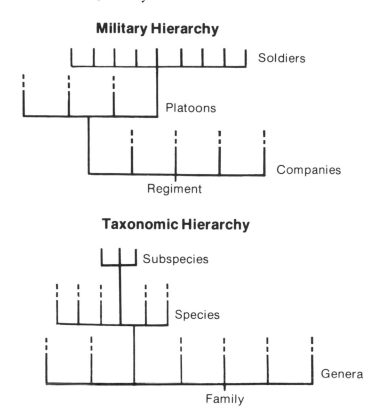

Figure 2-1. Hierarchical organization of military and taxonomic units. Broken lines show places where further subdividing has been omitted (e.g., all companies are divided into platoons, but the platoons of only one company are shown).

unit can only belong to one particular more inclusive unit—a genus can be in only one family, just as in the military hierarchy a regiment can belong only to one division.

The Linnaean system has proven most useful for organizing the vast numbers of diverse living things into manageable categories. Although nature is not precisely hierarchical,[3] the similarities of organisms can, in most cases, be approximated by a hierarchy. So all species of the genus *Canis* are more similar to one another than to any species of *Vulpes*, and dogs and foxes as members of the family Canidae resemble each other more closely than they resemble members of the cat family, Felidae.

Since the Linnaean system worked so well for species, genera, families, and so on, it is hardly surprising that Linnaeus and subsequent taxonomists attempted to extend the hierarchic system to deal with variation within species. This was done by adding a subspecific, or racial, name to the specific name. Just as a genus could be viewed as a collection of species, so a species could be a collection of races. Linnaeus accordingly characterized four races of man:[4]

Homo sapiens americanus: red, hot-tempered, erect.
  Hair black, straight, thick; broad nostrils; freckled faces; hairless on chin.
  Resolute, cheerful, free.
  Paints self with artful lines of red.
  He is ruled by custom.

Homo sapiens europaeus: white, optimistic, brawny (fleshy).
  Hair flaxen, long; blue-eyed.
  Nimble, of the keenest mind, innovator.
  He wears tight-fitting clothes.
  He is ruled by ritualistic tradition.

Homo sapiens asiaticus: pale yellow, meditative (gloomy), hardy.
  Hair dark, dark-eyed.
  Grave, proud, greedy.
  He wears loose-fitting robes.
  He is ruled by opinions.

Homo sapiens afer: black, sluggish, loose-limbed.
  Hair dull black, kinky; silky skin; flat-nosed; big lips.
  Women immodest concerning bosom; long nipples.
  Cunning, lazy, careless.
  Smears self with fat.
  He is ruled by authority.

Note that Linnaeus used *color* as his first distinguishing characteristic. While his comments on other characteristics would qualify him for Ku Klux Klan membership today, they were representative of the views of educated Europeans two centuries ago (who, of course, had relatively little contact with non-Europeans).

One hundred years after the appearance of Linnaeus' *Systema Naturae*, Charles Darwin published *The Origin of Species*, which, among other things, provided a novel explanation for the diversity of life forms that taxonomists had been classifying. These life forms had not been created all at once by God; instead, they had gradually evolved from organisms that had lived in the past. Darwin's work gradually focused attention on variation within species, for this was seen as evidence of evolution in progress—of the changes that would lead to new species.

Subsequent to Darwin's theory, taxonomists struggled to give evolutionary interpretations to their work. The taxonomic hierarchy was viewed as representing the hierarchic structure of a "phylogenetic tree"—that is, a diagram indicating natural evolutionary relationships (see Figure 2-2).

This trend peaked in the 1930s and 1940s when biologists such as Bernard Rensch, Theodosius Dobzhansky, George Gaylord Simpson, and Ernst Mayr revolutionized taxonomy by integrating it with ideas from genetics and other biological disciplines, creating an evolutionarily oriented "New Systematics." Geographic variation within a species was seen as an indication that it was about to split into two or more species. The concept of subspecies thereby assumed new importance, as subspecies were thought to be species *in statu nascendi*—in the state of being born. The concept is important to the understanding of human races because, with the growing prominence of subspecies in the zoological literature, anthropologists began to view *Homo sapiens* as a collection of subspecies. The terms "race" and "subspecies" were used interchangeably by taxonomists working with other animals, and it was only natural that students of humanity should adopt the same terminology. Indeed, the whole procedure cloaked the study of human "races" in an aura of scientific respectability, tying it to the activities of zoologists dispassionately describing subspecific variation in other animals—a trend that culminated in the publication of Carleton Coon's tome *Origin of Races*,[5] to which we have already alluded.

Unfortunately, it turns out, in retrospect, that zoologists eagerly describing new subspecies were dealing the scientific study of geographic variation a blow from which it is just now recovering. Attempts to divide species into subspecies tended to conceal rather than illuminate the nature of variation within species. During the flowering of the New Systematics, taxonomists (especially those working with much-studied groups such as birds and butterflies) went through an orgy of naming subspecies. Virtually any population that could be distinguished from one already named was promptly christened. The Latin names of subspecies, like those of species, had the name of the author appended to it—a clear incentive to would-be discoverers to find new subspecies in a world where virtually all the species of prominent groups had long since been named. For example, in the last century, an English entomologist named Butler received a specimen of a new species of brown alpine butterfly from North America and christened it *Erebia epipsodea*. Ever since, whenever that species, the most common and widespread "alpine" butterfly in America, is cited for the first time in a scientific paper, it is cited as *Erebia epipsodea* Butler. (Technically, our species should be cited first as *Homo sapiens* Linnaeus.)

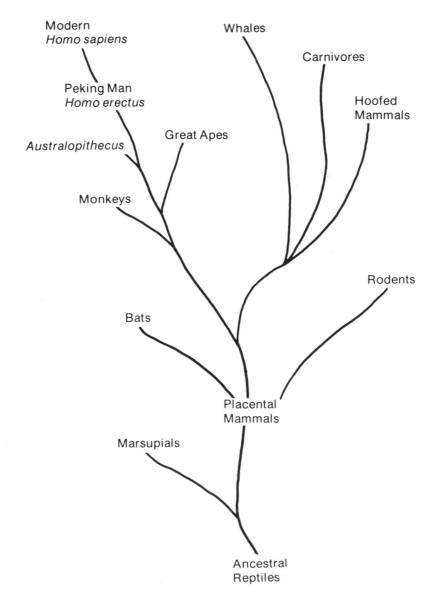

Figure 2-2.   A phylogenetic tree of the mammals (only some groups shown).

When in the early 1950s Ehrlich was studying geographic variation in *Erebia epipsodea*, he obtained from subarctic areas some specimens that had reduced spots on the wings. The populations represented by these specimens were described as a new subspecies, named in honor of the friend who had collected the sample: *Erebia epipsodea remingtoni* Ehrlich.[6]

Since it was recognized that most taxonomists had that common human desire to see their name in print, attempts have been made to define the degree of difference between populations that should be recognized with formal subspecific names. Various "percent rules" were propounded for what populations could be named, such as "if 75 percent of the individuals of one population can be distinguished from 95 percent of the other, then they are different subspecies."

The commonly accepted definition of subspecies was well expressed by the famous evolutionist Ernst Mayr: "The subspecies, or geographic race, is a geographically localized subdivision of the species, which differs genetically and taxonomically from other subdivisions of the species."[7] But in sexually reproducing organisms, *all* populations are genetically different, and since "taxonomically" can mean simply "in the opinion of a taxonomist," one can see that taxonomists were basically without guidelines except for the so-called percent rules. Moreover, the percent rules actually proved unworkable because they were dependent on the refinement to which measurements were made and on the numbers of characteristics measured.

Human Geographic Variation

The spree of naming subspecies among zoological taxonomists was also reflected in the attempts of anthropologists to come to grips with variations within *Homo sapiens*. Our species is, by any standard, an extremely variable one. There is striking geographic variation in skin color, hair form, head shape, tooth size, height, length of nose, and many other characteristics that have been studied. Faced with this richness of variation, anthropologists divided *Homo sapiens* into many races, although mercifully they usually did not give each a formal Latin name, as was the custom among biologists working with other organisms.

For example, Coon, Garn, and Birdsell[8] classified humans into six stocks: Negroid, Mongoloid, White, Australoid, American Indian, and Polynesian. They carefully warned students that "a stock is not a race but merely a convenience in classification; it is a lumping of races which seem similar to each other into broad categories." They defined a race as "a somatically [bodily, as opposed to genetically] unique population or collection of identical populations," and then listed a tentative classification of humans into thirty races:

1.	Murrayian	15.	Hamite
2.	Ainu	16.	Hindu
3.	Alpine	17.	Mediterranean
4.	Northwest European	18.	Nordic
4a.	Northwest European Prototype	19.	North American Colored
		20.	South African Colored
5.	Northeast European	21.	Classic Mongoloid
6.	Lapp	22.	North Chinese
7.	Forest Negro	23.	Southeast Asiatic
8.	Melanesian	24.	Tibeto-Indonesian Mongoloid
9.	Negrito	25.	Turkic
10.	Bushman	26.	American Indian Marginal
11.	Bantu	27.	American Indian Central
12.	Sudanese	28.	Ladino
13.	Carpentarian	29.	Polynesian
14.	Dravidian	30.	Neo-Hawaiian

Human racial classifications have been, as indicated by the "stocks" of Coon, Garn, and Birdsell, based primarily on skin color and to a lesser extent on hair type, which tends to vary in association with skin color. Once the primary division is made, statements may be made about other characteristics of the "races" delimited. Thus Negro and Caucasian races might be described as "usually of medium height or tall," while the Oriental race would, in contrast, be "mostly medium height or short." Of course, if humanity had focused primarily on stature in defining geographic differences among groups, there might have been the "tall race" (mostly dark or light skin color, occasionally medium), "medium race" (mostly light or medium skin color, occasionally dark), and "short race" (medium or, rarely, dark skin color).

Human populations respond physiologically and evolutionarily to the environmental conditions to which they are exposed. In this respect, they are like populations of most other organisms. Light-skinned human populations, for example, respond physiologically to exposure to large amounts of sunlight by increasing the pigmentation of the skin (tanning). Physiological responses tend to be relatively fast and reversible. Of more interest to us here are the relatively slow and usually irreversible evolutionary changes. These changes are caused primarily by what Darwin called "natural selection."

Natural selection is the differential reproduction of genetic types. Suppose, for example, that size differences in grizzly bears are caused in part by genetic (inheritable) differences among individuals. Suppose further that in Alaska large individuals are better able to stand the cold, survive, and reproduce. Then, in Alaskan populations of grizzly bears, the genes producing large individuals would become more common and those producing small individuals would become less common. In shorthand, biologists would say that there was natural selection for large size. The actual evolutionary process, of course, is more complicated, but the basic idea is very simple. Whenever inherited differences affect the comparative reproductive success of individuals in a population, natural selection (and evolution) is occurring. (Selection is discussed further in Appendix A.)

Sometimes widely scattered populations of one species may show a similar evolutionary response to the same environmental factor. For instance, dark skin color in people is generally (but far from perfectly) correlated with the presence of relatively intense ultraviolet solar radiation. It has been suggested[9] that the dark color provides protection against the harmful effects of solar radiation. The pigment melanin in the outer layer of the skin absorbs the ultraviolet component of the radiation, which has been implicated in the production of skin cancers.[10] On the other hand sunlight is also needed by the skin to transform the precursor of vitamin D into the vitamin. If too much sunlight is screened out, vitamin D deficiencies occur, resulting in abnormal calcium metabolism. In children the symptom of this is rickets, in adults defective bones. If too little is screened out, a toxic excess might occur. If these factors were the key ones, they would explain the situation that pertained before recent mass movements of people—dark-skinned people living where there was an abundance of solar radiation and light-skinned people where sunlight was in short supply.

These points provide a possible explanation for the broad pattern of darker-skinned people living near the equator and lighter-skinned people living near the poles. It does not, however, explain many of the details of the distribution of skin color. For instance, the Bushmen of southwestern Africa have relatively light skins, even though they are subject to relatively intense solar radiation in their desert homes. It may be that natural selection has produced a lighter skin there because of the need for these hunters to be inconspicuous in an environment where a black skin would stand out.[11] Then again, the answer may be entirely different—one that has not yet even been imagined.

Similarly, African pygmies living in deep forest shade for much of their lives also have dark skins even though they are hardly subject to intense solar radiation. Anthropologist C. Loring Brace[12] has suggested that this is because they have only been in the forests for a relatively short time, but camouflage (dark skins in a dark environment) or some other factor may be involved here also. There are many unanswered questions about human pigmentation: Why are the aborigines of northern Australia not as dark as the darkest Africans? Why are the Eskimos not as fair-skinned as the Scots? And so on. The descendants of Jews who migrated to Iran and Iraq two millennia ago are much darker than those who moved north or into less arid areas of similar latitude. Is this a result of natural selection for darker skins?[13]

Various patterns of migration may explain away some of these seeming anomalies, and the apparently rapid change in the Jewish populations may be due to interbreeding with indigenous peoples. In the last analysis, however, we will probably discover that the overriding factor in determining prehistoric geographic patterns of human pigmentation —indeed in determining most patterns of genetic differentiation of human populations—will have been natural selection. That is, persons with certain kinds of genes had more children than those with other kinds of genes—and these "successful" genes come to characterize populations. Remember, differential reproductive success is the essence of natural selection. There is evidence that, in general, natural selection is the key force in the evolution of nonhuman organisms,[14] and there is little reason to believe that the situation in human populations has been very different, at least until the last few hundred years.

Evolutionary explanations have been advanced for patterns of variation in many other characteristics of *Homo sapiens*.[15] For instance, a general tendency for warmblooded animals to be larger and to have shorter extremities in cold areas than in warm areas has long been noted by zoologists. Arctic foxes are large and have short ears; desert foxes are small and have long ears. Large individuals have less surface area per unit of volume than small individuals.* They are thus less susceptible to heat loss and therefore presumably more likely to survive in chilly climates. Similarly, long appendages increase surface area and are more susceptible to frost damage. Small size and long appendages are favored in warm climates where the problem of warm-blooded organisms is not to conserve heat but to dissipate it.

Examination of trends in human stature indicates that in a general way aboriginal peoples appear to have been subject to the same selective pressures. Eskimos, for instance, are heavy-set and tend to have short limbs, while desert peoples are often tall and slender, with long limbs. The ultimate in elongation to increase body area is seen in extremely tall Africans of the Upper Nile. African pygmies have solved the problem of increasing their surface/volume ratio in a different way—by becoming very small. Brace[16] suggests that this particular evolutionary strategy on the part of the pygmies is a response to their uncertain food supply and chronic protein deficiency. Small people, of course, require less food than tall people. The Nilotic Africans, in contrast, derive an assured high-protein food supply from their cattle. Thus the apparent evolutionary anomaly of the tallest and the shortest people in the world living in rather close proximity seems readily explained—although it is highly unlikely that definitive evidence supporting this or any other explanation will be found.

The color of human hair appears to be under much the same control as skin color, and varies quite closely with it. Hair is part of the skin and derives melanin from the same developmental system. Considerably less melanin is required, however, to darken the hair than the skin. Where a great decrease of melanin has occurred in the skin, as in Northern Europeans, the hair may be greatly depigmented, and people with light brown or blond hair occur frequently in the population (the significance of redheads is not known). But unless the skin becomes very light, the hair usually remains dark, which explains why most people have brown or black hair.

Hair form, on the other hand, appears to be related to the need for insulation. Woolly hair on the head is found where skin is darkest and is presumed to provide protection from the tropical sun. Hair, of course, also serves to cushion the effect of blows to the head. People of

* For instance, a 1-inch cube (volume = 1^3 = 1 cubic inch) has a surface area of 6 square inches and a surface/volume ratio of 6:1, while a 2-inch cube (2^3 = 8 cubic inches) has a surface area of 24 square inches and a surface/volume ratio of only 3:1.

European descent, who have a long history of substituting hats for the protective function of hair, have the highest incidence of baldness. This may, of course, be a coincidence; one wishes that the Peking men of China had left a rich record of cave paintings so something about the antiquity of hat-wearing in the Orient could be known.

Variation in the form of human face appears to be related to such things as the vulnerability of the nose to frostbite, the need for long nasal passages for filtering and warming air, the use of teeth as tools, and the amount of abrasive material in the diet. Australian aborigines, for instance, have the largest teeth of any human group and large jaws to go with them. They eat their meat partially roasted in the ashes of a fire, and consume raw and with no cleaning a variety of insects, lizards, nuts, roots, and berries. Like many hunters and gatherers, they too use their teeth as tools. Thus the grit in their food wears down their molars, and their use of jaws as pliers and vise wears down their incisors. It is hardly surprising that aborigine teeth are generally worn to the gums by what, for an American, would be middle age.

Tooth wear is very rapid among the Eskimos even though they have a culture technologically far advanced over the aborigines. Although they get far less grit with their diet and fashion many tools from bone and stone, their teeth are used constantly, especially in connection with making and maintaining their skin clothing. Even in the 1950s, after the introduction of European tools, an Eskimo woman in the central Arctic would often spend entire evenings chewing her husband's sealskin komiks (boots) to keep them soft and pliable. Thus it is reasonable to conclude that natural selection has produced large teeth in those groups of people for whom lack of substantial dental apparatus would be a distinct handicap.

Viewed characteristic by characteristic, therefore, patterns of geographic variation in some obvious features of humans make considerable evolutionary "sense."

Genetic Variation in Human Populations

Geographic variation in more cryptic characteristics has also been shown to be under selective control. For instance, certain human populations show a relatively high frequency of a kind of severe anemia characterized by deformation of the red blood cells, causing them to appear half-moon or sickle-shaped. The "sickle-cell" anemia is found predominantly (but not exclusively) in black Africans and their descendants. In order to understand the distribution of this anemia, a little background in elementary genetics is required.

Populations may differ from one another in the proportions of different kinds of individuals: blonds and brunettes, anemics and non-anemics, blue-eyed and brown-eyed, and so forth. They may also differ in the proportions of the genes controlling the development of different characteristics. Each person has tens of thousands of different genes.

Genes in individual human beings (and most higher animals) occur in pairs. One gene occurs on each of a pair of minute structures called chromosomes, which are found in the nucleus of each cell of the body. Each of the billions of cells of the body usually has exactly the same genes, so we can think of each individual having just two genes for each characteristic. In many cases two different genes occur in a population, say gene 1 (G^1) and gene 2 (G^2). In this case, three different kinds of individuals can exist in the population: those whose pair of genes in each cell are both gene 1 (G^1G^1); those with one of each (G^1G^2); and those with two genes of type 2 (G^2G^2). If the three kinds of individuals can be identified and counted, a little simple arithmetic can be used to calculate the proportion of G^1 genes in the entire population. Population geneticists call that proportion the *gene frequency* of G^1.[17]

In most people, the two genes that control the formation of hemoglobin carry coded information that leads to the production of hemoglobin A, the normal adult hemoglobin. Hemoglobin is the red pigment that transports oxygen from the lungs to the cells of the body. Only normal red blood cells are produced in such persons, whom geneticists call $Hb^A Hb^A$ individuals, indicating the presence in each cell of a pair of Hb^A genes. Those with sickle-cell anemia, however, have a different pair of genes, $Hb^S Hb^S$. These genes program the production of hemoglobin S, which differs from hemoglobin A in just one of the some 300 amino-acid building blocks of the protein molecule. This minor change in the basic structure of the molecule results in the sickle-shape red blood cells and fatal anemia of $Hb^S Hb^S$ individuals.

Since $Hb^S Hb^S$ individuals usually die before they can reproduce, why has natural selection not eliminated the Hb^S gene from human populations? The answer lies in the "carriers" of the sickle-cell trait, people who have one gene of each kind—Hb^{A}Hb^S individuals. Such individuals normally do not suffer from anemia; but if both members of a couple are carriers, about one-fourth of their children will get an Hb^S gene from each parent. Thus being Hb^{S}Hb^S, they will suffer the anemia. Carriers of the sickle-cell trait can be detected only by subjecting samples of their blood to an atmosphere low in oxygen, which produces the sickle shape in many of their red blood cells. About three-quarters of their hemoglobin is type A and about one-quarter type S.

What, then, do these carriers have to do with the distribution of sickle-cell anemia? The absence of anemia in Hb^{A}Hb^S individuals would not in itself be sufficient to prevent natural selection from reducing the frequency of the Hb^S gene to a very low level in the population. But it turns out that Hb^{A}Hb^S individuals are resistant to the attacks of one of the four species of malaria parasite that attack man, *Plasmodium falciparum*. Individuals with this protection are selectively favored over both Hb^{A}Hb^A and Hb^{S}Hb^S individuals. The sickle-cell carriers outreproduce anemics *and* normal individuals. This constitutes a pattern of natural selection in which both genes Hb^A and Hb^S are retained in a population that is regularly exposed to *falciparum* malaria.

Thus geographic variation in the frequency of Hb^S genes is highly correlated with the distribution of *Plasmodium falciparum*. Where that malarial parasite is found, one is likely to find sickle-cell anemia. There is evidence, for instance, that the introduction of Malaysian agricultural crops and practices into Africa some 1,500 years ago permitted Africans to move into tropical rain forests and brought them into greater contact with *falciparum* malaria. This increased selection pressure favoring the Hb^S gene led to the development of a large West African population in which the frequency of the Hb^S gene was .20 or greater.[18] Many Africans brought to the New World as slaves carried the gene, and it is still present (although at less than half the frequency) in the American Black population today. One would expect that as Africans moved to malaria-free localities and as malaria control was established in West Africa, the frequency of the Hb^S gene would be gradually reduced to a very low level and the frequency of individuals affected with sickle-cell anemia would become negligible.*

* Since in anemics, both of the genes must be Hb^S, the frequency of anemic individuals is the square of the frequency of the gene in the population. Therefore if the gene frequency is .2, $.2^2 = .04$, and four out of every hundred children will be sickle-

Other differences in human blood chemistry are controlled by known genetic systems. These divide people into different "blood groups" detectable on the basis of immunological tests. More than twenty such systems have been identified,[19] including the well-known ABO and Rh systems, both of which are of medical importance. The ABO blood group determines whether blood can be transfused successfully between two individuals.[20] The ABO system involves three genes: A, B, and O. Since each person has a pair of genes affecting the ABO system, six different combinations of these genes can be found in individuals. These combinations result in four blood groups, since in two cases different gene combinations produce the same blood groups. The gene combinations and resultant blood groups are:

Gene Combination	Blood Group
OO	O
AA	A
AO	A
BB	B
BO	B
AB	AB

There is great geographic variation in the frequency of ABO blood-group genes,[21] but the significance of this variation is unknown. No one knows why, for example, Australian aborigines differ greatly from Africans in the frequency of gene B.

Geographic variation also has been found in the frequency of numerous other blood-group genes and in a large assortment of genes that control the inheriting of such things as eye color, color blindness, the production of many enzymes, and the ability to taste the chemical PTC (phenylthiocarbamide).[22] Although the evolutionary significance of the geographic variation in the frequency of most of these genes is uncertain at present, there is every reason to believe, as noted above, that at least some of the observed variation in gene frequencies is a result of natural selection.

There is, however, some well-known geographic variation in physical characteristics of *Homo sapiens* that appears not to be under significant genetic control. For example, people who live in the high Andes

---

cell anemics. If the gene frequency is reduced to .0001—a reasonable expectation if Hb^{A}Hb^S genes are no longer favored—only one in a hundred million individuals will be sickle-cell anemics.

have expanded lung capacities, high red blood cell counts, and other physiological adaptations to help them cope with a shortage of oxygen. These appear, however, to be responses that can be elicited from any child born and raised at high altitude.[23]

With geographic variation so abundant in the physical characteristics of humanity, it is hardly surprising that *Homo sapiens* shows great variation in "mental" and cultural traits. Going all the way back to Linnaeus (remember the "optimistic" Europeans and the "hot-tempered" Native Americans), people have recognized geographic variation in human attitudes, personalities, abilities, and so on. Humans are a diverse lot, not just physically, but also mentally and culturally. Indeed, this enormous mental-cultural variability is perhaps the best defining characteristic of *Homo sapiens*. Chimpanzees make and use tools (and thus are presumably capable of abstract thought), dolphins can learn to communicate with people by "speech," and rhesus monkeys can learn to solve problems that stump many people,[24] but none of these organisms approaches the kaleidoscopic, multidimensional cultural variability of humanity.

Eskimos and Ifaluk Islanders in the Pacific lavish enormous time and attention on their children, while European parents often turn them over to parent surrogates at an early age, and the Ik of Africa habitually maltreat their children. Arabs approach each other closely when conversing, the English stand far back from one another, and Americans occupy an intermediate position. Nigerians developed a magnificent tradition of sculpture centuries ago that has never been approached in England or America, but the English and Americans (using mathematical notation developed by Arabs) invented steam engines, radar, airplanes, and a large variety of other devices of far greater sophistication than any manufactured devices arising in Africa. A rich Chinese culture bloomed while Britons were living in caves and painting themselves blue. The finest light cavalry in the world evolved among the natives of the American plains, people who had only been exposed to horses for a few centuries. The frequency of artistic and mechanical ability seems anecdotally to be very high among Eskimos; Africans are often "credited" with having an unusual sense of color and rhythm and having high athletic ability (the crediting usually being done by people who value high scores on Stanford-Binet intelligence tests as the ultimate in human achievement). Mental depression is more common among European whites than among African Blacks.[25] The degree to which this rich nonphysical variation in behavior and aptitudes is the result of natural selection operating to change the genetic characteristics of human populations is at present unknown, and is, as will be seen, extremely difficult to investigate.

The Subspecies Problem

If our species is such a prime example of a geographically variable animal, does this mean that it is in the process of splitting up into a batch of new species? Are the races of *Homo sapiens* each a species *in statu nascendi*? If they are, how many races are there? Zoologists faced this problem a quarter of a century ago. By the early 1950s, they had become uneasy about the expanding literature applying formal subspecific names. For example, in one species of North American pocket gopher, *Thomomys bottae*, more than 150 subspecies had been named. Such profligate naming was difficult to justify on the grounds that *T. bottae* was about to give birth to more than 150 new species, and it certainly did not enhance the main function of the formal system of scientific names originated by Linnaeus—that of communicating information. Rather, there was a loss of information. A zoologist, told that a specimen was *Thomomys bottae albicaudatus*, knew less than if he had been told that it was *T. bottae* from Provo, Utah—since *albicaudatus* is simply the name applied to individuals of *T. bottae* from around Provo. Similarly, many of the racial names applied in the finer fractionations of *Homo sapiens*, such as Dravidian and Carpentarian, communicate little to those not immediately and deeply concerned with the details of human racial taxonomy.

In 1953, zoologists E. O. Wilson (now of *Sociobiology* fame) and W. L. Brown published a classic paper, "The Subspecies Concept and Its Taxonomic Application,"[26] that once and for all put to rest the notion that subspecies or races are biological units. Wilson and Brown pointed out that with few exceptions the array of subspecies recognized within a species is simply a function of whatever varying characteristics of the animal the taxonomist chose to study. The essence of Wilson and Brown's criticism of the subspecies concept is that variation in different characteristics is generally *discordant*. That is, instead of being *concordant* and varying together, characteristics change from place to place in unique patterns, usually unrelated to patterns in other

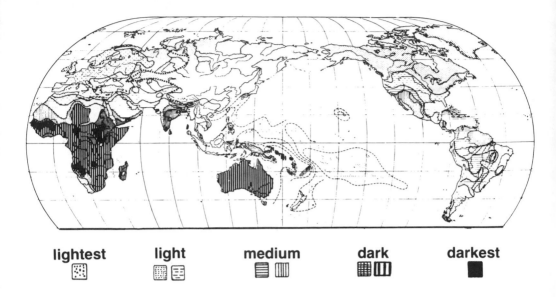

lightest **light** **medium** **dark** **darkest**

a. Distribution of Skin Color

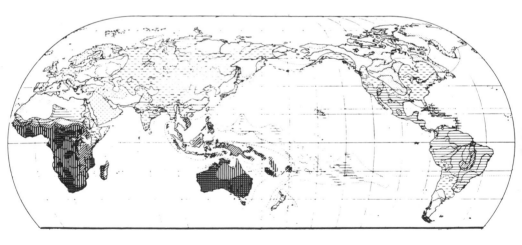

very long and narrow **long and narrow** **short and wide**

very short and wide

c. Distribution of Average Nose Form

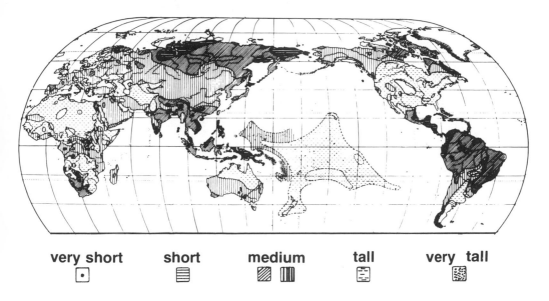

very short **short** **medium** **tall** **very tall**

b. Distribution of Average Height

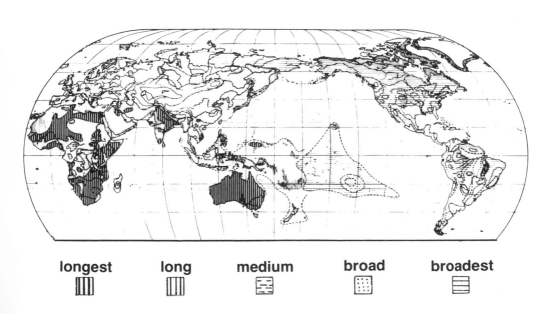

longest **long** **medium** **broad** **broadest**

d. Distribution of Average Head Shape

Figure 2-3. Discordant variation in human characteristics: (a) skin color; (b) average height; (c) average nose form; (d) average head shape. (Data from R. Biasutti, *Le Razze e i Popoli Della Terra*, 4th ed. Turin: Unione Tipografico, 1967.)

characteristics. Whereas, for example, wing length in a butterfly might vary in one geographic pattern in response to certain evolutionary pressures, the spotting on the wings might vary in quite another pattern in response to different selection pressures.[27] And variation in the frequencies of the genes controlling the production of forms of different enzymes might show a unique geographic pattern for each enzyme.[28]

Geographic variation has been more thoroughly studied in *Homo sapiens* than in any other organism. And, like the variation of other animals, human variation has been found to be largely discordant.[29] Notice in Figure 2-3 that the distribution of skin color and height show no similarities with each other or with the shape of the head or the nose (distributions illustrated in the Americas are for populations of Native Americans). Other discordant variation in characteristics can be illustrated just as readily, such as the distribution of A, B, and O blood-group genes compared with each other or with the genes involved in other blood-group systems.

How, then, could one create a biologically sound subspecific (racial) taxonomy of our variable species? Racial classifications of humans have already been constructed, based, as noted above, primarily on skin color. Are these in some sense "natural" divisions of humanity, biological units that deserve to be recognized as races? The answer is no. The discordance of human variation means there are no natural units within *Homo sapiens* that permit the species to be divided into four or forty evolutionary entities that can be described as races. If there were natural divisions among human races, one would expect concordant variation, with discontinuities (or at least sharp gradients) in many characteristics at the racial boundaries. But, as is shown in Figure 2-3, in most cases the pattern of variation in one characteristic seems unrelated to that in others—hardly surprising when we consider the probable causes of the patterns. As a result, geographic boundaries where constellations of human characteristics change together do not occur.

Any racial division of *Homo sapiens* therefore depends on which characteristic or characteristics are arbitrarily chosen by the classifier. Humankind, like most other widespread animal species, exhibits geographical variation *but does not consist of a collection of biological races*.[30] The racial approach to human variation is of historical interest to zoologists but is misleading in terms of what is now understood about evolutionary units within species. Most subspecies (races) are certainly not "species in the state of being born"![31]

Biologically there are no races of *Homo sapiens*. Any two geographic samples of *Homo sapiens* will be different from one another in very many characteristics, but humanity does not fall naturally into a series of differing groups. This is a key point. We are not saying that the collections of people living in different places are alike. On the contrary, we are saying that, statistically, all samples of *H. sapiens*, however defined, are different. But the presence of differences does not mean the presence of natural groups (see Figure 2-4).

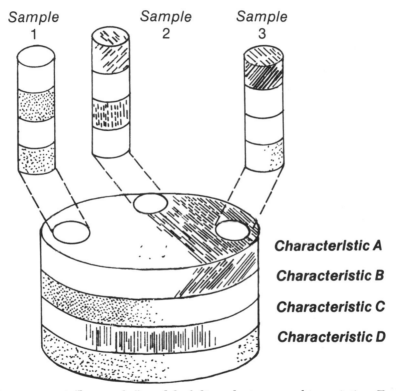

Figure 2-4.   A "layer cake" model of discordant geographic variation. Each of the four layers represents a different characteristic; the shading represents geographic variation in the characteristic. The "cores" represent three population samples. Each sample is different, as would be the case with three samples taken from other parts of the cake. But there is no way to divide the cake into three logical or "natural" racial subdivisions. Just because the three cores are different doesn't mean they come from a tripartite cake.

Consider an analogous case. Books vary, among other things, in size, shape, color, kind of binding, type style, design, paper quality, language, author, date of publication, price, publisher, and many features of content (subject matter, quality of writing, accuracy, style, presence or absence of libel, and so on). Classification can be very difficult for some of these characteristics. Is, for instance, Gore Vidal's *Burr* a novel, a popular history, a revisionist history, or a historical novel? Or is it political science? Often it seems impossible to decide among several categories. Is this book about biology, sociology, anthropology, psychology, or is it just a political tract?

The difficulties in classifying books "naturally" do not arise because there are too few differing characteristics, but because those characteristics vary *discordantly*. In addition, the characteristics of a book that most impress a person will depend on who that person is. Publishers and students may focus first on the book's price, a printer on its typography, a shipper on its size, a bookstore salesperson on whether it is hardback or paperback, and a librarian on content, author, date, and length. Anyone having experience with a library (even a sizable personal library) or a bookstore knows that while there are infinite ways of arranging books, no way is entirely satisfactory—it is always necessary to adopt some arbitrary scheme to deal with the variation.

So it is with human variation—and races are just arbitrary schemes for dealing with that variation. In this context, we may compare people who are fascinated with the relationship between "race" and the genetics of intelligence with bookbinding fanatics who would bombard the "National Academy of Librarians" with demands for research on the correlation between the color of a book's cover and the quality of its contents.

3

Races in a Social Context

The society is beginning to hold the black man in America as essentially responsible for many of its problems. For example, Negroes are thought to be the cause of high tax rates because of poverty programs and welfare payments. Ignoring the vast sums consumed by the Pentagon, the pork barrels, the boondoggles, whites are tending to speak of "them getting everything," and thinking of Negro claims for simple justice as a threat to the very warp and woof of American society itself. Relatively speaking, and here precise judgments are impossible to make, placing blame on the Negro while avoiding real threats may be the most dangerous shift in white America's thinking. The danger to whites is obvious: The exorcism of the demon could well come at the price of white freedom.
—Barry N. Schwartz and Robert Disch, *White Racism*, 1970

THAT THERE IS no biological reality to races will be small consolation to you if your children get inferior schooling because they are members of the "Black race" or if someone shoots you and your family because you are "gooks" or have "Jewish blood." There are other realities besides biological realities. In a social context, distinctions are generally made among people on the basis of tribal membership or national citizenship. Additional social distinctions may be based on purported biological (racial) differences, on financial position (class), on language or religion, or on combinations of these. In the United States, for instance, a person with any known Black ancestry usually is defined socially as a Negro, regardless of personal "color-coding." In the United States, to be a Negro is to be a member of a caste—no amount of education, no amount of financial success will permit an individual to leave the caste. A rich, light-skinned Ph.D. who admitted to having a black-skinned great-grandmother would be treated by

many if not most Americans as Negro. Senator Edward Brooke of
Massachusetts is always described as "Black" in spite of his light skin
color.

Races as Social Units

In Brazil, the status of a Negro is defined on the basis of the skin
color of the individual (not of any ancestor), combined with the class
of the individual. In Brazil, a "Negro" is any of the following:[1]

Poverty-stricken White
Poverty-stricken mulatto
Poor mulatto
Poverty-stricken Black
Poor Black
Black of average wealth

In contrast, a "White" is any of the following:

White who is wealthy
White of average wealth
White who is poor
Wealthy mulatto
Mulatto of average wealth
Black who is wealthy

Thus the concept of Negro is a very different one in Brazil from that
in the United States. In Brazil, it is possible for a Negro, through
personal effort, to overcome the substantial barriers of prejudice
thrown in his way and become White—or as it has been crudely put,
"Money whitens."[2]

The differing biological "realities" of Brazilian and American racial
groupings and the nonexistence of natural racial units do not, we
emphasize, justify the conclusion that races have little social reality. As
Senator Brooke would probably testify, being socially defined as "Black"
is *very* real. Remember, *Homo sapiens* is a "visual animal"; sight domi-
nates our sense. Defining people who "look different" as being outgroup
members has been a widespread, if not ubiquitous, feature of human
society. Indeed, even where the outgroup is essentially defined on
other than a visual basis, myths are often developed that give the
outgroup visual defining characteristics. Thus there are the well-known

set of facial features that is considered to identify Jews (a group defined primarily on the basis of religion) and the half-moons on the fingernails of Negroes attempting to pass as White in the United States (where Negro is defined not by present physical attributes but on the basis of known descent from at least one dark-skinned ancestor).

Even though races are not biological entities, then, they certainly are social units. People are classified into these units on the basis of an arbitrary grab-bag of attributes that may include real and imagined physical features of the individuals, their class, or their ancestors. It is this *social* racial unit that is involved in the IQ controversy, and it is this social unit to which the term "race" will be applied henceforth. Similarly, when we say "Black" or "White," the reference is to *socially defined races*, not to skin color per se.

Race, Slavery, and Genocide

Where physical differences are extremely obvious, as in the case of skin color, the actual differences tend to be exaggerated in the social stereotype.[3] Although the structure of prejudice has been very different in the United States and Brazil, in both countries the notion is firmly entrenched that dark-skinned people are "apelike." This is especially amusing, since of the there major features of the Negro stereotype, dark skin, kinky hair, and thick lips, only the first is shared with any apes. Gorillas are dark-skinned; chimpanzees vary—some are white-skinned, some black, some yellow. All apes have straight hair and thin lips. Indeed, white-skinned people tend to excel in that most apelike of characteristics—hairiness.[4]

The identification by some groups of people of other groups as inferior or less than human has for centuries justified practices ranging from possession of Black slaves to genocide. Shortly before 1700, there was a proliferation of theories on the inferiority of Negroes, a proliferation that accompanied the rapid increase in the slave trade at that time. The Age of Discovery brought to European attention the vast lands of the Western Hemisphere, which could be made to yield great wealth if only an adequate and secure labor supply could be found. That labor supply was found in the slaving complex of West Africa. The complex predated European involvement in the trade, but was

vastly expanded by Europeans in the sixteenth century to fill a growing demand for cheap labor in the West.

A theological problem arose, however, namely that the first obliga-
tion of a faithful Christian was to convert these people, not to kidnap
them. At this point, the argument that Blacks were subhuman, not
possessed of a soul, and therefore beyond the pale of ordinary human
consideration, began to be heard. Negroes were presented as nonhuman, sometimes even as monsters that could not successfully
interbreed with humans but had sexual intercourse with apes.[5]

Although slavery has been a widespread human institution since the
agricultural revolution, this trend of dehumanizing the slaves was
rather novel. In ancient societies, although slaves often suffered in the
extreme, they were not always drawn from a different racial group
from their masters and no questions were raised in regard to their
humanity.[6] Apparently, the necessity to dehumanize those whom
Europeans wished to hold in bondage arose from the emphasis of
traditional Western Christianity on the worth and significance of the
individual and his ultimate responsibility for his own destiny. Obviously, a person who is a slave and does not control his own actions
cannot be held accountable by God for his conduct during life. Hence,
there is an irreconcilable contradiction between the Christian concept
of salvation and the institution of chattel slavery. However, if a person
were not a Christian in the first place, this bar to his enslavement
would be absent. The very word "slave" is derived from the same
origin as our word Slav, referring to eastern European peoples who in
the Middle Ages were not Christian or who could be presented as non-
Christian.

It must be said, however, that the trend to dehumanize those whom
Europeans wished to exploit did not go unchallenged. Pope Paul III
(1534–1549) was strongly antiracist, proclaiming as the work of the
devil "the opinion that the inhabitants of the West Indies and the
southern continents . . . should be treated like animals that have not
reason, and be employed solely for our profit and service, on the
pretext that they have no part in the Catholic faith and are incapable
of adopting it."[7]

As theological debate gave way to scientific argument as the ultimate basis for authority in Western culture, the empiricists and
positivists adopted and continued the debasing arguments against
Black humanity begun by the theologians. Some scientists continue it
today.[8]

Just as it is necessary in Western culture to dehumanize those whom we would enslave, so it is necessary to strip the mantle of humanity from those we would kill—possibly for the same reason. Our religious scriptures, Old Testament and New, are replete with examples of and justifications for killing. Usually before killing, a way must be found to categorize the victims as nonhuman. This process begins with vocabulary. We cease to refer to potential victims in familiar, human terms, and we adopt new words, most recently "gooks," "dinks," "slopes," etc. Usually the change of vocabulary is enough to permit killing without psychological violation of the murder taboo, but in the most horrendous modern example of killing, the holocaust visited on the Jews by the Nazis, simply imputing evil to the word "Jew" was not enough. A whole pseudoscientific literature was created to dehumanize the victims, based mostly on specious measurements from physical anthropology relative to cranial indices and the like. In other words, it was necessary to take a group of people who were defined completely by social and cultural characteristics and invent physical differences in order to establish justification for their mass murder.

That the extermination of millions of Jews by Nazi Germany was a case of racism as well as of religious prejudice can be seen in the Nuremberg laws in which Jews were clearly treated as an inferior race from which the "Purity of German Blood" had to be protected.[9] This ultimate program led to the invention of the term "genocide," which was defined by the United Nations as:

any of the following acts committed with the intent to destroy, in whole or part, a national, ethnic, racial, or religious group, such as:
  a. killing members of the group;
  b. causing serious bodily or mental harm to members of the group;
  c. deliberately inflicting on the group conditions of life calculated to bring about its physical destruction in whole or in part;
  d. imposing measures intended to prevent births within the group; and
  e. forcibly transferring children of the group to another group.[10]

Today, the term "genocide" is frequently used in discussions of race, all too often simply as a label that groups try to hang on one another to discredit the opposition. It is heard especially often in connection with attempts to achieve population control. Hence, under the UN stricture against "imposing measures intended to prevent births within the group," a White welfare worker in Oakland who gives the address of an abortion clinic to a Black woman ends up in the dock with Heinrich Himmler. The connection may seem remote, but the charge is based on understandable anxiety. After all, a White scientist declares that Blacks are color-coded for inferiority and a White welfare worker takes steps that can lead to fewer Black births. Presto— genocide.

Fear of genocide among racial minorities is a natural result of the periodic behavior of dominant races. Consider, for example, the fates of the native peoples of the New World, past and present, at the hands of Whites. Some of the behavior of European migrants to North America toward Native Americans was clearly genocidal—clichés such as "the only good Indian is a dead Indian" attest to that. The Indian's land was stolen in a series of official maneuvers unparalleled in their perfidy, and many tribes had deliberately inflicted on them "conditions of life calculated to bring about [their] physical destruction in whole or in part."[11] As Vine Deloria put it, "The truth is that practically the only thing the white men ever gave the Indian was disease and poverty."[12]

In South America, there have been numerous campaigns to exterminate Indian tribes occupying land desired by others. There are, for instance, only an estimated 1,000 Aché Indians left. These gentle Indians living in the forests of Paraguay have been the victims of merciless genocidal pressure. Paraguayan anthropologist Chase Sardi says, "They are hunted, they are pursued like animals. The parents are killed and the children sold . . . and there is no family of which a child has not been murdered."[13] Other tribes in Paraguay and Brazil are suffering similar fates. The peaceful Aché cannot comprehend the forces deployed against them, and many of them have lost all sense of social and personal identity in response to their persecution and the disruption of their lives. German ethnologist Mark Munzel commented, "I recorded many songs lamenting the end of the Aché, in which the singer regards himself as no longer an Aché and not even a human being, but as half dead."[14]

Genocide is not an activity restricted to modern industrial societies, although their technological capabilities for mass murder have given them opportunities not available to agricultural peoples. In recent years genocide has reared its head in several of the less-developed countries of the world. For instance, in early 1972 some 100,000 Hutu tribesmen in Burundi were systematically slaughtered by the Tutsi rulers of that country in revenge for a Hutu attempt to kill those rulers and set up an independent country.[15]

In the face of such continuing horrors, is not anyone justified in viewing with suspicion activities of one race that appear to involve restriction of births in another? Could it be true that "population control" and other jargon used in its place merely represents "a plot to commit genocide against Black peoples of the U.S. and the world"?[16] In view of the absolute necessity of limiting population growth if *any* of the world's problems are to be solved, this question must be confronted directly. Unfortunately, the accuracy of the population-control-equals-genocide accusation is difficult to determine. If most (or many) people involved in programs to supply birth control to Blacks are doing it in the hope of reducing the proportion of Blacks in the population, then the program is genocidal. Some individuals do think there are too many Blacks in the United States (or people of dark skin color in the world) and would like to see programs of population control initiated to reduce the numbers of "inferior" people—people who, for example, get low scores on IQ tests.

Race and Birth Control in the United States

The entrance of the United States government into the field of birth control through the extension of family-planning services to the poor aroused a controversy quite out of proportion to its potential effect on the national birth rate—particularly in the Black community, some of whose members did perceive the extension of the services to the poor as a policy of genocide against racial minorities.[17]

In the United States, birth rates have long been higher among the poor and among non-Whites (Blacks, Orientals, and Native Americans) than among the nonpoor and among Whites, but in recent years the birth rates of the poor and non-Whites have been declining even more rapidly than those of the population as a whole. In addition, the poor and non-Whites also have consistently higher death rates, especially among infants and children. Above the poverty level, the birth-rate difference between races diminishes, and the college-educated non-Whites have *fewer* children than their White peers.

Although there is conflicting evidence regarding desired family sizes among the poor, several surveys conducted in the 1960s indicated that they wished to have only slightly more children than middle-class couples, and non-White couples in most socioeconomic classes wanted fewer children than comparable Whites did. This was especially true among the younger couples in their prime childbearing years.[18]

At the same time, in the early 1960s, the incidence of unwanted children among the poor and near-poor was estimated to be as high as 40 percent. For nonpoor couples, the incidence was about 14 percent.[19] The reason for this disparity between desires and actual reproductive performance appears to have been less the lack of knowledge of contraceptives than the patterns of their use. The poor who used birth control tended to use less reliable methods than did members of the middle class and used them less effectively.

Because poor people usually cannot afford contraceptives, and because no family-planning information or services were provided through welfare health services until the late 1960s, most poor people were until then deprived of effective methods of birth control.

Between 1965 and 1970, fertility among the poor and near-poor declined by 21 percent, doubtless due in part to the new family-planning services that by 1970 were reaching an estimated 1.5 million women. The greatest fertility decline occurred among non-White women below the poverty level. As the family-planning services have expanded, non-White fertility has continued to drop since 1970. By 1974, Black women under 25 expected to have essentially the same number of children as White women their age: an average of 2.2.[20]

Despite the tendency of Black militants to regard the provision of birth-control information and services to the poor as a policy of "genocide" against Blacks, the government's present program is basically intended to benefit the poor, and poor children in particular. In this connection, it is unfortunate that the government chose to label its policy a "population control" measure, which it is not; rather, it is a logical and long-overdue extension of both the family-planning movement and the welfare program.

In the 1920s, 1930s, and 1940s, racism in the United States thrived at a level difficult for today's young Americans, Black or White, to comprehend. It was a period of numerous lynchings, forced sterilizations, and hideous "research" projects like the infamous Tuskegee Study in which Black males with syphilis were left untreated. And it was a period of an outpouring of racist literature clearly genocidal in intent. However, it is important to note that the Black community was not uniformly against family planning then, nor is it uniformly against it now. In 1922, the great Black leader W. E. B. DuBois endorsed birth control for Blacks, saying it was "science and sense applied to the bringing of children into the world" and that of those who needed it "we Negroes are first."[21] In 1932, he further expressed his distress at Black ignorance of birth control and came down squarely on the side of quality not quantity of children.[22]

In more recent years, Black militant opposition to birth control has been balanced by, among others, Martin Luther King, Jr. In accepting the Margaret Sanger Award in Human Rights, he stated:

Negroes have no mere academic nor ordinary interest in family planning. They have a special and urgent concern. . . . The Negro constitutes half the poor of the nation. Like all poor, Negro and White, they have many unwanted children. This is a cruel evil they urgently need to control. There is scarcely anything more tragic in human life than a child who is not wanted.[23]

Black women have very often spoken out in favor of access to birth control and abortion—frequently putting themselves in opposition to Black men. Carolyn Jones has written, "Young black women who have watched their own mothers and grandmothers struggle to raise a family alone, are no longer willing to listen to the blackman's cry of genocide."[24] Shirley Chisholm, the great congresswoman from Brooklyn, described the portrayal of legalized abortion and family-planning programs as genocide as "male rhetoric for male ears. It falls flat to female listeners and to thoughtful male ones."[25]

On the other hand, it might be claimed that those who attempt to *prevent* the extension of family-planning services either to ghettos or to poor nations are acting genocidally. The world's present socioeconomic structure ensures that the underprivileged of any nation will suffer first and most from their own increased numbers, so much so that increased death rates may well wipe out any gains made resulting from a high birth rate. It is indisputable that top priority must be given to changing the socioeconomic structure of the world;[26] but until that is done, encouraging large families among ghetto Blacks, poor Whites, or peasants in Bangladesh is one of the surest ways to "keep the niggers down."

In the 1960s, those who saw family planning in ghettos as a genocidal plot against the Blacks often claimed that American behavior in Vietnam was also genocidal. As with family planning, intent is also the key question when it comes to evaluating the claim. It would seem that the behavior of the United States and its South Vietnamese allies toward the Montagnard tribesmen, at least, was genocidal under the strict definition. It seems unlikely, however, that destroying the Vietnamese as a people was ever an intentional part of American policy, even though to a certain degree that was its effect. Our destructive impact was not only through the enormous casualties inflicted, but also through the ecological destruction of much of Vietnam[27] and, perhaps most important, through the destruction of Vietnamese culture.

Whether or not there was genocide in Vietnam, the downgrading of a physically recognizable outgroup as inferiors was probably an important factor in American behavior. American servicemen were taught contempt for the "gooks," "slopes," and "dinks" and for their way of life. Antique racial myths about disrespect for life in the Orient, the ability of Orientals to stand suffering, and their sneakiness and barbarism in warfare pervaded U.S. policy in Indochina and permitted policies that equaled in callousness our treatment of Native Americans during the Indian Wars. Indeed, for casual brutality to women and children in a situation of no resistance, the My Lai massacre may exceed the most infamous massacres of American Indians at Sand Creek and Wounded Knee. That anti-Oriental racism, like anti-Black racism, pervades American society can be seen clearly in the semi-hero treatment accorded Lt. Calley by large numbers of Americans and the special privileges granted him by then President Nixon.

Racial Mythology and Discrimination

Of course, slavery and genocide are only the most extreme fates that may await those defined as "inferior" races on the grounds of "color-coding" or other social criteria. One could cite examples *ad nauseam* of less extreme racial discrimination—the horrible treatment given Japanese-Americans in the United States during World War II as contrasted with the treatment of German-Americans; the British treatment of dark-skinned immigrants; the Israeli prejudice against dark-skinned Jews and Arabs; the Syrian harassment of Syrian Jews; the Japanese treatment of the Ainu; the Soviet treatment of their yellow-skinned minorities.

Although people generally attempt to distinguish other races by physical characteristics, their prejudices against them are usually based on imaginary intellectual or cultural traits. Thus one hears from bigots that Blacks are stupid, lazy, childlike, entranced by primitive musical rhythms, lacking artistic talent, but possessing great athletic ability. Jews are greedy, pushy, and loud, but smart. Japanese are treacherous and unoriginal, but hard-working. Southern Europeans are dirty and eat garbage, but cheerful. Occasionally these statements contain elements of truth. For instance, people in the Tropics often are "lazy" compared with people in more temperate regions—and with good reason. They suffer more from malnutrition from an enormous variety of debilitating parasitic diseases. Malaria, probably still the most important disease of humans, is now largely confined to the tropics. Hookworm is much more common in the tropics than in temperate regions, and where it occurs in temperate regions—for instance in the southeastern United States—it causes "laziness" in people with the pearliest of white skins and WASPiest of pedigrees.

Other putative racial traits are simply the product of the world view of bigots. No one who has viewed the Benin bronzes of Nigeria, the decorations of a New Guinea spirit house, or a fine example of an aboriginal "X-ray" bark painting could contend that esthetic sense is not just as much "at home" inside a black skin as a white one. The art of other cultures may have varying degrees of appeal to individuals in our own culture (just as do different styles of Western art), but art it undeniably is. It is tragicomic to hear White Rhodesians attempt to explain away the magnificent ruins at Zimbabwe, remains of a great Black civilization, with such nonsense as "It must have been built by Arabs." And only those not familiar with, say, the Eskimos, Masai, or Aborigines would look down on the achievements and abilities of these peoples. They might have difficulty dealing with our technology, but we would perish almost immediately in their environments.

Whites are prone to point to the achievements of Western science and technology as evidence of the innate superiority of their race. In this context, the distinguished human geneticist Curt Stern quoted a statement by Lord Raglan:

"It has been said against the African Negroes that they never produced a scientist; but what kind of a scientist would he be who had no weights and measures, no clock or calendar, and no means of recording his observations and experiments? And if it be asked why the Negroes did not invent these things, the answer is that neither did any European, and for the same reason—namely that the rare and perhaps unique conditions which made their invention possible were absent."[28]

And, of course, neither the bigots nor Lord Raglan questioned whether the invention of science and technology was truly humanity's greatest cultural achievement, or merely a colossal mistake destined to be its *last* cultural achievement.

Scientific Racism

One of the most prevalent of all the racial myths—one that has great sociopolitical importance in the United States and increasing significance in such countries as France—is the myth that IQ tests show that Blacks are genetically inferior in intelligence to Whites. This myth is given credence by the support of a few members of the scientific community today, and by many scientists of the past. Indeed, there is a long history of attempts by Western scientists to "prove" the innate superiority of their race over all others. (Remember that in general scientists have always tended to be at least as enmeshed in the common wisdoms of their culture as any other members of society, and their work, even in their own areas of expertise, is often more reflective of these wisdoms than of dispassionate judgments.) Accordingly, in 1865, the great liberal English evolutionist Thomas Huxley, sometimes referred to as Darwin's bulldog for his brilliant defenses of evolution by natural selection, wrote:

It may be quite true that some negroes are better than some white men; but no rational man, cognisant of the facts, believes that the average negro is the equal, still less the superior, of the average white man. And, if this be true, it is simply incredible that, when all his disabilities are removed, and our prognathous relative has a fair field and no favor, as well as no oppressor, he will be able to compete successfully with his bigger-brained and smaller-jawed rival, in a contest which is to be carried on by thoughts and not by bites. The highest places in the hierarchy of civilisation will assuredly not be within the reach of our dusky cousins, though it is by no means necessary that they should be restricted to the lowest.[29]

It is to Huxley's credit that, in spite of his culture-bound view, he believed that "no human being can arbitrarily dominate over another without grievous damage to his own nature . . . no slavery can be abolished without a double emancipation, and the master will benefit by freedom more than the freed-man."[30]

Huxley's view of Black inferiority was typical of Victorian scientists and was supported by numerous scientists in the late nineteenth and early twentieth centuries. This scientific racism did not go unnoticed by politicians. Making use of it, the famous racist Senator Theodore Bilbo of Mississippi claimed in 1944 that

Historical and scientific research has established three propositions beyond all controversy:

First, The white race has founded, developed, and maintained every civilization known to the human race.

Second, The white race, having founded, developed, and maintained civilization, has never been known, in all history, to lose that civilization as long as the race was kept white.

Third, The white man has never kept unimpaired the civilization he has founded and developed after his blood stream has been adulterated by the blood stream of another race, more especially another race so widely diverse in all its inherent qualities as the black race.[31]

Bilbo was right in one respect—people of his bent could indeed quote a raft of "historical and scientific research" demonstrating the inferiority and lack of achievement of dark-skinned peoples.

Although the tide of scientific racism has ebbed in the last few decades, racism persists in some corners of the scientific community today. And it persists not just in gibbering tracts like the George Report, but also in the writings of otherwise distinguished and reputable scientists.

The brilliant British geneticist C. D. Darlington is world renowned for his studies of chromosomes, the tiny bodies in the nucleus of the cell that carry the genes. His belief in genetic determinism and his fascination with race and class pervade his writings on *Homo sapiens*. In his view, those individuals, classes, and races that reach positions of power do so primarily because of their possession of the proper genes: they "derive their dominant position from the fitness of their genetic character to the conditions they find or make for themselves."[32] This statement from another upper-class Englishman written a century after Huxley could in itself be taken as a powerful bit of evidence for the extreme importance of environmental factors in shaping mental characteristics!

Even some anthropologists have contributed to the effort to "scientifically" justify the Whites' dominance in the world and the Whites' prejudice against the Blacks. Carleton Coon, in his long and confused book *The Origin of Races*, described his thesis that "over half a million years ago, man was a single species, *Homo erectus*, perhaps already divided into five geographic races or subspecies. *Homo erectus* then evolved into *Homo sapiens* not once but five times, as each subspecies, living in its own territory, passed a critical threshold from a more brutal to a more sapient state."[33] Needless to say, Coon (a light-skinned man) discovered that it was the Negroes who made the transition from brutal to sapient last. From our early discussion of the nonexistence of biological races in humankind, one can immediately see that Coon's thesis is preposterous. It is based on selected evidence and misinterpretation of modern evolutionary thought. And, as critics were quick to point out, even if there were five biologically distinct subspecies of humans, Coon's thesis is still preposterous! For five separate subspecies of a species to make the same major evolutionary step (from brutal to sapient) independently and in parallel would strain the laws of probability, to say the least—since different populations even when exposed to similar selection pressures rarely respond identically.[34]

Coon's book is awash with a biological determinism and a naiveté about human culture that seemed quaint even in the early 1960s. For example, on the basis of an anecdote about interbreeding patterns in sheep, he states:

Some of the very soldiers, sailors, and marines who nearly created a new race in the Pacific Islands in World War II are opposed to the mingling of races in their native states. This is not inconsistency—it is simply biology.[35]

Or consider his statement:

High blood pressure is particularly frequent in urbanized Negroes both in America and in Africa. In terms of animal behavior, all this evidence—much of it quite new and not yet fully digested by the medical profession—seems to indicate that individuals vary widely in their inherited ability to resist the evil effects of large amounts of interaction, and that a higher ratio of individuals who can withstand it has arisen, by natural selection, in some populations than in others. These differences are not racial *per se*, but some races have been exposed to more of this kind of pressure than others.[36]

There are, of course, equally plausible environmental explanations for a high incidence of high blood pressure in Blacks; for one, they are under consistently greater social stress. The phenomenon is still not thoroughly understood. But the above statement of Coon's is followed on the next page by a hypothesis about selection favoring "individuals who have both a stress tolerance and superior intelligence."

It is not surprising, in spite of their speciousness, that Coon's conclusions are widely cited by those unable or unwilling to see through them—for instance, in the George Report and in more pretentious works such as *The Geography of Intellect* by social scientists Nathaniel Weyl and Stefan Possany.[37]

In the 1970s, scientific racists seem to have largely abandoned attempts to show that Blacks are genetically inferior on the basis of physical evidence (since none exists). Instead, they have returned to a pattern that prevailed in the early part of this century. As evidence of the innate inferiority of Blacks, these racists have focused on the gap in average IQ test scores that often occurs when the tests are administered to Blacks and Whites. The history of this recurrent pattern of scientific racism provides a fascinating study in the sociology of science.

History and Heresy in the IQ Game

Scientifically, Shockley and Jensen notwithstanding, the claim that Blacks are genetically inferior to Whites in intelligence is just plain silly. In our racist society, it is also just plain dangerous. So is the notion that White, upper-class scientists can investigate the Jensen hypothesis dispassionately. The idea that science can somehow proceed in a social and political vacuum, with the scientist being objective, is certainly quaint, but not one that would be supported by any serious student of science or society. It has been shown, for example, that the conclusions of Black vs. White IQ studies can be predicted from the background of the investigator. Upper-class scientists tend to conclude that Blacks are innately inferior intellectually.[38] One need only look at the history of the uses of IQ testing to see numerous additional examples of how this particular kind of science can be perverted. Conscious or unconscious advocacy by some scientists of the innate superiority of their "race" or class is as old as science itself. Systematic attempts date back at least to Francis Galton, who in 1869 in his book *Hereditary Genius*[39] concluded, curiously enough, that upper-class Englishmen had the best heredity of all—even though he failed to devise tests that would distinguish them from run-of-the-mill Englishmen.

Nor have psychologists been immune to the disease of jumping to unscientific conclusions about hereditary superiority and inferiority. Edward L. Thorndike, described by Jensen as "probably America's greatest psychologist and a pioneer in twin studies of the heritability of intelligence,"[40] stated in 1905: "In the actual race of life, which is not to get ahead but to get ahead of somebody, the chief determining factor is heredity."[41] Thorndike's genes obviously got him ahead of everybody in his studies of heredity, since his statement was published five years before Morgan's chromosome theory and thirteen years before Fisher established the statistical theory that made it possible to estimate heritabilities,[42] which are crucial to arguments about the genetics of intelligence.

Modern IQ tests all trace back to the work of French psychologist Alfred Binet. He realized that Galton and others before him had been on the wrong track when they had attempted to correlate such things as sensory acuity with success in Western society. Binet's test was designed to measure such traits as memory, problem solving, and verbal reasoning, which the French school system was designed to reward. These tests were first put to use when Binet and his associate Theodore Simon were hired in 1904 to identify retarded children in the schools of Paris.[43]

The first large-scale political use of IQ testing was not against Blacks but against another clear and present danger to WASP domination of American society—waves of immigrants from eastern and southern Europe. Psychologist Henry Goddard, at the invitation of the United States Public Health Service, administered, through translators, some IQ tests to immigrants at Ellis Island. Goddard discovered, astonishingly, that of the testees 79 percent of the Italians, 80 percent of the Hungarians, 83 percent of the Jews, and 87 percent of the Russians were "feeble-minded."[44] Goddard's efforts and those of his followers led to a great increase in the number of aliens prevented from entering the country because of "feeble-mindedness."[45] Curiously, even in the 1970s, similar results were being reported in California school systems where Chicano children whose first language was Spanish were being given IQ tests in English!

These immigrant IQ testing "results" seem ludicrous today, and yet a point made recently by psychologist Leon Kamin[46] bears repeating. In 1923, psychologist R. Pinter went to some pains to point out in his text *Intelligence Testing: Methods and Results*[47] that in six separate studies of Italian-American children, their median IQ was 84—a full 16 points below the U.S. average. In response to this deficit, should the National Academy be petitioned to do research on the genetic inferiority of Italian-Americans (as it recently has been for Blacks)? Or do hereditarians think that Italian-Americans have become genetically smarter in two generations?

Although Binet did not consider his intelligence test a measure of innate capacity, that notion quickly emerged with the work of Lewis Terman at Stanford University. Terman modified the Binet test for use in the United States, publishing his version in 1916.[48] In his book, Terman declared that "high grade moronity" or "borderline" mental deficiency were

very, very common among Spanish-Indian and Mexican families . . . and also among negroes. Their dullness seems to be racial, or at least inherent in the family stocks from which they come. The fact that one meets this type with such extraordinary frequency among Indians, Mexicans, and negroes suggests quite forcibly that the whole question of racial differences in mental traits will have to be taken up anew and by experimental methods. The writer predicts that when this is done there will be discovered enormously significant racial differences in general intelligence, differences which cannot be wiped out by any scheme of mental culture.[49]

Terman then went on to deplore the fact that society could not be persuaded to stop such people from reproducing, ". . . from a eugenic point of view they constitute a grave problem because of their unusually prolific breeding." He considered such people "uneducable beyond the merest rudiments of training. No amount of school instruction will ever make them intelligent voters or capable citizens . . . judged psychologically they cannot be considered normal."

It is ironic indeed that a half-century later, again at Stanford, Shockley, an electrical engineer, should start a crusade to resurrect such antique views partly on the basis that scientists are unwilling to consider "the theory that intelligence is largely determined by the genes and that races may differ in distribution of mental capacity" because it "offends equalitarian environmentalism."[50] Shockley even has had the temerity to compare himself with Galileo and Darwin,[51] apparently blissfully unaware that the "heretical" position he holds was for some time the solid orthodoxy of science—an orthodoxy strongly associated with his own university, and an orthodoxy demolished when its tenets did not stand up to careful scrutiny.

Psychologist H. J. Eysenck, another prominent subscriber to the theory that Blacks are genetically stupid, also suffers from the delusion that hereditarianism is something new. The first chapter of his book *The IQ Argument* is titled "The Jensenist Heresy" and includes the statement, "More recently, social scientists, educationists and others have condemned a *novel heresy,* called 'Jensenism' by the *New York Times.*"[52] Were the matter not so serious, it would be tempting simply to be amused at a handful of scientists having discovered (and seemingly misunderstood) simple genetics, exhuming a hoary fallacy, and parading it as a statement as bold and new as the defense of a heliocentric solar system by Galileo! We hope we will be spared their rediscovery of phlogiston.

Eugenics, Racism, and IQ

The discovery of Mendel's work and the resultant rapid expansion of genetics in the early part of this century coincided with the early flowering of mental testing. It is understandable that attempts were made to co-opt both for social purposes—attempts best illustrated by enthusiasm for eugenics (the improvement of humanity by controlled breeding). A eugenics movement was started in 1904 by geneticist Charles B. Davenport. Early on, it had support both from distinguished geneticists and from rich WASPs anxious to maintain their dominance over an increasingly non-WASP nation.[53] The eugenic notions of Davenport and his friends seem preposterous in the light of modern genetic knowledge,[54] but they provided abundant ammunition for racists. After all, if one race is superior to another and the goal is to improve all of humanity, then obviously the breeding of the superior race should be encouraged and that of the inferior race discouraged.

The careers of prominent racists like Madison Grant were inextricably intertwined with the eugenics movement.[55] Grant believed, for example, that "the amount of Nordic blood in each nation is a very fair measure of its strength in war and standing in civilization."[56] He was extremely concerned with the possibility of the dilution of that precious blood by immigration or, horror of horrors, interbreeding. The eugenicist-racists held to the peculiar view that non-Nordic blood easily overpowered Nordic blood in mixtures—apparently they thought Nordics were weak-blooded![57]

It should be noted that geneticists have always hoped that their science could lead to some form of "betterment" for humanity—and that many of the greatest geneticists, among them H. J. Muller, retained a strong interest in eugenics long after publicly repudiating the pseudoscientific and racist eugenics *movement*. Today some degree of betterment *is* achieved through genetic counseling—helping people deal with the risks of bearing abnormal children (this is done only when the genetics of the situation are reasonably well known). This mild form of eugenics is pretty much the limit of what is considered scientifically and socially legitimate today. As geneticists L. L. Cavalli-Sforza and Walter Bodmer have written, "The scope for eugenics is severely limited for both theoretical and practical reasons."[58]

By the 1920s, the geneticists' support for the eugenics movement had largely evaporated in the light of growing understanding of the complexity of genetics and gene-environment interactions. Biologists such as T. H. Morgan and Raymond Pearl openly condemned the increasingly racist propaganda, joining, among others, the great anthropologist Franz Boas and the distinguished anatomist Burt Green Wilder in opposing racism in general and the idea that Blacks were inferior in particular.[59]

Lest one get the impression that outspoken scientists of the early part of this century were all on the racist side, it is important to note that Boas and Wilder, for example, did not confine their views to the scholarly literature. Wilder, for example, was appalled by the racism of Owen Wister, author of *The Virginian*. Wister, in a book called *Lady Baltimore*, had declared that while the skulls of Blacks and Whites were readily distinguishable, those of a gorilla and a Black had a "kinship which stares you in the face."[60] Wilder first tried by correspondence to get Wister to retract his statements, and then corrected Wister in *Alexander's Magazine*.

Wilder also battled in the scientific literature with his racist scientific colleagues, as did Boas. Boas recognized that combating racism in scientific journals was not enough, however. As historian Edward Beardsley put it,

Greatly concerned to widen the influence of his views, in the early twentieth century Boas began an assault on middle-class white racism that was extraordinary for a man so heavily engaged in strictly professional tasks. His ideas were presented in various forms, in newspaper and periodical articles, book reviews, and a major book of his own. The periodical pieces appeared or were noted in such journals as *Everybody's Magazine, Van Norden's Magazine, Charities and the Commons,* and *The Century,* and his articles in the *New York Sunday Times* extended his range even further.[61]

Both Boas and Wilder often appeared before civil rights groups and did everything they could to persuade Blacks that they were not doomed to inferiority. Boas and Wilder were true radicals, going against the popular racism of the day. They and those who stood with them in that period gave scientists a tradition they can be proud of, a fine counterweight to the views of racist scientists.

IQ Against Blacks: The First Round

In view of the strength and popularity of the racist eugenics movement, it is not surprising that poor performance of Blacks on IQ tests administered to draftees in World War I was interpreted as "proof" that they were innately inferior. The tests showed that the average mental age for Blacks in the army was 10.4 years, while that of Whites was 13.1 years.[62] The army test results were interpreted in a totally hereditarian and racist manner in a book by Princeton psychologist Carl C. Brigham.[63] He concluded not only that Blacks were deficient in "native or inborn intelligence" when compared to Whites, but that Whites from southern Europe ("Alpines" and "Mediterraneans") were genetically inferior to Whites from northern Europe ("Nordics"). He baldly concluded, "Our own data from the army tests indicate clearly the intellectual superiority of the Nordic race group. This superiority is confirmed by observation of this race in history."[64] Brigham warned: "The decline of American intelligence will be more rapid than the decline of the intelligence of European national groups, owing to the presence here of the negro."[65] He went on to suggest immigration restrictions and eugenic measures appropriate to prevent the "deterioration of American intelligence" and "insure a continuously progressive upward evolution."

Brigham's book, its interpretations of the army tests, and its policy suggestions were received very favorably by the psychological establishment—a striking contrast to Pope Urban VIII's reaction to Galileo's *Dialogue on the World Systems*. But then, as Leon Kamin points out, the year Brigham's book was published, Lewis Terman was elected president of the American Psychological Association[66] and Robert Yerkes, an ardent mental tester, eugenicist, and leader in psychology, had written the foreword to Brigham's book, *A Study of American Intelligence*. In that foreword, Yerkes declared, "The author presents not theories or opinions but facts. It behooves us to consider their reliability and their meaning, for no one of us as a citizen can afford to ignore the menace of race deterioration."[67] The book was well received and was a major contributor to the mass of "scientific" support for restricting immigration in the 1920s because of the "innate inferiority" of non-WASP immigrants.

But even while Brigham's work was being put to political use, other scientists began to question his interpretations of the army test results. They noticed, for instance, that not all groups of Whites performed better than all groups of Blacks. In general, Whites from northern states did better than Blacks from northern states, who in turn did better than Whites from southern states. Blacks from southern states scored lowest of all. Within states, Whites almost always did better than Blacks, the only exceptions being Kentucky and Ohio, where Blacks outscored Whites on the so-called Beta tests (given to those eliminated from the Alpha test because of relative illiteracy). Some representative median scores on the Alpha tests were:

	Black	White
Mississippi	10.25	41.20
Missouri	33.25	59.55
Ohio	48.30	67.25
Total	28.40	61.25

Thus, while the test scores of Blacks were considerably lower, psychologists were struck by the obvious environmental correlations. After all, if Blacks are irredeemably inferior to Whites, how could Blacks from Ohio score higher on the Alpha tests than Whites from nine other states? How could one explain that Ohio Blacks outscored Whites from twenty-seven states on the Beta tests?[68] The answer seemed obvious. In the southern states, then as now, the standard of living was lower, as was per capita expenditure on educational systems. Furthermore, the tests stressed verbal skills and used academic rather than vernacular terms. In short, they were loaded in favor of the socially advantaged in particular and Northerners in general.

Further work seemed to bear out an environmentalist interpretation of the results. IQ tests were given to Black and White youths in various cities. In Nashville Whites did much better than Blacks, in Chicago Whites did a little better, and in New York the scores were equal. In Los Angeles, Black scores averaged 104.7, slightly above the White test group and far above southern Blacks, who averaged around 75. Full-blooded Native Americans scored about 70, and Mexicans in the Southwest scored around 78.[69]

These results were questioned by the hereditarians. Perhaps, they said, the brightest Blacks went north, wishing to escape the oppression in Dixie. On consulting southern school records, investigators found that the average IQ of emigrants before they left the south was essentially identical with that of the rest of the Black school population.[70] They also found that the IQs of immigrant Black children in New York schools were positively correlated with the length of time that they had been in New York—the longer the children lived in that city, the higher were their scores. Furthermore, later migrants had higher scores than earlier migrants, so the positive correlation of IQ with northern time-in-residence could not be explained by earlier migrants being a more select, smarter group.

All of these results were inconsistent with a hereditarian hypothesis and consistent with an environmentalist one. As a result, in the 1930s social scientists largely reversed themselves, and most of them discarded genetic differences as an explanation of the Black-White test-score gap. Columbia University psychologist Otto Klineberg declared in 1935, "Intelligence tests may therefore not be used as measures of group differences in native ability. . . . These differences may be satisfactorily explained . . . without recourse to the hypothesis of innate racial differences in mental ability."[71] Even C. C. Brigham, the man responsible in 1923 for the extreme hereditarian interpretation of the army test scores, wrote in 1930:

For purposes of comparing individuals or groups, it is apparent that tests in the vernacular must be used only with individuals having equal opportunities to acquire the vernacular of the test. . . . Comparative studies of various national and racial groups may not be made with existing tests. . . . In particular one of the most pretentious of these comparative racial studies—the writer's own—was without foundation.[72]

The "Jensenist heresy" is, we repeat, an antique orthodoxy, discarded long ago by many of its creators. And the history of that scientific racist orthodoxy is hardly obscure—it is described in some detail, for example, in Ruth Benedict's superb book *Race: Science and Politics*, first published in 1940 and widely available in paperback.[73] Benedict's book is highly recommended to all those interested in racial problems—especially to those with dreams of propounding new heresies!

Thus psychologists and geneticists in the 1920s and 1930s retreated from positions of scientific racism that could not survive in the face of increasingly sophisticated knowledge about genetics and mental testing. But, as we have seen, the concerns that were so popular in part of the scientific community prior to 1930 linger on in the writings of Shockley, who is explicit about them, and others like Jensen, who are not quite so explicit. Jensen's statements are especially important, because he has impressive credentials as an educational psychologist. In Jensen's famous *Harvard Educational Review* article, he states:

Certain census statistics suggest that there might be forces at work which could create and widen the genetic aspect of the average difference in ability between the Negro and white populations in the United States, with the possible consequences that the improvement of educational facilities and increasing equality of opportunity will have a *decreasing* probability of producing equal achievement or continuing gains in the Negro population's ability to compete on equal terms. . . . Much more thought and research should be given to the educational and social implications of these trends for the future. Is there a danger that current welfare policies, *unaided by eugenic foresight*, could lead to the genetic enslavement of a substantial segment of our population? The possible consequences of our failure seriously to study these questions may well be viewed by future generations as our society's greatest injustice to Negro Americans.[74]

Jensen's statement may seem to reflect only a heartfelt, if misguided, concern for a possible genetic deterioration of the "Negro race." But the statement itself surely produced a smile on the face of Madison Grant's ghost, to say nothing, for example, of some assorted racists in Louisiana. In 1955, when a lawsuit was brought to integrate Louisiana public schools, the main argument used in court by the segregationists was that "white teachers could not understand the Nigra mind" and consequently could not teach them effectively. Various scientists who believed in White supremacy were quoted in support of the segregationist case.

In 1968, just *five days* after Jensen's ideas were splashed all over

Virginia newspapers, precisely the same arguments were used by the segregationists fighting suits in the Federal District Court to integrate Greensville and Caroline County schools in Virginia. This time, Jensen's theories of White mental superiority were heavily quoted by the racists in support of their views.[75] Apparently, the Jensenist "heresy" seemed not so heretical in Virginia—a state not noted for the speed with which it embraces heterodoxy!

William F. Brazziel, a psychologist with extensive teaching experience in the South, was among the first of many to question the message of Jensen's paper. Writing in the next issue of the *Harvard Educational Review* about, among other things, the use of Jensen's writings by the Virginia racists, Brazziel stated:

It will help not one bit for Jensen or the Harvard Educational Review editorial board to protest that they did not intend for Jensen's article to be used in this way. For in addition to superiority in performing conceptual cluster tricks on test sheets, the hard line segregationist is also vastly superior in his ability to bury qualifying phrases and demurrers and in his ability to distort and slant facts and batter his undereducated clientele into a complete state of hysteria where race is concerned.[76]

The well-known newspaper columnist Joseph Alsop was apparently as unimpressed by the weasel words scattered through Jensen's paper as were the segregationists. He said, "There is no use being mealy-mouthed about it. Dr. Jensen is really saying that in *addition* to the handicaps wickedly imposed by prejudice and discrimination, the average black American begins the race of life with a detectable genetic handicap."[77] But in what other way could an intelligent layman interpret a paper that cites numerous studies showing that on the average Blacks have lower IQs than Whites, goes to great lengths to demonstrate a high heritability of IQ, and then concludes: "The techniques for raising intelligence . . . probably lie more in the province of the biological sciences than in psychology or education"?[78]

Why Does Racism Persist?

It takes little stretch of the imagination to understand why the notions that the earth was flat and that the sun revolved around it were so persistent. They, after all, tend to be the hypotheses formed by children, hypotheses that are later destroyed by experience with the accumulated knowledge of our culture. Society corrects a fallacious world view.

The situation with racism is not very different, in that children form hypotheses about different races and are quick to judge others unfavorably. However, societal attitudes more often than not support the childish prejudices rather than correct them.

Incipient racial prejudice first rears its ugly head in the behavior of 3- and-4-year-olds who use ethnically related terms, not always consistently or completely accurately, to label and evaluate (usually to derogate) others. Children learn societal values early and well: both Black and White preschoolers prefer Whites and deprecate Blacks.[79] By school age, children evaluate their own group positively—Blacks prefer Blacks and Whites prefer Whites.[80] Clear increases in prejudice of Whites against other groups (Blacks, Chinese, Mexicans, Jews) are recorded during the school years.

How do children come to manifest prejudice? Their thoughts, feelings, and attitudes about minority groups do not come out of the blue. They come from the social and cultural contexts the children grow up in. Children pick up cues given by adults, especially their parents, by other children, and from the mass media. But more than passive acceptance of commonly held attitudes is involved in ethnic prejudice: in many regions (the South, for example), each member is *expected* to adhere to these attitudes, and pressures and penalties are brought to bear on those who deviate.

Where the cultural value is one of racial equality, that, too, is transmitted to children. In the 1930s, children living in a cooperative housing project occupied by people with a strong belief in the equality of races showed none of the racial prejudice manifested by other children.[81]

But social and cultural materials are filtered through the personal, psychological makeup of each individual. Certain personality characteristics have been described as occurring in the strongly prejudiced, including low self-esteem, a certain rigidity and inflexibility, greater conventionality in values, a status and power orientation in relationship to other people. People with these traits are called "authoritarian personalities."[82]

It has also been found that when faced with frustration, people bottling up inside them a flood of hostility and aggression direct their hostility onto vulnerable minority groups in the form of prejudice.[83] It is assumed that ethnic minority groups become the target because they are visible, of low status, and socially sanctioned as targets of aggression.

In short, society manufactures racists, and continues to do so in spite of the massive evidence that racism is not only unsupportable scientifically but maladaptive. The promotion of xenophobia within tribal groups may once have had survival value, but it is clearly not conducive to the health of large, complex, technologically advanced societies.

Why, then, does racism persist? An easy answer is that the racists profit from it. In the United States, for example, Blacks own only one-tenth of the businesses they would own if Blacks were represented among businesspersons in proportion to their representation in the American population.[84] The amount of Black control of business enterprises, both those serving the public at large and those serving the Black community, is pathetically tiny, and the system as it now functions perpetuates the anti-Black bias. It is, for instance, very difficult for a Black businessman to obtain credit, a situation not helped by the vanishingly small portion of the financial institutions of the nation controlled by Blacks.[85] Blacks also tend to be excluded from craft unions and desirable positions in industrial unions.[86] Whites therefore profit disproportionately from the economic activities of the nation and are in a position to maintain their dominance. Sociologist Harold M. Baron summed up the situation:

In [the American] capitalistic economy black people are cut off from the sources of power, wealth and influence that come from the control of corporate enterprises. In a society such as ours where wealth and ownership are the most enduring sources of power, such exclusion will limit the strength and opportunities of a group in many noneconomic areas of the society.[87]

It would be convenient, then, to lay the blame for continuing racism on the money-grubbing slumlords, "blockbusting" real-estate agents, greedy White businessmen selling overpriced goods to ghetto residents, White union members afraid for their jobs, and so on. But, although these elements doubtless contribute to the perpetuation of American racism, they seem to be only part of the story. Much of the rest of the story may be a mix of the dominance of sight among human senses and of a syndrome that our civilization has been trying to escape for the last 200 years—social class as birthright.

As already indicated, human beings like to make visual distinctions —and indeed go to great lengths to establish such distinctions. A moment's reflection on the role of clothing in society—uniforms, academic regalia, dress styles, and so on—reveals the extremes to which groups of people will go to achieve visual differentiation. When individuals feel they belong to a subgroup in society, a group defined by job, social class, financial position, religion, sex or what have you, there is a tendency to make that membership visually evident. It is not surprising, then, that an obvious physical difference like skin color should be commonly "read" as socially meaningful (and that the converse should occur—that imaginary physical differences should be created for groups defined on other bases).

Until the Democratic Revolution of the last quarter of the eighteenth century and the early years of the nineteenth, the notion of social class as birthright was never seriously challenged. In the prescientific age, the model for comparison was the hierarchy, with the many and the bad occupying the lower tiers and the good and the few at the apex. This is the way Dante arranged heaven and hell, and the way the prescientific mind analyzed the world. This way of thinking has many vestiges. On the surface, the Parliament of England still reflects a nation divided into Lords and Commoners. And racists, scientific or otherwise, still see humanity divided into inferior and superior races distinguished by color (just as in the Middle Ages the inferior peasantry were always portrayed as swarthy and dark-haired while nobility was always light and blond).

The prescientific view of society had certain things to commend it. Not the least of these was that people did not feel obliged to deny the existence of inequality or to explain it away. Inequality was not considered undesirable. The idea of social class as birthright permeated custom and law. The most potent determinant of one's level in the social hierarchy was the "bloodline." The human pedigree was a carefully guarded piece of property, and every nation in Europe had its College of Heralds that kept the pedigrees straight, along with the attendant rights and coats of arms for those who benefited from this hereditarianism.[88]

The Democratic Revolution did much to wash away the idea of innate worth and privilege. The much misunderstood declaration that "all men are created equal" was Jefferson's challenge to the prescientific sociology, which recognized men not as individuals but as members of hereditary categories with different rights and privileges.

Bonaparte declared that every one of his soldiers carried a marshal's baton in his knapsack; that is, advancement could be based on ability.

His egalitarianism may well have traced to his being forbidden from rising above the rank of captain when he entered the French army. Napoleon's pedigree barred him from senior command. It is interesting that his army, or a considerable portion of it, was utterly trounced by a Haitian insurrectionary named Toussaint L'Ouverture, who was Black. According to one reasonable interpretation, Napoleon's inability to deal with the Haitian revolt was the first step on the road to Waterloo. Maybe he assumed that Blacks were color-coded for defeat.

As science began to play an increasingly large role in human affairs, it was only natural that some individuals would attempt to use scientific methods to confirm prescientific views of innate worth. Today's hereditarians are, in fact, representatives of a long tradition of attempting the impossible—the establishment of qualitative distinctions through the use of scientific measures.

As the nineteenth century progressed, quantification began to replace qualitative argument in determining the nature of things. The hierarchic model for nature and society gave way to the continuum. One problem with the continuum as a model for understanding the universe and all of its parts is signaled by its very name. There are no clear dividing lines, no points of graduation from one condition to another. In the spectrum of light, there is no identifiable point where red turns to purple. Similarly, there is no identifiable dollar amount that divides rich from poor, and yet rich and poor seem qualitatively distinct.

The problem is created by our overly high expectations of quantitative measures. If a large sample of American families was examined from widely diverse positions on the income continuum, families and individuals would be found with pride, ambition, self-esteem, and love. Others would be found to be bickering, shot through with greed, or indolent. It is quite likely that these qualities would be remarkably evenly distributed along the income scale, that is, that income would be a poor measure of attributes that many consider to have overriding importance. We cannot, however, test the relationship of these attributes to income because there are no objective measures of decency, sloth, pride, self-esteem, or love. This is not to say they lack meaningful existence, just that at the moment (and possibly forever) they are unmeasurable.

That worth cannot be measured has not, however, dissuaded the measurers. Over and over again in the last century and a half, pseudoscience has marshaled its measuring sticks in the service of maintaining old, qualitative systems of categorization, which the very measurement destroys. Once an IQ continuum is created, the categories of smart and stupid disappear. The prescientific view of innately superior and inferior humans has outlived the failure of science to find anything measurable in groups of "lesser" human beings that would validate their assumed inferiority. After all, in the case of Blacks, all one had to do was look at their skin and one knew they were different. And if they were different in such a basic, perceptible characteristic as skin color, must not that skin color be related predictably and measurably to their generally inferior condition?

So at the bicentennial of the intellectual demolition of ideas of group inferiority and superiority, we still find the measurers, armed with IQ tests, searching for truths they know are there. After decades of trying, they are undaunted by their failure. Racism and racists are, indeed, persistent.[89]

4

Intelligence and Intelligence Tests

Since questions that did not predict progress in reading, arithmetic, and composition were purposely omitted from the intelligence test, it is not surprising that a high IQ score predicts school and college grades. . . . The causal relation between IQ and eventual success has been turned on its head. It is argued that teachers and lawyers have higher intelligence than cab drivers or house painters because they possess biologically better nervous systems, rather than because the circumstances of their rearing familiarized them with the language and class of problems presented on the IQ test and nurtured the motivation to solve those problems.
—Jerome Kagan, *Social Policy*, 1973

STARTING AT BIRTH, most Americans are constantly measured and their abilities constantly assessed. If born in a modern hospital, an infant is weighed and measured, and its vital functions (including breathing effort, muscle tone, heart rate, reflex irritability, and color) are assessed by a single numerical score before it is ten minutes old. A great deal of information about the body is thus summarized in three numbers. In a society obsessed with measurement, it is not surprising that efforts are also made to assess mental functioning and to summarize it in a number, which then becomes part of the description of a person.

Scores allow comparisons between individuals, whether the comparison be in height, blood pressure, running speed, or performance on a driver's license exam. There is usually no difficulty in judging who is the tallest child in a group or who won a race without taking precise measurements, but such comparisons include only people who are present at that particular time. They might not be an accurate reflection of a person's standing in some other group. If assessments were based only on comparisons of people with those around them, one would conclude that a 6-foot 3-inch basketball player was short if the average height of the team were 6 feet 8 inches.

Not all measurements become an important part of an individual's description. For example, body temperature is not a prominent statistic—perhaps because there is little variation from one healthy human being to another or because it fluctuates with the time of day and the health of the person. On the other hand, blood pressure exhibits more variability from person to person, and while it often is part of a medical description, it is unimportant in an individual's general description and is not prominently involved in social decisions.

Throughout history and from culture to culture, societies differ in the attributes they value and the social criteria by which they assess each person's adequacy. Piety and good works were emphasized by the Calvinists; courage, chivalry, and bravery in battle earned a man status and prestige in medieval Europe. On the American frontier, endurance and toughness were valued. In contrast, skill at hunting and storytelling tend to be highly prized among Eskimo men, and obesity is valued among Tonganese women. Industrial society has prized, among other things, the ability to solve problems. Although mental agility has not always been valued as highly as it is today, most languages contain words for cleverness and foolishness, implying that there is a widespread and enduring belief in the existence of some ability to adapt to new situations, to solve problems, and to cope intellectually with the demands of life. Psychologists have tried to summarize and quantify these abilities, which they collectively call intelligence.

What Is Intelligence?

Intelligence means so many different things that it defies a simple dictionary-type definition. It is more accurate to talk about intelligent behavior than about intelligence, for the very use of the noun "intelligence" suggests it is a "thing" rather than an abstraction inferred from actions to describe the way people behave. But there are difficulties even with this approach, for there is no behavior that by itself can be called "intelligent." Any activity, whether it be philosophizing or dish-washing, can be performed intelligently or stupidly. The term "intel-ligent" is not restricted to performance on highly abstract problems, but is applied to competent handling of such an enormous array of tasks that it is impossible to list them.

In light of these difficulties, the essence of intelligence has remained elusive. Alfred Binet, the father of intelligence testing, thought that the tendency to maintain a definite direction in thinking and to make adaptations for the purpose of attaining a desired end was at the heart of the concept. The American psychologist David Wechsler, who con-structed several widely used intelligence tests, defined intelligence as the capacity to act purposefully, think rationally, and to deal effec-tively with the environment. But no definition of intelligence has been adopted universally. In general, definitions stress either ability to adapt to the environment, the capacity to learn, or the ability to think abstractly.[1] Like the word *love*, *intelligence* remains a term we all have a feel for but cannot quite pin down.

What is the structure of intelligence? Is there one general intelli-gence, or are there many different special intelligences? Do people show peaks and troughs in different abilities? Is intelligence merely the sum of many component abilities? Should some abilities be considered more important than others in the definition of intelligence—or should they all be weighted equally? How many different abilities are there?

One common view of intelligence concerns a capacity to compre-hend, reason, and solve abstract problems. These capacities generally involve language, and consequently verbal skills are given more im-portance in defining and measuring intelligence than nonverbal skills. There is some agreement that there exists a general or overall intel-ligence—people who are very bright tend to do well on many tasks and in many (but not by any means all) situations. In addition, there are special abilities (or intelligences)—some people have fantastic numerical skills, being able to do complex arithmetic problems almost instantly without paper and pencil; others are talented in manipulating and visualizing geometric relations and transformations. No clear an-swer exists as to how many special abilities or groups of abilities can be identified. In the late 1930s, the American psychologist, L. L. Thurstone, using complex statistical analyses, identified seven special abilities—verbal comprehension, word fluency, number ability, spatial ability, memory, perceptual speed, and reasoning. But these special abilities can in turn be further subdivided. In fact, each researcher of the structure of intelligence comes up with a different number of abilities. The net effect is a bewildering array of described abilities, ranging from 2 to 120. Small wonder, then, that despite the common-sense view and the statistical findings that suggest multiple abilities, many social scientists work with a theory of general intelligence.

To avoid the problems inherent in defining intelligence, psychologists have adopted a pragmatic position. The purpose, the *raison d'être*, of intelligence tests has been defined not by some theoretical notion of intelligence, but by the success tests have in predicting present and future performance in academic and related areas. *Intelligence, then, is whatever the tests measure, and the adequacy of tests resides in the ability to make accurate predictions.*

If the definition of intelligence remains elusive, if scientists and others cannot agree on the nature of intelligence nor on the underlying processes involved, is the concept worth retaining? How can one presume to measure what cannot be defined? In physics, scientists work comfortably with the concept of gravity, yet in the final analysis they do not understand the process involved—that is, how it works. They can measure the effects of gravity, and many consistent relationships concerning gravity have been described. Both the concept of gravity and the concept of intelligence are useful because they allow prediction and help scientists to make sense of a large body of empirical findings, findings based on experiments or observations rather than on theories. But when concepts like intelligence and gravity are treated as things rather than as abstractions, scientists give the appearance of having explained sets of observations when they have really only given them a label.

Measurement of Intelligence

Without a clear definition of intelligence and in the absence of an understanding of the mechanisms and the processes by which intelligent acts are done and decisions made, intelligence is defined comparatively. Persons who perform better at an array of problem-solving tests are judged to be more intelligent than those who do less well.

There are several dangers inherent in using such a definition of intelligence. Who turns out to be intelligent depends upon the problems (often called "items" by psychologists) selected for the intelligence test, and upon the sample of people used for comparison. For example, tests such as the Stanford-Binet and the Wechsler, the tests most commonly administered to individuals, generally contain many different kinds of items. Although there is no theoretical guidance to help in their selection, experience has provided strong guidelines to ensure that the test accomplishes what its designer intended. One of the key guidelines is whether or not the score on the test permits the making of reasonably accurate predictions about behavior society considers important—for instance, the chances that a student will do well in school. If the scores do that, then IQ tests serve a useful purpose, regardless of what "intelligence" really is.

The assumptions underlying the design of an IQ test reveal the test author's view of intelligence and, by inference, the author's view of what society considers important. Since the test score becomes part of a person's description, and influences what gates are opened for that person in the educational and vocational world, the assumptions merit close scrutiny. The popular Stanford-Binet test, for example, is based on four broad assumptions.

The first assumption is that intelligence is a *general ability* and should be manifest in diverse tasks. Many different types of ability are assessed, although no single question on the test or no single ability is important in and of itself. For example, being able to recall a string of ten numbers in the reverse of the order in which they were heard (an actual problem on the Stanford-Binet) is not a very useful skill. However, it has been found that people generally considered "bright" or "clever" in our society can recite the numbers backward, while others have difficulty, and therefore such tasks are included in an intelligence test. Because it is assumed that intelligence pervades many areas of intellectual functioning, tests are designed so that those who score well on a given item will also tend to score well on the test as a whole. In Table 4–1, some typical items used in the Stanford-Binet are described.[2]

Asking for definitions recurs at different age levels of the test. For instance, at age 5 the words a child is asked to define are generally common nouns such as *ball* and *hat*. By age 8, words such as *roar* and *eyelash* are included. Twelve-year-olds are expected to define *brunette* and *revenge*. Adults are asked to define such words as *tolerate* and *lotus*. Also at different age levels, knowledge of similarities and differ-

TABLE 4-1

Typical Items from the Stanford-Binet Intelligence Test

Age 2	Age 5	Age 11	Adult
1. Formboard: putting cutouts back in a board.	1. Completing a drawing of a man.	1. Drawing geometric designs.	1. Defining vocabulary.
2. Finding hidden object after seeing it hidden under one of two boxes.	2. Folding paper into a triangle.	2. Discerning verbal absurdities in a story.	2. Ingenuity or problem solving involving simple arithmetic.
3. Identifying parts of body.	3. Definitions of words.	3. Defining abstract words.	3. Giving differences between abstract words.
4. Building a tower with two blocks.	4. Copying a square.	4. Reproducing exactly a heard sentence.	4. Arithmetical reasoning.
5. Picture vocabulary.	5. Deciding whether two pictures are same or different.	5. Drawing inferences from a story.	5. Interpreting proverbs.
6. Word combinations from spontaneous speech.	6. Putting two triangles together to make a square.	6. Describing similarities among three objects.	6. Orientation to directions (north, south, east, west).
			7. Giving differences between words.
			8. Defining abstract words.

ences in meaning are tested: for example, *bird* and *dog* (age 6), *ocean* and *river* (age 8), *winter* and *summer* (age 15), *poverty* and *misery* (adult).

Nonverbal problems also appear, especially at the younger ages. For example, the 3-year-old is asked to sort different colored buttons, the 5-year-old is asked to fold a rectangular sheet of paper into a triangle after he or she has observed an adult do the task, the 7-year-old is required to copy a diamond shape, the 9-year-old is asked to anticipate how a folded sheet of paper with a piece cut out of it would look if it were unfolded, and the 13-year-old is asked to remember and reproduce a chain of nine beads containing three shapes in a fixed order (e.g., □○◯⬜○□○⬜○).

In addition to assuming that intelligence is a general ability, the Stanford-Binet IQ test assumes that intelligent people learn from everyday experience. Testing is supposed to identify ability independent of environmental advantage. Throughout history and in different cultures, educational, occupational, and financial rewards, together with status and prestige, have been assigned on the basis of wealth or social class: only the rich or wellborn had the advantages; others were doomed to poverty and ignorance. It is functionally impossible to measure ability independent of the environment in which it was nurtured; however, designers of tests have tried to find items that minimize cultural and environmental advantage. There are two possible strategies: one is to present totally unfamiliar problems and see how rapidly and competently the tasks (such as memorizing nonsense syllables) are mastered. A second strategy, and one adopted in the Stanford-Binet, is to try to find tasks to which everyone in a specific culture has been exposed. For example, asking testees to play one of Mozart's piano sonatas would be unsuitable, since many people have never learned to play the piano. Knowledge of the days of the week and how to count blocks (both actual items on the Stanford-Binet) meet the criterion of wide cultural exposure much better; yet, again, previous cultural exposure to these tasks is unlikely to be equal among all groups within the culture.

Folding paper to make a triangle or copying a drawing of a square or a diamond is probably even better. Not only are these shapes familiar to all segments of society, but these tasks are extremely difficult to teach before the child is developmentally ready. But there are other cases, such as with vocabulary, where it is harder to argue that most people in the culture have had equal exposure. Words such as "juggler" or "lecture" are probably not heard as often in rural areas as they are in suburban or urban areas. While most existing IQ tests seem to show that urban and suburban children score better than rural children of the same age, it is possible to construct a test using items of general information that favor rural children. In 1929, psychologist Myra Shimberg made up two information tests—one favored urban schoolchildren, the other favored rural children.[3] Children from the cities were better at answering questions such as "How can banks afford to pay interest on the money you deposit?" while rural children did better on items such as "Of what is butter made?" "Name a vegetable that grows above ground," and "How often do we have a full moon?"

Recently, Adrian Dove devised the "Chitling Test of Intelligence"[4] as a half-serious idea to demonstrate that if the language and concepts of Blacks in the Watts area of Los Angeles were used in a test, most Whites would perform poorly. Part of the Chitling Test is shown in Table 4–2. That most college students have difficulty with the questions on this test suggests that common experience is in fact difficult to define. At least some of the differences in intelligence supposed to exist between urban and rural children or Blacks and Whites are due not to genuine differences in ability to profit from the environment, but from cultural biases found in tests, that is, from the choice of test items that occur more frequently in middle-class urban environments.

There has been some attempt to devise IQ tests that show less cultural bias than the traditional ones. Most of these rely on a minimum of language in giving instructions and in the answers required. For example, in the Goodenough-Harris Drawing Test, children's drawings of a man or a woman are assessed for the amount of detail and basic structure portrayed (Figure 4–1). Pueblo Indian children, who score lower than White children on almost all tests, score 20 points higher than White children from New Mexico on the Draw-a-Horse test, a variant of the Draw-a-Person test. These findings suggest that cultural values influence the salience of objects in the environment, and therefore tests are never assessing underlying intelligence *per se*, for performance is always influenced by the *content* of the item.

A third assumption of the Stanford-Binet is that mental competence increases with age. Older children solve more problems, know more information, and reason better than younger children. Increasing competence with age has been summarized in the notion of *mental*

TABLE 4–2
Sample Items from Dove's Chitling Test of Intelligence

The following 15 items are taken from an "intelligence test" developed by Adrian Dove, a social worker in Watts. The test is slanted toward a non-White, lower-class experience. The whole test has 29 items. According to Dove, a score below 20 suggests a low ghetto IQ. Dove says, "As white middle class educators put it, you are 'culturally deprived.'"

---

1. T-Bone Walker got famous for playing what?
   - (a) Trombone
   - (b) Piano
   - (c) "T-Flute"
   - (d) Guitar
   - (e) "Hambone"
2. Who did "Slugger Lee" kill (in the famous blues legend)?
   - (a) His mother
   - (b) Frankie
   - (c) His girlfriend
   - (d) Billy
3. A "Gas Head" is a person who has a _____.
   - (a) Fast-moving car
   - (b) Stable of "lace"
   - (c) "Process"
   - (d) Habit of stealing cars
   - (e) Long jail record for arson
4. If a man is called a "Blood," then he is a _____.
   - (a) Fighter
   - (b) Mexican-American
   - (c) Negro
   - (d) Hungry hemophile
   - (e) Redman or Indian
5. If you throw the dice and "7" is showing on the top, what is facing down?
   - (a) Seven
   - (b) "Snake eyes"
   - (c) "Boxcars"
   - (d) "Little Joes"
   - (e) Eleven
6. Jazz pianist Ahmad Jamal took an Arabic name after becoming famous. Previously, he had some fame with what he called his "slave name." What was his previous name?
   - (a) Willie Lee Jackson
   - (b) LeRoi Jones
   - (c) Wilbur McDougal
   - (d) Fritz Jones
   - (e) "Cheatin' Charles" (the "Boxcar Gunsel")
7. Cheap chitlings (not the kind you purchase at a frozen food counter) will taste rubbery unless they are cooked long enough. How soon can you quit cooking them to eat and enjoy them?
   - (a) 15 minutes
   - (b) 2 hours
   - (c) 24 hours
   - (d) 1 week (on a low flame)
   - (e) 1 hour
8. "Down Home" (the South today for the average "soul Brother" who is picking cotton in season from sunup until sundown) what is the average earning (take-home) for one full day?

(a) $0.75
(b) $1.00
(c) $3.50
(d) $5.00
(e) $12.00

9. If a judge finds you guilty of "holding wood" (in California) what's the most he can give you?
(a) Indeterminate (life)
(b) A nickel
(c) A dime
(d) A year in the County
(e) $10.00

10. "Bird" or "Yardbird" was the jacket that jazz lovers from coast to coast hung on _____.
(a) Lester Young
(b) Peggy Lee
(c) Benny Goodman
(d) Charlie Parker
(e) "Birdman of Alcatraz"

11. A "hypo" is a person who _____.
(a) Always says he feels sickly
(b) Has water on the brain
(c) Uses heroin
(d) Is always ripping and running
(e) Is always sick

12. Hattie Mae Johnson is on the County. She has four children and her husband is now in jail for nonsupport, as he was unemployed and was not able to give her any money. Her welfare check is now 236.00 dollars per month. Last night she went out with the highest player in town. If she got pregnant, then nine months from now, how much more will her welfare check be?
(a) $ 80.00
(b) $ 2.00
(c) $ 35.00
(d) $150.00
(e) $100.00

13. "Hully Gully" came from _____.
(a) "East Oakland"
(b) Fillmore
(c) Watts
(d) Harlem
(e) Motor City

14. What is Will Mae's last name?
(a) Schwartz
(b) Matauda
(c) Gomez
(d) Turner
(e) O'Flaherty

15. The opposite of square is _____.
(a) Round
(b) Up
(c) Down
(d) Hip
(e) Lame

Answers. 1. d, 2. d, 3. c, 4. c, 5. a, 6. d, 7. c, 8. d, 9. c, 10. d,
11. c, 12. c, 13. c, 14. d, 15. d.

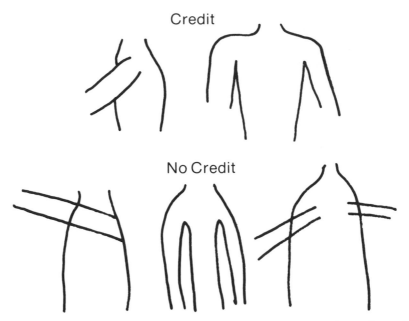

Figure 4-1.   Illustration of scoring of drawings done by children taking the Goodenough-Harris Drawing Test. (Adapted from D. B. Harris. *Children's Drawings As Measures of Intellectual Maturity.* New York: Harcourt, Brace, 1963.)

age. In fact, the alignment of mental and chronological age originally formed the basis of the IQ score. When mental age and chronological age correspond, the child has average intelligence. Retardation is indicated by a mental age significantly lower than the chronological age, and children with superior intelligence have mental ages in advance of their chronological age.

To ensure that his intelligence test reflected more advanced functioning with age, Binet selected only items that could be successfully passed by progressively more children as they became older. Singing in tune or being able to discriminate pitch would therefore not be suitable, for there is no systematic improvement with age. A good item at the 9-year level consists of showing two simple geometric designs for ten seconds, then asking people to reproduce from memory what they saw. Older children do better than younger ones: approximately 5 percent of 6-year-olds, 50 to 60 percent of 9-year-olds, and 90 to 100 percent of 11-year-olds are successful. Each item is assigned to the age level where between 50 and 70 percent of children pass it.

In the Stanford-Binet test, items are arranged in age-scales: at six-month intervals between ages 2 and 5, at twelve-month intervals between ages 6 and 14, and two adult scales. Each subtest is arranged so that not only is each item age-appropriate, but each age-level scale consisting of six subtests must be passed by approximately half the children of the appropriate age.

The fourth important assumption of the Stanford-Binet and many other tests is that males and females should perform equally well. Consequently, questions are selected so that there is no difference in overall score earned by the two sexes. It turns out in practice to be difficult to make each question satisfy this requirement—so in the test some items favor boys (usually those involving spatial orientation) and some favor girls (often verbal exercises). At each age level, however, the test is designed so that sample groups of males and females get the same average scores.

In the better-known tests, there are, therefore, some safeguards in the selection of items to ensure that what is measured is not based solely on the whim of the test constructor. While the theoretical underpinnings of intelligence testing remain weak, the requirement that tests predict socially important and academically related behavior, together with the methodological and statistical requirements that surround the selection of test items, gives the tests a usefulness, albeit limited, in our society.

Intelligence tests by no means assess all important intellectual abilities. Conspicuously absent are problems requiring *creative solutions.* Instead, the answers to the questions are clearly right or wrong, a necessity for objective scoring. The time constraints in administering an intelligence test (rarely are more than two or three sessions of forty-five to fifty minutes used, and often there is only a single session) are such that only problems with readily obtainable solutions can be used. In real life, many problems yield only to long-sustained attacks. It is not uncommon, for example, for scientists or executives in industry to work many months on a given problem. Finally, in a testing situation, the questions are always posed to the person being tested—the testee rarely if ever has to pose questions. This can be contrasted to the type of intelligence needed by a detective, for instance, who in order to solve a case must be able to raise important questions. These abilities, creativity, sustained problem-solving, and question-raising, are just a few of the intellectual abilities not assessed by a conventional IQ test.

Administering and Scoring an IQ Test

In administering an IQ test such as the Stanford-Binet, the tester first tries to put the child (or adult) at his or her ease. In the course of chatting, the tester decides where to start the test. He or she has to find the *basal age*—the age-scale at which the child can pass all the subtests. All the age-scales except one have six subtests (see Table 4–1, for example), each of which contains three or four items of a similar kind. To pass a subtest, it is necessary to answer correctly most, but not necessarily all, of the items. The test manual indicates what constitutes a pass for each subtest. For example, the 7-year age-scale contains a subtest on similarities of two things. Four items appear on this subtest, but the child is only required to pass two of them in order to be credited with success.

Having located the basal age, the tester continues to administer each of the subtests on all the age-scales until the child has failed all of the subtests (but not necessarily all of the problems on all of the subtests) on a particular age-scale. This is called the *ceiling*, and at this point the testing is terminated.

In scoring the test, the basal-age scale defines the number of years (and months) credited to the child. For each additional subtest passed, 2 months of credit are given. All these credits are summed to yield the mental age. For example, suppose a child passes all the subtests for age 5, passes four out of six for age 6, three out of six for age 7, one of six for age 8, and none for age 9. The basal age is 5 years, to this are added 8 months credit for age 6, 6 months for age 7, and 2 months for age 8, yielding a total mental age of 6 years 4 months.

Originally, the mental age (MA) was converted to IQ (intelligence quotient) by the following formula:

$$IQ = \frac{\text{mental age}}{\text{chronological age}} \times 100$$

In the above example, if the child was 6 years 4 months old,

$$IQ = \frac{6 \text{ yrs } 4 \text{ mos}}{6 \text{ yrs } 4 \text{ mos}} \times 100 = 100$$

If the child was 5 years 10 months old,

$$IQ = \frac{6 \text{ yrs } 4 \text{ mos}}{5 \text{ yrs } 10 \text{ mos}} \times 100 = 109$$

If the child was 7 years 6 months old,

$$IQ = \frac{6 \text{ yrs } 4 \text{ mos}}{7 \text{ yrs } 6 \text{ mos}} \times 100 = 84$$

Today, IQs are not calculated in this way. Instead, the mental age of a child is compared to the mental age of others of the same chronological age. Tables of norms and IQ scores have been constructed so that it is possible to locate a person's IQ score from information about mental age and chronological age. In practice, the original calculation $\frac{\text{mental age}}{\text{chronological age}} \times 100$ and the modern calculation yield highly similar results.

Other major intelligence tests do not use mental age as the basis for scoring performance. For example, the Wechsler tests score the number of correct answers and, using tables, convert that into an IQ.

IQ As a Comparative Measure

An IQ score gives information about the ranking of a given individual compared to others of the same age and the same culture. An IQ of 100 indicates average performance—50 percent of the population perform the same or better and 50 percent perform at or below the same level. An IQ of 148 indicates a performance better than that of 99.8 percent of the population. An IQ score therefore differs from inches, meters, kilograms, or ounces, which give the exact length or weight of an object. An IQ score does *not* give an absolute measure of anything. A 4-year-old, a 12-year-old, and an adult with the same IQ score possess different information, solve different problems, and reason in different ways. An 8-year-old with an IQ of 75 passes more items on an IQ test than a 4-year-old with an IQ of 120 or a 3-year-old with an IQ of 140.

Even when children of the same age are compared, an IQ score tells little about their particular intellectual strengths and weaknesses. Ten 5-year-olds with the same IQ could produce ten different patterns of items passed. In the better IQ tests, examination of the profile of responses does yield to the skillful tester relevant information concerning peaks and troughs of intellectual competence, but this information does not appear in the summary IQ scores.

The IQ score is, above all, an age-relevant comparison making use of age standards of performance. What defines average, superior, or inferior performance is based on the performance of a very large sample of children or adults. The Stanford-Binet has been standardized three times—in 1916, 1937, and 1960. The 1960 sample, comprised of 4,500 children, was carefully chosen to be representative of the population. Included in the sample were people from different geographic regions; urban, rural, and suburban communities; different social strata within communities; and Blacks as well as Whites. *Norms* were calculated from this standardization sample—that is, the scores were organized from lowest to highest, so that one could see how frequently each score was earned. Because of the way the items were selected the results form a bell-shaped curve; most children received scores in the middle range, a smaller number got medium-high or medium-low scores, and very few showed extremely high or extremely low scores.[5]

By convention, the average score for each age group is called IQ 100, and due to the statistical properties of the bell-shaped curve, the cutoff points between average, medium-high, and medium-low scores are defined so that the average section contains 68 percent of the group. The cutoff points are 16 IQ points apart (in some tests, they are 15 IQ points apart).

The advantage of having norms is that children of different ages can be compared to each other, even though they obtain different numbers of correct answers. As long as they occupy similar positions in relation to their age-mates, they are judged equal in IQ. In addition, the norms enable comparisons of a given child with *all* potential age-mates, not just with age-mates in the same neighborhood.

The potential for comparison with the general population can be very important. For example, in an upper-middle-class suburb, teachers in a nursery school were concerned that one of the girls was slow—compared to the other children in the class, she seemed one or two years behind in mental and physical skills. A psychologist administered IQ tests and found the child entirely in the normal range, with an IQ over 100. She needed neither to be retained in nursery school an additional year nor to be given remedial help. Yet the teachers' observations were also correct—the child's performance was lagging behind that of her classmates. It turned out that the average IQ in that nursery school was 135, and from years of working with such children, the teachers had acquired biased notions concerning average development.[6]

An IQ score has meaning only when the test is given under standard conditions to people who *are drawn from the same general population on which the test was standardized*. Grave errors and terrible abuses have resulted from administering the tests to people for whom it was not intended, as in the cases of the immigrants and the Chicano children described earlier.

The standardization sample is important, for it specifies the groups for whom the items are appropriate. One would not conclude that Australian aborigines had lower intelligence than Americans because they could not identify the average height of American men nor interpret the proverb, "Don't judge a book by its cover." Americans would not want to be judged, in turn, by items appropriate for the aborigines, such as interpreting from a trace of a paw print in the desert what animal had passed by, how long ago, and the state of its health. An intelligence test assesses an individual's adaptation to his or her own environment, and the standardization sample specifies the cultural and physical environment on which the test is based.

Types of Tests

Not all IQ tests are alike. Some are administered on a one-to-one basis, and some are administered to groups. Intelligence tests for individuals, such as the Stanford-Binet and Wechsler scales, are administered by trained psychologists in a clinical-type setting, where the tester not only records the answers given by the testee, but also records information concerning the testee's mood, the amount of effort exerted, whether the testee is tense or relaxed, and so forth. Furthermore, in the course of testing, the tester has an opportunity to repeat misunderstood items (following carefully specified directions).

Group tests are generally paper-and-pencil tests given to many people at the same time. Frequently, they are not given by a person specially trained in test administration. They take no account of the mood or attitude of the person taking the test, have no provision for correcting any misunderstanding of the tasks, and usually depend on the ability to read and write. In the extreme, group tests may be administered in the most absurd of conditions. In one case, the SAT (Scholastic Aptitude Test) was given to a group of students, some of whom had to arise at 5:30 A.M., get to their schools at 7:00, to ride school buses for two hours to arrive at the testing site at 9:00, for a test commencing at 9:30. Other students had only a ten-minute walk from their homes. The test was not administered according to instructions from the Educational Testing Service. Because of administrative confusion, one group of students went to the wrong room and then were sent late to the proper room. All in the second room were given an extra ten minutes to finish, giving the late-comers less than the prescribed time and the earlybirds more—on a timed segment of the test![7]

Group tests may serve a useful function when large numbers of people have to be tested in a short period of time, but there is an increased chance of inaccurate scores. As a gross screening device, they can be justified only if *all* the testees who achieved very low scores or very high scores are given individual tests before being placed in special programs or before other action is taken based on the test results.

What a person is capable of doing and what he or she might be able to do if given appropriate training are two different things and should not be confused. This is the distinction between achievement and ability. We do not expect a predental student to know how to extract teeth, nor a starting electrician's apprentice to know how to wire a house. But we do expect that they each have *potential* ability to do these things and to profit from instruction and experience. Tests that measure potential capacities, that predict what an individual might accomplish, are called *aptitude* or *ability tests*. Tests that measure what one can do now are called *achievement tests*. Intelligence tests are general aptitude (ability) tests because they are designed to predict performance over a broad range of situations. A school test in science is an achievement test, for it measures what the student knows on the basis of the instruction given.

Predicting School Performance and Occupation from Measures of Mental Ability

Today, the major justification for the use of intelligence tests is their power to predict something important about future success in school and school-related areas, such as occupation. The score on an IQ test predicts future school performance with moderate success.

In discussing how accurate such prediction is, a statistical device known as the *correlation coefficient* is commonly used. Correlation coefficients are used to measure the degree of relationship between two varying quantities (variables). A coefficient of 0 means that there is no relationship at all—for instance, knowing the day's rainfall in San Francisco allows one to predict nothing about the Dow-Jones stock average. A correlation coefficient of +1 means there is a perfect relationship, such that knowing one variable (e.g., size of a cube of gold) means you can predict exactly the value of the other variable (e.g., weight of the cube). Similarly, a coefficient of −1 means there is a perfect negative (inverse) relationship—such as between the amount of water in a glass and the remaining capacity of the glass. A correlation coefficient can be +1 or −1 or any value in between. The higher the absolute value, the greater the relationship. The nearer the value is to zero, the less relationship exists.

For most purposes, a correlation coefficient of .5 or .6 (positive or negative) is required before the relationship would have practical predictive value. Suppose, for example, IQ were found to correlate at a level of .3 with success in a course in biology. Slightly more high-IQ students would do better in the course than low-IQ students, but many low-IQ students would do well, and many high-IQ students would do poorly. Therefore, the IQ score would be essentially useless for making predictions about individuals.[8]

How well does the IQ score predict school performance? In one large and thorough investigation, the IQ of ninth-grade students obtained from the Stanford-Binet test score was a moderately good predictor of achievement in the tenth grade. The correlation coefficient between ninth-grade IQ and tenth-grade reading comprehension was .73; between IQ and English usage, .59; between IQ and biology, .54.[9] In another study,[10] a group test of intelligence given to seventh-graders predicted teachers' grades for the children somewhat better for Black students (correlation between IQ and grades was .64) than

for Whites (correlation .50) and somewhat better for girls (.66) than
for boys (.50). On the other hand, IQ does not predict nor correlate
well with nonacademic subjects, such as handwriting (.21), manual
work (.18), and drawing (.15). Moreover, predictions over long intervals are not as good as predictions over short intervals. For example, in
one study, third-grade Stanford-Binet IQ scores correlated .74 with
school performance in sixth grade, but kindergarten IQ scores correlated .57 with scores on a reading test six years later.[11]

It will come as no surprise that achievement tests of reading and
mathematics also predict school performance as judged by teachers'
grades and classroom performance. The reader might well ask why
expensive and time-consuming IQ test scores are used in predicting
school performance when the less expensive group achievement tests
could be used instead.[12] If we seek to predict the grades of students
within a classroom or a school, then achievement tests can be used
profitably. However, when students of different educational backgrounds are to be compared, aptitude tests are preferred over achievement tests because they are designed to depend less on exposure to a
particular curriculum and to give pupils from different schools an
equal chance. Consequently, for college admission, the Scholastic Aptitude Test (SAT), a general ability test, is used rather than an achievement test.

A point often overlooked in discussing prediction of school or occupational success from IQ scores is that although the reported correlations hold for groups, using an IQ score to predict an individual's
performance is very risky. Motivational and personality factors are
very important in determining that performance. Diligent, hardwork-
ing, achievement-oriented students with average IQ scores often have
a better school record than those who score higher on aptitude tests
but who find schoolwork irrelevant, or who are lazy. The IQ test does
not give us a measure of these motivational attributes. For example, in
the Terman studies of gifted children followed over a period of forty
years,[13] it was found that most of them were extremely successful—
they attended and graduated from college, they published books,
plays, scientific articles, and so on. However, some of these gifted
children flunked out of college—despite their high IQs. At the other
end of the scale is a follow-up study of children classified, on the basis
of their childhood IQs, as average (IQ 100–116), low (IQ 85–95),
and very low (IQ below 70). At age 50, sixty-five percent of the group
classified in childhood as having very low IQs were entirely self-

supporting, and their average IQ had risen from 60 to 82. This would not have been predicted from their childhood scores. More than 90 percent of the other two groups were self-supporting.[14]

IQ, then, can be used with moderate success in predicting school performance of children. At best, however, we are dealing with probabilities, not certainties. Children with high IQs are more likely to experience success in school, gain admission to college, and complete college than children with lower IQs. But IQ seems to measure only one factor that enters into school success. Personality and motivational variables as well as environmental opportunities and encouragement are not assessed by the IQ measure, yet they also contribute to school success. And, of course, *school success is only one form of success in our society.*

That IQ scores also correlate with occupational level should not cause any surprise, for certain levels of education (which themselves are correlated with IQ) are prerequisite for entry into many occupations. The average correlation of IQ and socioeconomic status of adults is almost .60.[15] Other indices of occupational success, such as income, also are correlated with IQ. Within a given occupation, men with higher IQs have been found to make more money than men with lower IQs, even when they had the same amount of schooling and were in the same line of work.[16]

Stability and Constancy of IQ

Test scores must be trustworthy if they are to be useful for predicting future behaviors and outcomes. A score is considered *reliable*, or trustworthy, when it is reproducible and consistent—that is, repeated administration of the test yields highly similar outcomes. When the time interval between two tests is short, psychologists talk about the *stability* of the test score. When the time interval is longer (say six months or more), they talk about the *constancy* of the scores.

STABILITY OF IQ

No single score gives a precise characterization of a person. The score obtained gives only an approximation, for there is always some influence of unsystematic variables, such as lapses in attention, guessing, good or bad luck in encountering tasks. It is essential to know the extent of influence that such chance variables have on IQ scores if any practical decision such as assignment to special classes or admission to college is to be based on IQ. Imagine, for example, that John had an IQ score of 118 on a test, and that an IQ of 120 was the prerequisite for admission to a special gifted-child program in school. John should be excluded only if one could be confident that the IQ score of 118 was accurate and that upon retest he would not score an IQ of 128. Similarly, an IQ score can only be successful in predicting future performance if the measure is stable and does not fluctuate widely from one administration of the test to another. On the Stanford-Binet and the Wechsler, the short-term stability of the IQ scores is very high. Over a one- or two-week interval, two parallel forms of the test correlate about .90. Even group tests show high short-term stability.[17]

When IQ tests are given, there are always some errors of measurement. Good tests have low measurement errors, and repeated tests give similar results. Poor tests have high measurement errors (and therefore low short-term stability). For both the Stanford-Binet and the Wechsler, the *standard error of measurement* determined statistically from repeated testing is found to be 5 IQ points. IQs are therefore usually reported as a range five points on each side of the actual numerical score. A child whose tested IQ is 105 is reported to have an IQ between 100 and 110. In general the standard error of measurement is larger for bright children than for below-average children. In other words, repeated tests of children with high scores give more variable results. Even when the standard error of measurement is reported, it is *not* certain that a repetition of the IQ test would yield a score within the stated range of 10 IQ points. The standard error of measurement is calculated so that 68 percent of the time, a repeated score lies within these limits, but in 32 percent of cases it is outside the limit. Ninety-six percent of the time the repeated test score lies within ±10 IQ points, that is, within a range of 20.

It should be apparent that *the exact IQ score cannot be taken too seriously. It usually can be pinpointed only within a 10-point range, and even then it is wrong nearly a third of the time.* It also is clear that attempting to interpret slight differences in IQ between children is a waste of time.

CONSTANCY OF IQ: CONSISTENCY AND CHANGE

Parents often have a sense of impending doom when learning their child's IQ. Doesn't the score determine their child's future? Isn't this the description of his or her mental capacities? Just as brown-eyed toddlers become brown-eyed adults, so bright children become bright adults. Right? Not necessarily. The evidence concerning the constancy of IQ—or the lack of it—should assuage much anxiety.

By studying groups of children who have been tested repeatedly as they grew older, it was found that the IQ score at age 2 is only modestly correlated (.4) with adult IQ. The older the child, the more closely the early test score resembles the eventual adult score. The correlation of IQ at age 4 with adult IQ is .6, and by age 10 the correlation reaches .9, where it remains through adolescence. These results seem to suggest that IQ is essentially fixed during the elementary school years. By and large, this fits with our everyday observations that bright 8-year-olds tend to do well when they are in high school, and in college it is more often the very bright freshman who graduates *cum laude* four years later.

Closer study of test scores of given individuals shows, however, that the IQ score frequently fluctuates from testing to testing, as shown in Figure 4–2. Attempts to relate changes in IQ to particular changes in a child's life (such as illness or divorce of parents) have generally been unconvincing.

In all careful studies, some IQ scores change by large amounts. In one recent study of eighty normal, home-reared, middle-class children, the average change in IQ between age 2½ and age 17 was *28.5 IQ points*, with one in three children showing a progressive change of *30 IQ points*, and one in seven shifting 40 IQ points.[18] The shifts in IQ generally were not random fluctuations about a constant value but represented directional trends over childhood, such as those shown in the figure.

But while there may be frequent fluctuations in an individual's IQ score over time, the general ranking among peers need not alter a great deal. If a 6-year-old child with an IQ of 136 scores 145 at age 8 and 158 at age 11, that child still remains in the top 1 percent of the population despite a 22-point shift in IQ. Similarly, it is possible that a preschooler with an IQ of 92 might score 114 at age 9 and at both times be classified as average in intelligence.

Different ways of analyzing the same data yield different conclusions. Correlations provide favorable evidence for constancy of IQ;

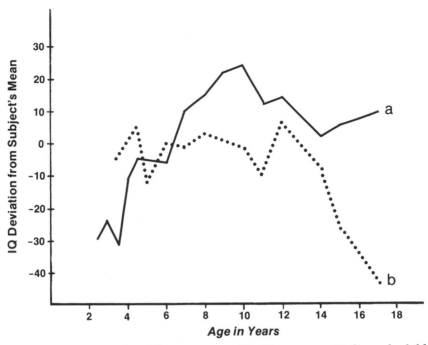

Figure 4-2.   Examples of inconstancy in IQ. The average IQ for each child
was calculated over the whole period, and the change from each child's mean
is graphed. Child (a) shows an increase of 24 IQ points at age 10, and a
decrease of 30 IQ points at age 3, compared to his own average score.
Child (b) shows a deficit of 44 IQ points at age 17 compared to his average
childhood IQ. (Adapted from McCall, Appelbaum, and Hogarty, "Developmental Changes in Mental Performance.")

bright people generally remain bright, average people average. The
magnitude of the changes, however, tends to favor the hypothesis of a
variable IQ. Individual IQ scores often change 20 or more points over
long periods of time.

All the data showing high correlations between IQ during the school
years and IQ during adulthood (or adolescence) are based on children
who remained in basically the same environments throughout the
years. *We do not know whether the stability of the environment is
responsible for the apparent constancy of IQ reflected in high correlations.* An understanding of the social issues concerning intelligence depends on being able to assess the environmental impact on intellectual
abilities. Naturally, then, psychologists have resorted to a variety of
strategies for sorting out environmental determinants of IQ.

One such strategy has been to consider what happens to the IQs of children whose environments have changed. Recall the studies of southern-born Black children who moved north. When they entered school in the North, they scored lower than the northern-born children, but their scores improved over time. The more years they spent in the northern school, the more their IQ scores improved. In contrast, Black children born in the North and attending schools there showed little IQ change from first grade to ninth grade. Clearly, the improvement in IQ of the southern-born children was in some way due to the change in their environments.[19] One might conclude that the tests were prepared by Northerners, and that the longer children lived in a northern environment, the more like the tests' creators they became!

One widely cited study of the effects of environmental change is by M. M. Skeels,[20] who placed a small sample of retarded orphanage children with an average IQ of 64 (range 35 to 85) in an institution for mentally retarded adults. The children, all under the age of 3, quickly became favorites of the attendants, who spent time playing with, talking to, cuddling, and teaching the children. The retarded women also interacted warmly and lovingly with the children, much like adoring aunts. The children stayed as "house guests" with the retarded women for an average of eighteen months (range six to fifty-two months). In order to appreciate the changes that occurred in the IQs of this experimental group of orphans, a comparison group of children who remained in an unstimulating, understaffed orphanage during their preschool years was later selected from the records of the same institution. The group consisted of twelve children on whom there were IQ records at about age 1½ and again at about age 4. The results are shown in Figure 4–3. The group that remained in the orphanage *lost* an average of 20 IQ points, a result commonly reported for children in very unstimulating environments. On the other hand, the group that moved to the more stimulating and responsive environment of the institution for mental retardates *gained* an average of 28 IQ points. Approximately two years later, when eleven of the thirteen children in this group had been adopted, their average IQ was 96, whereas the average for the contrast group who remained in institutions was 66. As adults, all who had been adopted were self-supporting, most of them having completed high school; most of the comparison group were still institutionalized.

The Skeels study is not without problems. There were more boys than girls in the group that remained in the unstimulating orphanage and more girls than boys in the group that changed settings (and

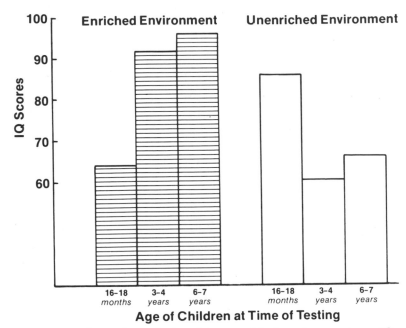

Figure 4-3. Effects of enriched and impoverished environments on IQs of children. The enriched environment consisted of a warm, responsive home for retarded women; the impoverished environment was an understaffed orphanage. (Data from Skeels, "Adult Status of Children with Contrasting Early Life Experiences.")

other research suggests the two sexes may not be equally influenced by the environment when it comes to intellectual development). Furthermore, not enough is known of the background variables concerning the children's parents to know whether the two groups were equally matched. Despite these problems, it is reasonable to conclude that dramatic improvements in the environment can bring about large increases in intelligence. Various studies have shown that a higher IQ persists as long as the child remains in an enriched setting.

The federally funded compensatory education programs also represent changed environments. Our aim here is not to give a complete account of their successes and failures, but to discuss one of the most successful programs that demonstrates that a planned enrichment program during infancy and childhood years can bring about long-lasting changes in IQ.

Psychologist Phyllis Levenstein[21] studied several groups of preschool children of low-income, low-IQ parents and provided some of these children with an enriched environment, while the others were left in an unchanged environment to act as a control group. Levenstein argued that a more effective strategy than taking the children out of their homes for enrichment would be to alter the home environment. In this way, the effectiveness of the program would not be confined to the limited hours of the intervention itself. The environmental modification consisted of a trained visitor making half-hour visits twice a week to the child's home for seven or eight months each year. The visitor stimulated interaction between mother and child with a kit of toys and books, which were left with the family. Some families received this program of enrichment for one year, others for two years. A control group was selected that did not receive any type of enrichment. The IQs were assessed before the program started and at its conclusion. Additionally, the children's performance some years later when at school was recorded.

As in other enrichment studies, the program had a dramatic effect in increasing IQ, when the assessment was made upon termination of the program. Average gains of 28 IQ points were recorded for the group with two years' enrichment, and 19 IQ points for the group with one year's experience. The control group, however, showed an average *loss* of 6 IQ points. Unlike some of the other intervention programs, the gains in IQ were not eroded over time. As can be seen from Figure 4–4, by the time the children were in the second grade, several years after their enrichment program had ended, their IQ scores still remained considerably above those of the children who had not been in the program. The children's performance on standard achievement tests of reading and arithmetic were in accord with their IQ scores—somewhat above average, and significantly above that of the unstimulated control group. The point is clear—not only can environmental modification bring about an increase in IQ while the program of enrichment is going on, but if the environment has in some way been permanently altered, as in the Levenstein program, the gains are maintained many years later.

It is clear that moving children from unstimulating to stimulating environments *can* bring about sustained changes in their IQ scores. IQ scores are not constant over time unless the environment is relatively constant in the amount of stimulation it provides. It should be noted, however, that not all intervention studies have been uniformly successful. For example, the summer enrichment programs of Head

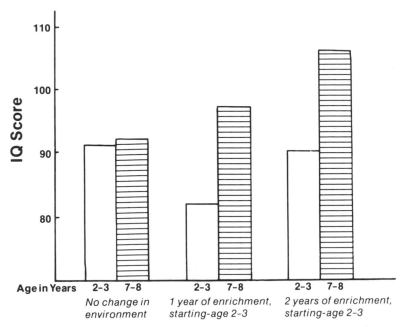

Figure 4-4.   IQ scores before entering an enrichment program and several years after the program ended. (Data from Levenstein, "VIP Children Reach School: Latest Chapter.")

Start have not been successful in modifying intelligence, in part because of the short period of enrichment, in part because the environment was not permanently changed, and in part because there was no quality control of the programs. The main point, however, is that some massive environmental enrichment programs have had success in raising IQ scores.

Until now, we have considered change in measured IQ as a function of changes in the external environment. Instability in IQ scores also results from personality and motivational factors. Investigators at the Fels Research Institute[22] analyzed changes in IQ and related these to changes in personality variables. They selected two groups of thirty-five children whose IQs during the ages 6 to 10 years were most unstable. One group showed increasing scores over this time, while the other group showed decreasing scores. There were more boys than girls in the group of IQ gainers. From behavioral ratings taken at home and at school, it was found that the gainers tended to be independent, competitive, and verbally aggressive. In general, they worked hard at school and exhibited concern for intellectual mastery both in their leisure-time pursuits as well as in school. When confronted with problems, they actively attacked them, in contrast to the losers in IQ, who tended to be passive and to withdraw from difficult situations.

A number of studies identify anxiety as being related to performance on IQ tests and school achievement tests. In general, the more anxious the child, the worse the performance on tests. While it is not possible to determine unambiguously whether anxiety is a cause or a result of the poorer test performance, research[23] on elementary school children tested over a five-year period found that increases in anxiety were associated with reductions in performance. Increasing anxiety had the same effect on students with high and average IQs. Changes in IQ, then, can be related to changes in personality and motivational variables as well as to changes in the external environment.

If educational decisions for individuals are to be in any way based on IQ, a sensible policy would be to insist on at least two IQ scores, including one very recent test. The mistaken notion that IQ is fixed, that it is unchangeable, all too often contributes both to anxiety about testing and to a lack of effort in improving the educational environment of those who could profit most from such enrichment.

How Early Can I Know If My Child Is a Genius?

How do intellectual abilities develop? At what age can a child's intelligence be assessed? While infant intelligence tests are available, some researchers think they are inappropriately labeled, since the tests obviously must be in a quite different form from tests for older children and adults. In fact, many of the infant tests recognize explicitly the minimal overlap in content with later IQ tests and are therefore called "tests of infant development," and developmental quotients (DQ) are calculated instead of IQs.

One of the best infant tests was developed by psychologist Nancy Bayley. The Bayley Scales of Infant Development provide a basis for evaluation of children in the first two and a half years of life. The test consists of two scales. The Mental Scale assesses the infant's ability to react to changes in the environment, memory, learning, problem solving, verbal communication, and the early ability to form classifications. A sample of this test is presented in Table 4–3.

TABLE 4–3
Sample Items from the Bayley Mental Scale
Shown with Average Age Placement

Age Placement	Item Description
3 days	Responds to sound of bell
3 weeks	Responds to voice when person is out of view
2.0 months	Visually recognizes mother
5.2 months	Lifts up cup to obtain toy he has seen hidden underneath it
7.6 months	Cooperates in games like Peek-a-Boo
10.4 months	Attempts to imitate scribble
12.5 months	Imitates words (e.g., Mama, Dada)
15.3 months	Shows shoes (clothing or toy) on request
21.9 months	Attempts to mend broken doll, by putting head on or near neck (in any position)
28.2 months	Understands two prepositions and executes sentences like, "Put the block on a cup; put it *in* the cup," etc.

The Motor Scale provides a measure of the infant's control over his or her body, including large muscle coordination and finer manipulatory skills of the hands and fingers. A sample of the motor scale appears in Table 4–4.

TABLE 4–4
Sample Items from the Bayley Motor Scale
Shown with Average Age Placement

Age Placement	Item Description
3 days	Moves head to side when placed on tummy
3 weeks	Holds head erect for 3 seconds when held against shoulder
3.8 months	Sits with slight support
6.6 months	Sits alone steadily
8.9 months	Picks up small pellet with precise movement involving thumb and forefinger
9.7 months	Pat-a-cake clapping at the midline
13.3 months	Throws ball to tester
16.4 months	Walks down stairs with help
28.1 months	Jumps from second step

If you compare the items in Tables 4–3 and 4–4 with those in Table 4–1, you will see that the skills evaluated by the Bayley Scales are different from those typically assessed in an IQ test for older children and adults. Consequently, it should be no surprise that while infant tests have satisfactory short-term stability, they are *unsuccessful* at predicting adult IQ. In other words, infant tests reflect current functioning accurately, but fail to make accurate long-term predictions.

Because of this, Bayley[24] has argued that intelligence should not be considered as an integrated or simple capacity that grows from birth in steady increments.

It can be asked, however, whether there are any items of the Bayley Scales that predict later intellectual functioning. The more intellectual (symbolic) items tested at age 2 modestly correlate (.40) with later IQ. Furthermore, if tests given at neighboring ages are combined, then the correlation with adult IQ rises. For example, a composite infant score from 18, 21, and 24 months correlates .55 with later IQ.[25]

Thus infant tests, as they exist today, are poor predictors of later IQ. The major difficulty is that the limited repertory of behavior available to the infant consists initially of coordinating responses to environmental changes. Only later, when more symbolic thinking emerges at around 18 months, do infant tests make useful, though modest, predictions.

The Development of Intelligence During Childhood and Adolescence

Intellectual growth as measured by IQ tests proceeds rapidly during the first twelve years or so, then slows down, showing continued but more gradual growth over the next ten years. Information on intellectual growth comes from studies in which the same individuals have been observed and tested over a period of many years.

A major problem with charting developmental changes in mental abilities is that the nature of intelligence and the composition of IQ tests change with age. Jean Piaget, a Swiss psychologist, and his collaborators have provided the most thorough account of the changing nature of intellectual processes. Piaget believes there are four periods in intellectual development, each one differing in the fundamental processes involved in thinking.[26] During the first few years of life, in what Piaget calls the *sensorimotor stage*, children learn to coordinate motor movements with the sensations experienced. They gradually build an elementary notion of cause and effect and become aware of the effects their actions have on the environment. The most important accomplishment, however, is the emergence of symbolic thought, which frees infants from the concrete here-and-now and allows them to deal with the world of absent objects and the world of possibilities. The toddler acquires the ability to picture mentally an object or action that is not perceptually present (representation). Imitation is an example of the symbolic activity of toddlers. The child can reproduce the behaviors of a person who is not present, showing that he engages in internal symbolic representation. Other rudimentary symbolic activity can be seen in play and in the child's understanding simple words and commands. The child also begins to construct notions of reality, based on his actions and perceived outcomes on the environment. Many of the accomplishments of this period are not usually thought of as intelligence in the traditional sense, but according to Piaget they are the foundation for more abstract thinking and problem solving.

By the age of 18 months to 2 years, language and symbolic processes have developed, marking the advent of the second stage, that of *pre-operational thinking*. During this stage, the child learns the rudiments of thought and begins to create and use mental symbols, to reason, and to employ memory. However, the child's thinking is constrained by egocentrism—an inability to take the viewpoint of others—and by an ability to focus on only one aspect of complex information at a time. This is revealed in contradictions in thought that the child does not even notice.

Concrete operations, the third stage, between 6 and 12 years, marks the onset of what we would call logical thinking. Piaget argues that a limited number of mental operations underlie all the developments of this period. Children come to be able to carry out classifications systematically, to arrange objects in a logical series, and to understand the basic notions involved in numbers. Most adults in our society function at this level.

The fourth and highest stage of thinking is that of *formal operations*, typically reached between 12 and 17 years, and most clearly manifest in the thinking of scientists. At this stage, the adolescent is able to consider hypothetical outcomes and to reason with them. In addition, he or she is able to figure out how to use all possible combinations of a given set of events, and is able to cast thought into "If . . . then . . ." propositions, so that conclusions can be deduced from premises.

This review of Piaget's voluminous work is necessarily sketchy (Piaget has written more than forty books on the development of children's reasoning and thinking). However, it should be apparent that inconstancy in IQ may be due to different rates of entering the four stages of development. Supporting this possibility, evidence from IQ tests shows that there is more variability in group data at ages 6 and 11 or 12,[27] and that individuals at these transitional ages often mark a major change in the rate of intellectual development. The overall IQ growth curve, smoothed to fit the average performance of many subjects, does not show this evidence.

Adult Development

Contrary to popular belief and early research findings, intellectual ability does not decline as rapidly or as profoundly during the mature adult years as was once feared. Adults tested during childhood or adolescence and then retested twenty-five or more years later do not decline in all abilities.[28] In fact, as shown in Figure 4–5, vocabulary and general information scores show an improvement during the middle years, while nonverbal performance tests in general, and time-limited tests in particular, show some declines with age. The amount of gain and decline in mental abilities during the adult years is related

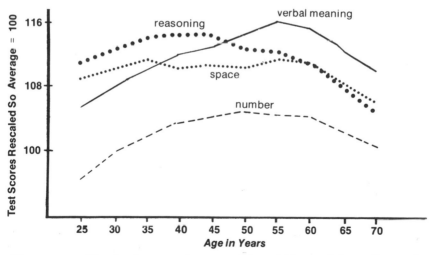

Figure 4-5.   The developmental course of four different abilities during the adult years. (Adapted from K. W. Schaie and C. R. Strother, "A Cross-Sequential Study of Age Changes in Cognitive Behavior." *Psychological Bulletin*, 70:671–680, 1968.)

to the amount of education and the nature of occupational employment. Those in stimulating, intellectually demanding occupations show gains in IQ, while those whose work demands little intellectual effort are more likely to show declines. This work factor may account for the finding that, when large groups are studied, the mental abilities of men generally show increases during adulthood, while those of women often stay stable or decline somewhat.

IQ tests, then, show a reasonable degree of repeatability, correlate with such things as scholastic achievement and occupation, and seem to be tapping what most members of the dominant Western culture subjectively define as intelligence. In this sense, "intelligence" is a concept much like "weather." One can scale intelligence from high to low and weather from good to bad and devise various tests to help with the scaling. But the choice of the tests and the preconceptions of the test designer necessarily limit the meaning of the score. If a weather quotient (WQ) were devised based primarily on the number of sunny weekends, it might correlate best with business in a resort, while a WQ heavily weighting the amount of early summer rainfall might show the highest correlation with farm profits in the area around the resort.

Like most analogies, this one should not be pushed too far— especially since the components of weather, in contrast to those of IQ, are well known and measurable. The key point is that both intelligence and weather are useful concepts, and various indices have been or could be devised to describe them. Indices like IQ and WQ should not, however, be confused with physical or biological measures like the temperature of a body of water or the length of a butterfly's wing. Both of the latter could be measured by different investigators using different kinds of equipment, with the expectation that the results would be essentially identical. Temperature and length have well-defined theoretical contexts. If measurements of the water temperature taken with two different instruments at the same time were consistently different, we would suspect a systematic error in one or both of the instruments—not that they were measuring different things.

IQ scores are different *in kind* from measurements of continuously varying characters of organisms such as weight, length, metabolic rate, and so on, because they lack a universally agreed-upon unit and depend instead on each test instrument. Two different tests can yield different IQ scores, not because of a systematic error in one instrument, but because the tests might be measuring different things.

The Impact of IQ

In the last decade, IQ testing has generated considerable public concern. Such testing is intimately tied up with individuals' feelings about their own worth, and, perhaps more important, the worth of their children. After all, in the scale of IQ test scores (which most laypersons unfortunately equate with the more general notion of intelligence), there is a clear "good" end and "bad" end. How does a parent feel, for example, when told that his or her child is of less than average intelligence? Parents in our society know that measured intelligence is the gatekeeper to higher education and higher occupational status.

For a long time, attempts were made to keep IQ test scores secret, but the principal result of this was that an aura of mystery developed about them. Many parents seemed to feel that buried in school records was a magic number that would tell them whether their children were smart or dumb—and what their futures would be. Recently, that secrecy barrier has cracked, and parents have been eager to be informed about their children's scores[29]—as they are now legally entitled to be.

The new openness about IQ scores has led to a de-emphasis on testing in some areas and especially to less dependence on group testing.[30] It seems, however, that at least three factors will keep IQ testing prominent on the American scene. One is the prevailing attitude that scholastic achievement is a major factor in "success." As long as most of society feels that a prominent university professor (whose insecurities and lack of exercise may bring on a fatal coronary at the age of 50) is more "successful" than a relaxed and competent gardener, plumber, or housewife, tests that predict scholastic achievement are likely to remain important.

The second factor is that those who are members of the educational field naturally value the things they do well, and will continue to promote those values and ways of assessing them. The educational establishment is unlikely to discard tests of vocabulary and exercises of reciting numbers backwards and adopt tests of manual dexterity, empathy, or contemplativeness. And they will be encouraged to maintain such attitudes by the third factor—that testing is *big business*. The design, production, administration, and evaluation of tests constitute a major American industry—and industries from automobile manufacturing to nuclear power generation are notoriously unwilling to consider seriously their negative impacts on society. In the testing game as in the peddling of cosmetics, the bottom line is what counts.

Since societal attitudes seem unlikely to change quickly and testing thus will probably be with us for a long time, what recommendations can be made to help limit its abuse? The obvious first one is the wide dissemination of information about the *assumptions* built into not just individual tests but the testing process itself. If Johnny has a low IQ score, that may mean he won't be successful in college. But this is only a disaster if Johnny or his parents *assume* that one must go to college in order to be a successful human being.

A second recommendation would be the elimination of most mass testing, and the restriction of individual testing to carefully and professionally administered tests and to relatively special cases where some sort of prediction is required. Most people should never take an IQ test, but unfortunately most still do. Parents would be well advised to check the IQ scores in their children's school files. While an IQ score is hardly a measure of a child's worth, *it may be treated as such by the school system.* If there is any question about a child's score or its use, intervention by the parent may be warranted.

5

Is IQ Inherited?

From a scientific standpoint or from one of valid inferences about social policy, the problem of assaying the genetic components of IQ test differences seems utterly trivial and hardly worth the immense effort that would need to be expended to carry out decent studies.

—R. C. Lewontin, *Annual Review of Genetics*, 1975

B<small>EFORE</small> we can satisfactorily discuss questions of the inheritance of IQ* and the genetics of IQ differences between races, a brief review of the principles of genetics is necessary. "Like begets like" can be thought of as the basic law of inheritance—a law that has been recognized by people for millennia. Cats invariably have kittens, never puppies or calves. Dogs have puppies, not human babies or chicks. Clearly, in some manner the characteristics of the offspring are influenced by the characteristics of the parent. Historically, however, unraveling the mechanism of this influence did not result from studies of differences *between* species like dogs and cats, but from studying differences *within* species—such as those between blue-eyed and brown-eyed people. Herdsmen discovered early on that if they kept as breeding stock those animals that had the most desirable characteristics, the quality of their herds would improve.

---

* From here on, the terms "IQ" and "intelligence" will be used as a shorthand for "score on a properly administered standard intelligence test such as the Stanford-Binet or the Wechsler."

Traits and Genes

Scientific attempts to unravel the nature of the hereditary mechanisms began with studies of the inheritance of exactly the kinds of traits that interested herdsmen, traits like weight, strength, speed, milk production, and docility, which varied from cow to cow, from horse to horse, or from dog to dog in imperceptible steps. The first systematic assaults on the mysteries of genetics dealt with such continuously varying traits, now technically called *quantitative* characteristics. And, indeed, early geneticists often studied quantitative characteristics of *Homo sapiens*, because the existence of pedigrees was more common in humans than in most groups of animals.[1]

A large and politically important body of literature developed on patterns of quantitative variation from generation to generation. By 1900, however, knowledge of the mechanisms of heredity had not advanced one whit beyond the speculations of Charles Darwin, who had guessed, quite incorrectly, that units of genetic transmission called "gemmules," which contained tiny, precise copies of each part of the body, were gathered by the bloodstream from throughout the body to be transmitted through the sex organs.

Unbeknownst to those attempting to unravel the problem of heredity with work in quantitative genetics, its solution had, in fact, been published in 1865 by the Austrian monk Gregor Mendel. But then, as now, a major factor in how a scientist's ideas are accepted is where the work is published, and Mendel unfortunately chose the *Annual Proceedings of the Natural History Society of Brunn* (in Austria—now Brno, Czechoslovakia). This is roughly equivalent to a physicist today putting the statement of an important theory in the *Transactions of the Missouri Dairyman's Association*. Mendel's work was ignored until the turn of the century, when it was "rediscovered."

Mendel's first key contribution was, in retrospect, disarmingly simple. He chose not to study continuously varying characteristics, but those whose variation was discontinuous. For instance, he noticed that the pea plants in his garden were either tall or short, but never of medium height.* He found that when he crossed tall with short, all of the offspring were tall. He then found that when he crossed these

* In most organisms, height varies continuously, and for them Mendel's analysis would not work.

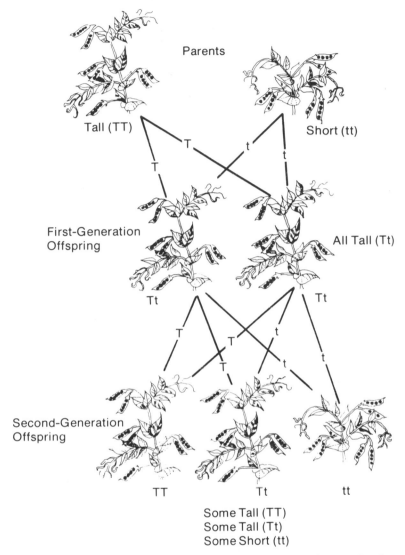

Figure 5-1. Inheritance of height in pea plants. Note that each plant in the first-generation offspring must receive a T gene from one parent and a t gene from the other. In the next generation, each plant may receive either a T or a t gene from each parent, so that three different gene combinations, TT, Tt, and tt, can occur. These combinations will occur in roughly the proportions 1:2:1, and since TT and Tt plants are both tall, the ratio of tall to short plants in the second generation of offspring will be about 3:1.

offspring, about three-fourths of their offspring (the "grandchildren" of the original plants) were tall and about one-fourth were short.

Mendel's second key contribution was his hypothesis to explain this pattern, which included the disappearance of shortness in the progeny of the original crosses and its reappearance in the next generation. He assumed that each original tall pea plant had two factors, TT, determining its tallness, and each short plant had two factors, tt, making it short. He further hypothesized that each plant donated one of its factors to its offspring, and that if the offspring received *at least* one T factor, the offspring would be tall. That is Tt individuals as well as TT individuals would be tall. Mendel's scheme is shown in Figure 5-1. Note that all of the first generation offspring are tall because they all received a T from each of their tall (TT) parents. It is only in the next generation that a tt combination is possible, and short plants reappear. Mendel's explanation of the pattern of inheritance of height in pea plants is precisely that accepted by geneticists today. The different factors are now called different *genes* (or, more precisely, different *alleles* of the same gene), and gene T is said to be "dominant" over gene t.

We now suspect that inheritance of quantitative characteristics is normally controlled by many different genes, operating either independently or in some degree of association with one another. The interactions of these genes with each other and with the environment are extremely complex. Even with enormous strides made by genetics in the last three-quarters of a century, it is usually impossible to produce a precise analysis of the pattern of inheritance of quantitative characteristics—as can now be done readily for traits controlled by alleles of one or a few genes.[2]

Genes and Environments

Of course, there is more to the passage of characteristics from generation to generation than genetics. The environment is also involved. Suppose, for instance, that farmers in a district had for generations bred their cattle from the best milk producers, and milk yield had gradually increased over time. A logical explanation would be that gradual genetic improvement of the stock was responsible for the increase.

This is, however, just one "logical" explanation that, without further testing, cannot be separated from the following "logical" explanation. All the cows in the herd have exactly the same genes for milk production and always have had them. Some cows, however, by accident had always given more milk than others; they may, for instance, have been born at more advantageous seasons or have had better treatment. These superior cows were selected for breeding. But their offspring were genetically identical to all others in the herd as far as genes for milk production were concerned. Hence, the gradual improvement in per cow yields over generations may not have resulted from genetic alterations but from the farmers' increased knowledge of how to care for cows.

Unless it is possible to standardize environments and carry out appropriate experiments, which of these two explanations is correct cannot be determined. Indeed, each could be partially true. If, however, the relevant environmental variables could be identified (which for many quantitative characteristics is often very difficult) and controlled generation after generation, the genetic hypothesis could be tested. Then, if in this controlled situation breeding from high-yielding individuals produces a gradual increase in milk yields, the hypothesis that all cows have identical genes for milk production would be shown to be incorrect (in scientific jargon, the hypothesis would be said to have been "falsified").

In modern genetics, the actual observed characteristics of an organism—the height of a pea plant, the milk yield of a cow, the IQ test score of a person—are called the *phenotype*. The observed phenotype is the result of the interaction of a genetic "blueprint" called the *genotype* with the environment in which the individual organism matures. We now know that the genotype is a body of information coded in the sequence of building blocks of extremely long molecules of deoxyribonucleic acid—DNA. And we also know that the information in the DNA acquires meaning only when it is "translated" by an environment.

This is a key point—even in Mendel's experiments, the environment was "doing its thing." A tall pea plant is only tall in an appropriate environment. All the T genes in the world won't do a thing if a TT seed is planted in cement. If Mendel had not planted TT and tt plants in similar environments, he would not have founded the science of genetics—for a TT plant growing in extremely poor soil will be shorter than a tt plant in normal soil. To talk of heredity in isolation from environment is to ignore the lessons of modern genetics. The old question of "Is it nature or nurture?" was the wrong question. Today one must ask, "How in this case are nature and nurture interacting?"

Studies of the quantitative genetics of many characteristics in many organisms—notably economically important plants and animals—have produced a considerable body of information on nature-nurture interactions. One of the earliest studies was an experiment by the Danish geneticist W. Johannsen. He planted the largest and smallest beans produced by an inbred line of bean plants in an experimental garden and discovered that the plants growing from the small beans produced beans just as large as those coming from the large beans. This experiment indicated that the differences among the beans were caused by differences in their environments, and that there was no genetic variability for size of beans in Johannsen's bean plants.[3] Inbreeding had removed significant genetic variation from the line.[*] Thus a population can be phenotypically variable yet genetically uniform.

Conversely, a population can be without phenotypic variability in a given environment, even though it is genetically variable. To see this, consider a classic experiment by the British developmental biologist C. H. Waddington. He worked with common fruit flies, *Drosophila melanogaster*. Like most insects, these flies have a characteristic grid of strutlike veins that support their wing membranes. Waddington noted that *all* of the flies in his stock bottles had a complete cross-vein at a certain position on the wing. Thus in the stock bottle environment, not only was there no sign of genetically controlled variation at the cross-vein, there was no variation at all! He found, however, that by subjecting an immature stage of the flies to a temperature shock (sudden change of temperature), some individuals appeared that lacked the cross-vein (cross-veinless phenotype). By breeding from those individuals, Waddington eventually was able to select out a strain that had a high frequency of cross-veinless individuals *without the temperature shock*,[4] showing that there had indeed been variability present in the genetic information that was the "blueprint" for producing the cross-vein. As we will see, understanding the "masking" and "unmasking" of

---

[*] Inbreeding, the mating of relatives, is one way to reduce genetic variability.

genetic variability in different environments is critical to any analysis of the genetics of IQ differences among populations.

Heritability

Most of the work of quantitative geneticists, of course, has been done on characteristics that vary within populations. Genetics is a science concerned with the inheritance of differences, and quantitative geneticists have concentrated on those characteristics that not only vary but that can be changed by artificial selection.* That is, they are interested in characteristics whose averages change from generation to generation in a uniform environment when nonaverage individuals are used as the breeding stock.

One of the main questions that quantitative geneticists have tried to answer for the animal breeder is "How fast can I increase the weight of my pigs (egg production of my chickens, speed of my race horses) if I carry out a certain program of artificial selection?" One of the tools devised to answer this and related questions is a statistic called "heritability." Although technically complex, in principle the statistic is very simple to define.[5] It is the amount (given as a proportion) of the observed variation in a trait that is caused by differences in the genotypes of the individuals in the group studied.[6] In practice, it is used as an indication of the degree to which differences in the trait will be inherited.

Heritability, H, can range from 0 to 1. In the Johannsen bean example, for bean size, heritability was zero ($H = 0$) because a selection experiment showed that the genotypes of all the beans were identical.

How does one go about estimating the heritability of a characteristic? Again, although there are complexities, the basic principles are simple, and several procedures can be used. One of the most straightforward is the type of experiment done by Johannsen. In a carefully standardized environment, individuals with extreme scores for a characteristic are selected from the original population and used as the parents for the next generation. For example, the heaviest swine in the

---

* Natural selection is the differential reproduction of genotypes in a natural situation. When people purposely create a differential, such as by causing a prize bull to have hundreds or thousands of offspring, this is artificial selection.

herd are used as breeding stock. When the offspring population has matured, it is measured and the average measurements of original and offspring populations are compared. If the two averages are very similar—that is, if the next generation of the herd of swine is no heavier than the last—then H = 0 or very close to 0 (small differences being attributed to random chance events such as undetected environmental fluctuations, which are usually lumped together under the term "experimental error"). If the next generation of swine is, on the average, heavier, that would indicate some degree of heritability of weight. The greater the difference between the original and offspring population averages, the higher the heritability estimate.[7] This is a logical procedure since if individuals with extreme measurements are selected as parents, the offspring population would be expected to have measurements similar to the parent group in proportion to the degree to which genetic factors are involved. The more genetic variability there is in the original population, the easier it is for selection to create differences between the average scores of two consecutive generations.

This expected genetic resemblance among relatives is the key to another common method of estimating heritability. Suppose you wished to know whether race horses could be selected for higher speed, but you didn't want to wait for the years needed to perform a selection experiment (or didn't want to go to the expense). You might reason this way. In general, if speed is influenced by genetics, related race horses ought to be more similar in speed than horses selected at random from among all race horses. You could then go to the racing records and determine the top speeds of, say, 100 pairs of thoroughbreds who are unrelated, and another 100 pairs who are brothers. Using an appropriate statistical measure, you might find that the brothers were much more similar in speed than the unrelated horses, and you might conclude that this was a sign of a high heritability of speed.

But would your conclusion be justified? After all, the brothers might be more similar because they were raised in the same stables with the same diets and the same trainers. Perhaps some stables are better than others, and simply being stable mates would cause brothers to resemble each other in speed more than random pairs. Or perhaps stables don't vary much in the quality of care provided, but brothers tend to race more in the same area of the country, and race tracks may differ in how "fast" they are. Here we see the kind of problem that plagues the geneticist trying to determine heritability when environments are beyond control. The argument can always be raised that similarities among relatives are caused by similar environments and not by common genes. To a degree, that problem can be avoided by careful matching of individuals and environments. For instance, in the horse study, one might take the unrelated random pairs from the same stables. But even then the possibility of undetected similarity in the environment of relatives will remain (e.g., Might trainers tend to treat brother horses more alike than unrelated horses?).

This problem must be considered in any comparison of human siblings or of parents and offspring. In either case, *if* the environments of relatives are *not* more similar than those of random individuals in the population, then the degree of similarity among relatives should be a measure of heritability. But in the world of heritability of human characteristics and especially of IQ, that is one colossal "if."

Suppose you have no interest in selectively breeding human beings, but were curious as to whether differences in height were highly heritable. How would you go about determining whether they were? One way would be to compare siblings and random individuals from the same generation. But siblings are generally raised in the same home and thus can be expected to receive more similar diets than nonsiblings. And various studies relate diets and development—severely undernourished people don't grow as tall as well-nourished people. What to do? One thing would be to make careful dietary inventories of families and then attempt to pair nonsiblings on the basis of the similarity of their diets. If this were done perfectly, so that their diets were as similar as (but not more similar than) those of siblings, then the confounding of diet with genetics would be removed. But the pairing procedure would be expensive and cumbersome—if not impossible—and it is likely that other environmental factors in addition to diet (such as amount of exercise and amount of sunlight) might have important influences on height.

TWINS AND ESTIMATING HERITABILITY

There is a simpler approach. Some human beings do not differ genetically—identical twins.[8] Such twins result when a single fertilized egg, that is, a zygote, divides and produces two zygotes, each with identical DNA complements. Twins resulting from this process are called identical and are rather rare (about 1 set per 250 births). In contrast, most twins are "fraternal"—resulting from the simultaneous formation of two zygotes by fertilization of two eggs by two sperm.[9]

Fraternal twins occur about once in every 125 births. Although they share the same womb and are born at the same time, fraternal twins are no more similar genetically than siblings born at different times.

Here we can see a good way to estimate the heritability of height. *All* of the difference in height between identical twins is *by definition* environmental. Height differences between fraternal twins could be environmental or genetic, or both, in origin. Should the height difference between fraternal twins turn out to be, on the average, the same as that between identical twins, we would seem to be justified in concluding that there is no heritability for height ($H = 0$).[10] For if genes were playing a significant role, the identical twins should be more alike in height than the fraternal twins. But if the identical twins are more alike in height, does this demonstrate that there is a significant heritability of height? Unfortunately, it does not. There remains the ever present problem of correlated environments. There is ample reason to believe, for example, that identical twins live in more similar environments within the family than do fraternal twins. If that is the case, the greater height similarity of the identical twins could be purely environmental in origin. In view of the more similar environments of identical twins, we must conclude that comparisons of identical and fraternal twin pairs will throw light on the heritability of IQ.

IDENTICAL TWINS REARED APART

There does, however, seem to be one way to get around these difficulties. Suppose it were possible to determine the similarity of IQ test scores of many pairs of identical twins separated at birth and reared separately. If the experiment were done correctly, the correlation coefficient calculated from the pairs of scores of the separated twins would be a direct estimate of the heritability.* This makes intuitive sense—after all, individuals with identical genotypes are being raised in different environments. And any association among the IQ scores of the separated pairs must then be due to the effects of their identical genes influencing IQ, which is what is meant by the term "heritability of IQ" in common usage.

Since identical twins themselves are quite unusual, it is not surprising that very few pairs of such twins raised separately have been discovered. Those few that have been found and studied, however, have been given great weight in the determination of the heritability

---

* In this case, heritability in the broad sense is meant, including nonadditive genetic variance and gene-environment variations.

of IQ. Studies have been reported of 121 pairs of separated identical twins.[11] The best-known of these studies was done by a famous British psychologist, Sir Cyril Burt.[12] He investigated 53 pairs of identical twins reared apart.[13] It was largely on the basis of Burt's work that Jensen estimated the heritability of IQ to be extremely high ($H = .81$),[14] and it was on the basis of Burt's studies and related work that many geneticists and psychologists have considered the heritability of IQ to be of substantial but uncertain magnitude.

The reason for the uncertainty was that Burt's studies and other studies of separated identical twins did not conform to the strict requirements necessary for the IQ correlations to be considered an estimate of heritability. For example, in a proper experiment, the environment of each twin would have to be selected at random from all the possible environments available in the population for which we wish to measure the heritability. That such random assignment of environments did not occur is evident, since in the vast majority of cases one of the twins was raised by a biological parent.

While this defect makes an actual estimate of H impossible, surely it would have been correct to assume that the high correlation of IQ scores in the separated identical twins is a sign of considerable heritability of intelligence. After all, if a boy raised by a Liverpool dock laborer had essentially the same IQ test score as his identical twin brother raised by a professor at Oxford, would this not be evidence of the strong influence of the genes?

Seemingly it was. The all too common (and often unavoidable) mistake of accepting the results of detailed investigations without subjecting the experimental techniques to sharp scrutiny was made by various scientists, and the notion that IQ had a significant heritability acquired wide currency. However, since Burt's work was central to the growing political argument over genetics and IQ, it was recently subjected to a searching reexamination by Princeton psychologist Leon J. Kamin.[15] Kamin discovered a large number of flaws in Burt's studies. For example, in his numerous statistical manipulations of IQ scores of twins, Burt often did not use the "raw" scores (i.e., the scores actually obtained from the tests); instead, he used subjective "adjusted assessments [of IQ]." Furthermore, "the test results, which generally covered other children in the school as well, were submitted to the teachers for comment or criticism; and whenever any question arose, the child was re-examined"! Burt did not state, for example, whether the teachers were aware of the performance of the identical twins when they criticized the test results. Could they, for example, have considered quite different scores from identical twins grounds for re-examination?

The failure to use raw scores would in itself very nearly be grounds for disregarding Burt's research. It is axiomatic in such work that the investigator does everything possible to exclude experimenter bias. If possible, for example, tests given to identical twins should be administered by people who are unaware of the purpose of the study and unaware of the existence of the other twin. Any knowledge of the other twin's performance at the time of the test administration, or any adjustment of scores by people who knew the other twin could destroy the objectivity of the study. Consider, for example, another study: when both twins were tested by the same person, the average IQ difference was 8.5 points; when there were different testers, the average difference was 22.4 points.[16]

In reexamining Burt's papers, Kamin found that it was impossible even to determine which tests were administered to the twins, let alone to sort out the various potential sources of investigator bias.[17] Burt's raw data from his various studies are lost, his procedures were not properly described in his papers, and suspicious numerical constancies and descriptive inconsistencies occur from paper to paper. For example, in 1955, Burt reported group-test correlations of .771 for twenty-one pairs of identical twins reared apart; in 1966, the group-test correlation for fifty-three pairs of twins was also .771. In 1955, he gave .944 as the correlation for eighty-three pairs of identical twins reared together; in 1966, the correlation for ninety-five pairs was also reported to be .944.[18] The probability of such consistent results with changing sample sizes is, in the real world, roughly 1.0 divided by the number of electrons in the universe. If you don't believe it, calculate the correlation of twenty-one pairs of numbers—any numbers—and then *try* to add thirty-two more pairs such that the correlation coefficient remains the same to the third decimal place. See how many trials it takes.

To top things off, in one article Burt and a co-author actually state that raw test scores were changed into "assessments" in order to "reduce the disturbing effects of environment to relatively slight proportions."[19] Hardly a reassuring statement from experimenters trying to evaluate "the relative influence of heredity and environment"!

Kamin's critique effectively removes Burt's publications from the realm of science. We have only mentioned a few of Burt's technical sins here—those interested in greater detail are referred to Kamin's excellent book or to Burt's own papers. Or they may consult the recent evidence that Burt's sins were not only technical, that his passionate belief that IQ was largely hereditary overwhelmed his training as a scientist and led him to such extremes as creating fictitious coauthors and publishing praises of his own work under pseudonyms. Since Burt's critical records were burned after his death it may never be known whether or not his twin studies were, in essence, a giant hoax.[20] Those not interested in going further might wish merely to ruminate on the idea of a society that awards knighthood for "science" of the caliber of Burt's. Even Jensen, who leaned heavily on Burt in drawing his conclusions about the inheritance of IQ in his 1969 paper (which began the current round of the nature-nurture controversy[21]) has been forced to admit that "unless new evidence rectifying the inconsistencies in Burt's data is turned up, which is doubtful at this stage, I see no justifiable conclusion in regard to many of [Burt's] correlations. Hypothesis testing depends on data of determinant reliability. Of this Burt's presentation of his own data unfortunately often gives us too little assurance."[22] Translation: GIGO—garbage in, garbage out.

IDENTICAL TWINS REARED APART: OTHER STUDIES

What about twin studies done by others besides Burt and his collaborators? James Shields, in *Monozygotic Twins, Brought Up Apart and Brought Up Together*,[23] reported on thirty-seven pairs of twins— the only other study approaching that of Burt in scale. There is no question about the scientific integrity of Shields's work. The raw data are presented in a detailed appendix, permitting other investigators to check Shields's analysis and interpretations and to further analyze his data—which the indefatigable Kamin has done in detail.[24] The most serious flaw in Shields's work has to do with whether or not the separated twins were reared in random environments. The degree to which this requirement of a proper study was violated by Burt cannot be determined due to his lack of adequate procedural reporting. The meticulous appendix in Shields's paper, in sharp contrast, permits evaluation of the degree of violation of the ideal of randomized environments.

It turns out that in many cases the environments of the two separated twins were obviously and highly correlated. In most cases, they were raised by relatives, and often by close relatives such as the mother and maternal grandmother. The children often lived in the same town, knew each other, knew they were twins, played with each other, and went to school together. For example, Bertram and Christopher's mother died the day after their birth. Their father's sisters raised them "amicably, living next-door to one another in the same Midlands colliery village." They were continually in each other's homes and went to the same school until they were 11. Foster and Francis were raised about five miles apart in the industrial suburbs of the same town by the mother and a paternal aunt. They dressed alike and attended the same school.[25]

Many of the female twins were also from highly correlated environments. Jessie and Winifred were raised by unrelated adoptive mothers, but within a few hundred yards of each other. They "were attracted to each other at the age of 2 . . . told they were twins after the girls discovered it for themselves, having gravitated to one another at school at the age of 5. In order to separate them Mrs. E. removed Jessie to another school but they continued to meet in the park. Just before their eighth birthday they found themselves in the same school again for administrative reasons. . . . They are very closely attached to each other." Jenny and Kathleen were separated at birth and raised by "paternal aunts, Jenny in a London suburb, Kathleen in a small seaside resort, where she was visited regularly by Jenny during the summer holidays for as long as they can remember." Joan and Dinah lived together for most of the time between 5 and 15. Christine and Nina, raised by the father and his sister "generally spent summer holidays together in each other's homes." Charlotte and Laura, raised by the mother and the maternal grandmother "lived as close neighbors in a coastal town attending the same school" from before age 9 to age 15 and "were closely attached and went around a lot together." Trixie and Anne were raised about a mile apart by the mother and the paternal grandmother and went to the same school. Adeline and Gwendolin were not separated until their mother died when they were 9.

As you can see, this is hardly the picture we once had of one twin raised in the home of a Liverpool dock worker and one in the home of an Oxford professor!

Two smaller twin studies, by H. H. Newman, F. N. Freeman, and K. J. Holzinger[26] (19 pairs) and N. Juel-Nielsen[27] (12 pairs) also suffer, among other defects, from the problem of correlated environments. This problem alone makes all of these studies worthless as sources of information on the heritability of intelligence. Since we cannot precisely specify what environmental factors are key to the

development of IQ, we can't falsify the hypothesis that the high correlations among separated identical twins are *entirely* due to correlations in their environments.[28] As David Layzer concluded after a
detailed mathematical consideration of heritability analysis:

Estimates based on phenotypic correlations between separated monozygotic
(identical) twins—usually considered to be the most reliable kind of estimates—are vitiated by systematic errors inherent in IQ tests by the presence
of genotype-environment correlation, and by the lack of detailed understanding of environmental factors relevant to the development of behavioral
traits.[29]

ADOPTION AND THE HERITABILITY OF IQ

If the separated twin studies that have been done cannot throw light
on the heritability of IQ, what are we left with? One possibility is
studies of adopted children. *If children are adopted at random,* one
would expect their IQs to resemble those of their biological parents
more than the IQs of their adoptive parents under a hereditarian
hypothesis (one that emphasizes genetic determination of IQ). The
reverse would be expected under an environmentalist hypothesis (one
that assumes IQ is largely determined by the circumstances in which a
child is reared). By examining the relationship of the IQs of adopted
offspring to the IQs of the biological parents, one should be able to get
an estimate of the heritability of IQ, and therefore test these hypotheses.

Several studies of adopted children have claimed to throw light on
the heritability of IQ. Ironically, the one most quoted as supporting a
hereditarian view was a long-term study by a prominent environmentalist, H. M. Skeels, begun in the 1930s and completed in the late
1940s in collaboration with M. Skodak.[30] In the final assessment, the
IQs of children tested at about 13 years of age were weakly correlated
(coefficient of .32) with the educational level of the biological mother
and not correlated (coefficient of .02) with that of the adoptive
mother—slight evidence on the face of it for some heritability of IQ.
These results have been widely and uncritically cited by those with a
strong faith in the potency of genes in determining intelligence.

A careful analysis of the Skeels-Skodak studies, however, shows this
interpretation to be without support. We are once again indebted to
Leon Kamin[31] for a detailed dissection of this work, and will only
touch on the high points of his critique. First of all, the hereditarians
strangely neglect to report the earlier results obtained by Skodak and

Skeels when the children were tested at around 7 years of age.[32] Then the children's IQs correlated with the biological mothers' educational level at a level of .24 and with the foster mothers' at a level of .20, correlations that do not differ significantly. Curiously, it would seem that at age 7 environment determines a child's IQ but at age 13 genes begin to have an effect!

How can this discrepancy be explained? One might claim that the genes for the IQ are only expressed after puberty—like the genes affecting baldness in men. But then hereditarians are always claiming just the opposite—that, for example, genetically determined IQ differences among social classes are observed in children under age 6![33]

Kamin's answer is simpler and much more persuasive. Only 100 children were tested in the final report, 139 in the earlier study. As is often the case in long-term studies, there had been drop-outs. If the drop-outs were not a random sample of the families in the study, then differential dropping-out could be responsible for the changes in correlation coefficients. And differential dropping-out is precisely what Kamin discovered. There was a tendency for college-educated adoptive mothers to stay in the study and for those who did not attend college to drop out of the study. This in turn made the adoptive mothers a more homogeneous group, but did not significantly affect the range of education of the biological mothers.[34]

There are several other difficulties with the Skodak and Skeels study as a source of an estimate for the heritability of IQ. One is the use of the number of years of education of the parents as a measure of their IQs. This implies, as Kamin points out, that

The difference between completing one and five years of grade school is exactly equal to the difference between completing high school and college—four years of education in each case. The assumption is thus made that the IQ difference between college and high school graduates is identical to that between grade one and grade five dropouts, and that the difference in intellect-fostering environments provided by parents is also identical in these cases. These assumptions seem ridiculous and are not supported by any data.[35]

It is obvious that the average educational levels of natural and foster mothers in this study differ greatly. Only 8 percent of the natural mothers completed college versus 51 percent of the adoptive mothers. The variation around the averages on the educational scale is thus likely to have very different meanings for the two groups, and the relation of that variation to what we're really interested in—IQ in the biological mothers and IQ-fostering environment in the homes provided by the foster mothers—is difficult to determine.

The flaw in these studies, from a hereditarian point of view, is, however, the same one that plagued the twin studies—correlated environments, in this case correlation between the environments of the homes of natural and adoptive mothers. The correlations of the IQs of the adopted children with their biological mothers can be explained, as Kamin points out, on the basis of selective placement. Children coming from homes where the mothers had higher educations tended to be placed in "better" adoptive homes. We repeat that a key requirement for an adoption study that produces significant information on heritability is that the adoptions be at random with respect to the IQ of the biological parents. If there is any tendency to place the children of "bright" biological parents with "bright" adoptive parents, a significant child/biological parent correlation of IQs does not necessarily indicate a genetic component of intelligence.

The hereditarian analyses of other adoptive studies have also been carefully examined and found to suffer from a variety of shortcomings similar to those found in the Skodak-Skeels work.[36] One is forced to conclude that adoption studies provide no convincing evidence for a substantial genetic component to variation in IQ. They do, however, in several instances indicate a substantial (if indeterminant) environmental component. For example, the IQs are known for sixty-three of the biological mothers in the Skodak-Skeels study. Their IQs averaged 86. The average IQ of their children was 106. This change, it is argued even by hereditarians, must be due at least in part to the superior adoptive homes (remember 51 percent of the foster mothers went to college as opposed to 8 percent of the biological mothers). The amount of improvement that can be assigned to the environment depends on what is assumed about the unknown IQs of the fathers. If, quite reasonably, they are assumed to be the same as the mothers', then the observed IQ improvement is difficult to reconcile with Jensen's estimate of .81 heritability of IQ.[37]

Even more intriguing is a result abstracted by Kamin from three other adoption studies. In some families, there are both natural and adoptive children. It is of considerable interest to compare the IQ correlation of the natural children, and of the adopted children, with the same parents. Under a hereditarian hypothesis, one would expect the first correlation, adoptive child/parent, to be very low, quite close to zero (assuming random adoption) and the second correlation, natural child/parent, to be quite high. In the first case only environment would tend to make the children and parents similar, in the second *both* environment and genetics would tend to cause similarity.

Kamin found that there was no significant difference among the correlations.[38] Also interesting is the observation that *both* adopted and natural children in families that adopt have lower correlations with the parents than natural children with the parents in nonadopting families. Thus the environment in adopting homes seems to be significantly different from that in nonadopting homes in some factor affecting how closely parents and children resemble one another in IQ. Furthermore, within adopting homes, whether or not the child is natural or adopted does not seem to affect his or her degree of resemblance to the parent. As Kamin says, "There seems to be no plausible hereditarian way to explain this finding."[39]

What Is the Answer?

Where does all of this leave us? It would seem that although in theory twin studies and adoption studies should throw light on the inheritance of IQ, *in practice* they have not.[40] With redesign (which undoubtedly would be socially unacceptable), they might do so, as might studies of the IQ correlations of children with their parents in cases where divorce split the family when the children were very young. Some genetic contribution to individual differences might be revealed by such studies. But at the moment we are left with one conclusion. There is no body of evidence that falsifies the hypothesis that $H = 0$. *In plain English, as far as we can tell today, all of the variation observed in IQ in the populations tested could be due to environmental factors only.* This also means, of course, that there is not a shred of evidence to support Jensen's contention that $H = .81$.

Note that we say that the *variation* in IQ could all be environmentally caused. This does not mean that genes have nothing to do with intelligence. The genetic program of a normal human being specifies that in the vast majority of environments an individual will develop with just one head containing a brain with an enormous potential for memory, for making associations, and so on. There is no significant genetic variation in the number of heads in different human groups, and there may be no significant difference in the genetically determined potential capacities of the brain. Saying that genes are involved in the production of intelligence or any characteristic of any organism is a simple tautology (one could not acquire a suntan without genes programming the development of a skin with the capacity to tan). It does not speak at all to whether differences observed among individuals or among populations in skin color, intelligence, or anything else are caused by differences in their genes.

Now, the question of the genetic determination or nondetermination of IQ differences is one fraught with emotion and political overtones. There is considerable evidence that committed hereditarians have, to put it charitably, sometimes permitted their zeal to overcome their judgment and care in reporting the literature.[41] If the hereditarians seem to have presented a selected and inaccurate account of the research bearing on genetics and IQ, why, you may ask, should not those critical of the hereditarian position also fudge their reports?

There is no way you can be certain that we have not led you up the garden path unless you are willing to go and check the original literature yourself. Indeed, the magnitude of the problems with and the flimsiness of the evidence for a significant heritability of IQ came as a shock to us. Yet our own checking of the literature as well as published reviews by others[42] show the Kamin critique to be quite robust. This does not mean that it has been demonstrated that all IQ variation in the populations studied is environmental. It can, indeed, be argued that some amount of it may be genetic simply because it seems unlikely that all of the genes affecting the development of the physical apparatus supporting complex behaviors would be identical in all people. But it is also quite probable that those systems can be so differently influenced by different environments that any genetic variation is utterly irrelevant. We cannot emphasize too strongly that a high heritability of IQ would not of itself tell us *anything* about how environmental change might change an individual's IQ.

Finally, we may ask what environmentalists would hope to gain from an assault on the notion that within the populations studied, IQ has a high heritability? To the uninitiated, the answer would seem to be "A great deal." After all, has not Jensen stated, "The fact of substantial heritability of IQ within the populations does increase the *a priori* probability that the population difference is partly attributable to genetic factors"?[43] The trouble is that, as we shall document in the next chapter, Jensen's statement is the purest nonsense—grounded in his apparent misunderstanding of heritability. Indeed, there is no *a priori* reason for the environmentalist to attack the notion that the heritability of IQ is high within both White and Black populations. For, counterintuitive as it is, if the heritability were .81 in both populations, that would say *nothing whatever* about the cause of differences in the average IQ scores of Whites and Blacks!

6

Group Differences
in Intelligence

All [test results] point to the presence of some native differences
between Negroes and whites as determined by intelligence tests.
—Audrey M. Shuey, *The Testing of Negro Intelligence*, 1958

At present there exist no methods of estimating differences in the
mean level of G (the genetic component of variation in IQ score),
and there is no evidence of any kind which suggests that negro
intelligence is, on the average, less than, equal to, or greater than
that of white people. These three hypotheses are not intrinsically
unplausible, but those who think they can be tested empirically
have been inadequately instructed . . . by their statistical colleagues.
—P. A. P. Moran, *New Scientist*, 1976

The world's greatest biologists: Huxley, Haldane, Keith, Millot,
Blumenbach, Garrett, Jensen and many others are agreed as to
Negro race inferiority.
Jefferson-Lincoln Americans, Inc.,
Case Against Racial Integration (New Orleans, 1976)

BLACKS are born stupid, even dumber than Poles. Jews are
smart. Country hicks are easily taken by city conmen. Women can't
handle mathematics well enough to be good scientists. Sound familiar?
They should. Society is shot through with prejudices about the comparative intellectual capacities of different groups. And "science" has
tried hard to confirm or disprove many of these folk conclusions.

This folklore raises three basic questions about group differences in
IQ. First, why should group comparisons be made at all? We will see

that they probably should not be. Second, what differences have been observed? The most frequently noted is that Black groups show average IQ scores below those of White groups. Third, are the IQ differences observed best interpreted as being caused by genetic or environmental differences among the groups? Here the evidence is overwhelmingly more compatible with an environmental interpretation than a genetic one.

The Use of IQ Tests in Comparing Different Groups

The purpose of assessing intelligence by means of an IQ test is to facilitate decisions and to provide some objectivity. The use of *individual* IQ tests theoretically enables merit to become the basis for decision making, rather than the traditional criteria of social class, sex, skin color, and age. While the results of testing for this purpose have fallen far short of the ideal, to date testing has probably been more successful than existing subjective means.

The comparison of individual IQs has been extended by many to a comparison of the average IQ of groups. What practical purpose does studying group differences serve? To know that the group of Phexes differs significantly in IQ from the group of Klanses (both fictitious groups) does not tell us much that is useful about Mary Smith, who is a Phexe—any more than the auto accident record of your age group tells us much that is useful about your driving ability. Mary's individual score conveys much more useful information about her, providing her score was obtained under appropriate conditions and that Phexes were represented in the standardizing sample. That she is a Phexe is of much less importance than what is known about her as an individual.

When all is said and done, it is impossible to escape the conclusion that most of the research on group differences in intelligence has been *motivated by a desire to affirm the superiority of one group over another*. That different groups are chosen at different times reinforces this view. Remember that when there was an influx of immigrants into the United States, it was in vogue to study groups with different national origins. For example, at a time when there was both overt and covert discrimination against the Italians, there were at least six studies within a decade comparing the IQ of Italian immigrants or their children with other Americans.[1] Today, most commonly the performance of Blacks on standard IQ tests is compared to that of Whites.

When group differences are examined, caution must be exercised. Within each of the groups, there is wide variation. While Danes are, on the average, much taller than Japanese, some Japanese are taller than most Danes. For most quantitative traits, especially for mental ability, there is relatively greater variation within any one group than the mean differences between any two groups. For example, the mean difference between two groups rarely exceeds 15 IQ points and is usually considerably less than this, while the normal range of IQ for 95 percent of any population is 60 IQ points. Consequently, knowing an individual's group membership gives very little practical information about that individual's IQ.

A second major problem in asking about group differences is that the single IQ score may obscure group differences in aptitude. For example, if the mythical Phexes excel in numerical and spatial abilities and the Klanses star on verbal items, and a scale of general intelligence is weighted equally with items from both fields, no significant differences between the two groups would be found. If, on the other hand, the intelligence test is weighted with verbal items, the average of the Klanses will consistently surpass that of the Phexes.

Group Differences

RACIAL DIFFERENCES

Blacks, on the average, score lower on IQ tests than do Whites. Whereas the average IQ for Whites is 100, the average IQ for Blacks is somewhat lower, ranging from 80 to 90, according to different studies on adults[2] and children.[3] It is frequently reported that Blacks score between 10 and 25 IQ points lower than Whites. However, when Blacks and Whites from the same part of the country and from the same social class are compared, the differences in IQ are smaller. For example, in a study of Black and White children from Boston and from the Baltimore-Philadelphia region,[4] Whites scored only 4 to 6 points higher on an IQ test than Blacks from the same region and social class. The difference in IQ between locales was much greater (10 to 12 IQ points). If the study had omitted an analysis by town, the traditional results favoring Whites by 15 IQ points could have been reported, since more Blacks lived in the Baltimore-Philadelphia area, and more Whites came from the Boston area.

Much of the early research in which the scores of Blacks were compared to the existing norms is misleading. For example, the average IQ of Black schoolchildren from Florida, Georgia, Alabama, Tennessee, and South Carolina was found to be 80.7,[5] while the norms of White children *nationwide* is 100. However, White schoolchildren from the same five southeastern states were not tested at that time, although it is known that the average IQ for Whites in that region is lower than the national average. Therefore, it is an abuse of statistics to argue, as many have, that such data are evidence for a 16- to 20-point difference between Blacks and Whites.

Recent research has found smaller differences in IQ between Black and White children, especially when social class is controlled. Prior to 1966 the Black-White IQ difference for lower-class children was 12 IQ points, and for middle-class children, 20 IQ points. The most recent studies show only a 6 point difference for lower-class children and approximately 9 point difference for middle-class children.[6] For adults, when the scores of military recruits from the Vietnamese War and World War II are compared,[7] the Black-White IQ difference has remained at approximately 23 points. This figure is probably an inflated estimate since social class is not controlled for, and there are proportionately more lower-class Blacks than Whites drafted for military service.

What about other groups? Can IQ tests discriminate between the rich and the poor, between men and women, between Jews and Catholics? Again we are prompted to ask, "Why is this interesting?" and "Who are we trying to put down?" But endeavors to make the discriminations have been undertaken.

SEX DIFFERENCES

The major individual IQ tests such as the Stanford-Binet do not reveal sex differences in IQ, simply because the test was deliberately constructed to eliminate items that greatly favored one sex over the other. As mentioned earlier, some items slightly favoring girls were balanced by a selection of items slightly favoring boys. Where there has been no attempt to erase sex differences, girls score somewhat better than boys, especially on tests relying on verbal skills.[8]

There is, however, considerable ambiguity in the question "Which sex is more intelligent?" It is more meaningful to ask what sex differences exist in the specific abilities that are measured on IQ tests. In an up-to-date and thorough review of sex differences,[9] it was concluded that girls show superior verbal abilities before the age of 3 and from adolescence on. Boys, on the other hand, excel at quantitative abilities, and at visual spatial abilities from adolescence through adulthood. Consistent sex differences are usually not found on mastery of concepts, in reasoning, or in memory.

CLASS DIFFERENCES

The United States is often claimed to be a land of opportunity, where every person willing to work hard and to save can make a fortune and perhaps achieve fame. However, the reality of the situation departs considerably from this idealized notion: America is clearly organized into social classes that are defined primarily, but not exclusively, by occupation (and the attendant wealth and status), education, and area of residence. The existing class situation within races is relatively open, allowing mobility both upward and downward to take place and preventing the hardening of the class system into a caste system.

Since IQ is related to occupation and education, it should cause no surprise that there is a relationship between IQ and socioeconomic status (class).[10] When the average IQ has been calculated for men in different occupations, men in the professions are generally 16 or more IQ points above the average office worker, and businessmen are about 8 to 16 points above, skilled tradesmen are at the national average (i.e., IQ 100), while semiskilled workers are usually slightly below, and unskilled workers considerably below.[11]

Two very important points should be remembered. First, there is a great deal of overlap in IQs among the different occupations. For example, IQs of 115 or above are found not only among accountants and teachers, but also among shipping and sales clerks, bricklayers, carpenters, and other laborers. Second, there is more variation in IQ at the lower end of the occupational hierarchy than at the upper end. In a large scale study, accountants showed a range of 30 IQ points (112 to 142), whereas among bricklayers there was a range of 42 IQ points. Children's IQs are related to their fathers' occupation, but the difference in IQ of the children of different social classes is significantly smaller than the difference between the IQs of their parents.[12]

Despite the modest relationship between IQ and social class, the "lower" classes make enormous contributions to the elite in our nation. Examine any group of professionals, top people in industrial management, top politicians, and so on, and you will find brilliant people of humble origins—people who had to be especially bright and tenacious to overcome their class handicap. The absolute contribution of brainpower to society by the lower classes is immense. And, of course, the upper classes produce their share of the not-too-brainy individuals.

Are there group differences in the various abilities tested in IQ tests? Harvard psychologist Gerald Lesser and his associates tried to answer this question by studying Chinese, Jewish, Black, and Puerto Rican children from New York City.[13] Half of each sample came from lower-class families and half from middle-class families. The children were given a variety of tests, including tests of reasoning, spatial, numerical, and verbal abilities. The major results of the study were clear-cut: differences in pattern of performance emerged among the four groups, as shown in Figure 6–1. Each ethnic group had its own distinctive profile.

Social class influenced the level of performance, with middle-class children scoring higher, on the average, than lower-class children, but it did not affect the pattern of results, as shown in Figure 6–2. The middle-class and lower-class members of an ethnic group showed the same pattern of relative strengths and weaknesses.

Social class or socioeconomic status, then, shows a consistent but modest relationship to intelligence in children and adults and in most "racial" or "ethnic" groups studied.[14] A similar relationship is shown in whether a person comes from an urban or rural environment, with children from cities outscoring those from farms by 10 or so IQ points, a difference that increases with age.[15] Despite the consistency in these basic findings, it is nonetheless clear that *the variation within groups is greater than the differences between them.* That there are high- and low-scoring individuals in every social class, in every ethnic group, and in both city and countryside is more important than the differences in group averages.

The Meaning of Group Differences: The Genetic Hypothesis

In this country, "race" or ethnic group membership and social status tend to vary together. If you are Black, the chances are relatively high that you belong to the poor and least-advantaged class. The odds are very small that you are a member of the upper classes. The urban-rural distinction is also intertwined with the social-class distinction, for a relatively high proportion of country dwellers are poor. Consequently, the explanations for Black-White, social class, and rural-urban differences in intelligence often follow similar lines.

One explanation of group differences is that the groups compared (the rich and the poor, the Blacks and Whites, etc.) have different genetic endowments. In the case of "races" or ethnic groups, gene frequencies are thought to have altered during times of cultural and geographic isolation. Among the social classes, the mobility in the open class structure of society supposedly allows the talented to rise to positions of prestige and status, those with lesser abilities to find their level, with the dullest sinking to the bottom of the heap, taking their bad genes with them. An obvious variant of this argument applies to the rural-urban differences: the brighter, more ambitious people carried their bright genes to the cities, leaving the less motivated and intellectually less endowed at home on the farm. In these ways, various groups may come to have different levels of innate ability.

GENES AND SOCIAL MOBILITY

What is the evidence on this issue? It is a simple matter to document that social mobility exists within races. For example, it is known that, if children in a family change social status as adults, the more intelligent usually move up in status, and the less intelligent move down.[16] It has also been found that the larger the difference in IQ between fathers and sons, the more likely it is that the son will alter his social class by moving upward if his IQ is higher or downward if it is lower.[17]

Whereas the evidence indicates social mobility to be based on ability, the converse, that high ability leads to social mobility, is not invariably the case; otherwise, there would not be a wide range of IQs found in each social class. In other words, there are countless thousands of people with very high IQs who do not occupy positions of high status. Surveys generally report that much talent is "wasted" in

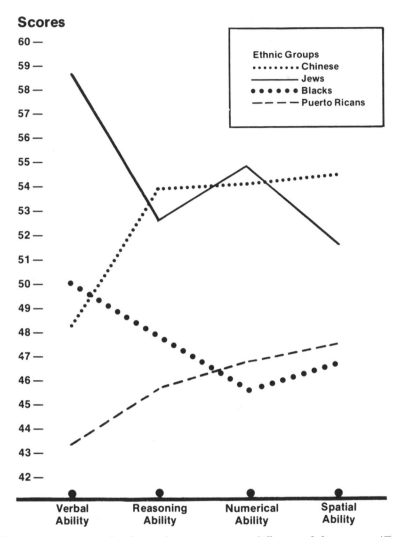

Figure 6-1.   Scores for four ethnic groups on different ability tests. (Data from Lesser, Fifer, and Clark, "Mental Abilities of Children from Different Social-Class and Cultural Groups.")

the lower social classes due to failure to complete high school and to obtain advanced education.[18]

What about the differences between farm and town dwellers? Is there evidence for selective migration—are those who leave the farm brighter than those who stay behind? Early studies, when rural emi-

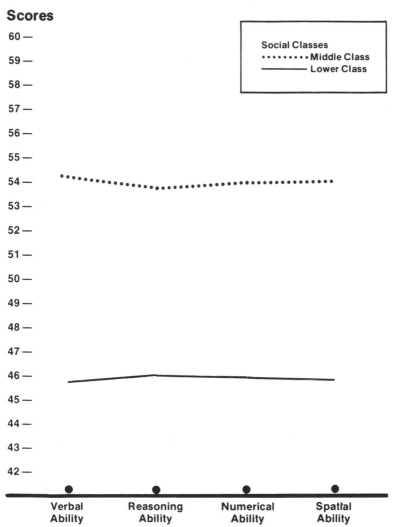

Scores

Figure 6-2. Social class differences for the combined ethnic groups on four mental abilities. (Data from Lesser, Fifer, and Clark, "Mental Abilities of Children from Different Social-Class and Cultural Groups.")

gration was a more important issue than today, suggest that migrants were of two types—the brighter and more ambitious people attracted by the opportunities offered by the cities, and the duller and less well adjusted people seeking escape from their failures.[19]

There is, then, a relationship between ability and social mobility, but it is far from perfect. And there is not one iota of evidence on whether "ability" in these cases is innate, environmentally produced, or a mixture of the two.

INNATE RACIAL DIFFERENCES IN INTELLIGENCE

Can genetic differences explain the "racial" differences in IQ? While natural selection appears to have produced geographic variation in a variety of physical characteristics, this does not mean that *all* genetically controlled characters are under different selection pressures in different populations. On the contrary, the amazing thing about different geographic samples of humanity (populations, "ethnic groups," "races") is the high degree of genetic similarity among the samples. Harvard population biologist Richard Lewontin[20] estimates that approximately 85 percent of human genetic diversity is found in individual variation *within* populations. Less than 15 percent of all human genetic diversity is accounted for by differences *between* human groups.*

How then can one assess the genetic interpretation of group differences? A variety of different methods exist, including studying racial admixtures and the effect of common environments on so-called different "races."

Racial Admixture. Suppose one so-called racial group has "good genes" for intelligence and another does not, then children from intermarriage should on the average manifest an intelligence midway between the means of the two "racial" groups. Thus one method of testing the genetic hypotheses of group differences has been to compare individuals who differ in their racial purity or admixture—that is in the socially defined racial groups to which their ancestors belonged.

No characteristic used as a measure of racial purity has ever been convincingly associated with IQ test scores. In early research using skin color as a basis for racial classification, only 2 or 3 IQ points differentiated light-skinned from dark-skinned Blacks,[21] and skin color correlated with IQ only very slightly (correlation coefficient a trivial .12 to .18). In a Canadian study of Blacks,[22] those classified as having mixed blood had higher scores than those considered to be pureblood Blacks, but, contrary to the genetic hypotheses, the group judged half-

---

* However, his estimates were based on known sets of genes and may not be applicable to complex behavior such as that involved in taking intelligence tests. Intelligence is presumably not under the control of such known sets but depends upon many genes whose mode of inheritance and within and between population variability (if any) is completely unknown.

Black averaged *lower* IQ scores than the three-quarters Black group.

When blood groups have been used to define races and racial admixture, interest has focused on whether "European genes"—blood-group genes showing very high frequencies in European populations and low frequencies in African populations—are related to high IQ test performance in Blacks. The answer is no. In samples of Blacks from Georgia and Kentucky,[23] it was *not* the presence of European (White) ancestry that predicted good intellectual performance. Similar results have been reported for both schoolchildren and college students. Further corroborating evidence comes from a study of gifted Black children (IQ more than 125), who were classified into four categories of race mixture on the basis of genealogical information supplied by their parents.[24] While the genetic hypothesis predicts that more high-IQ children should come from the sample that had predominantly Caucasian ancestry, the results did not confirm this expectation. Sixty-eight percent of the gifted Black children had more Black ancestry than White. These data can best be explained by assuming no genetic difference in IQ between Blacks and Whites. Despite these results, Shockley has gone so far as to suggest that there is a 1-point increase in IQ for every percentage point of "Caucasian ancestry" in Blacks.[25]

Can the offspring of interracial marriages tell us anything about innate intelligence and race? Genetically, the racial mixture is the same when there is a Black mother and White father as when there is a White mother and a Black father (assuming the criteria for defining Black and White are the same in both cases). The environments, however, are likely to differ for the children of these two groups, since the child normally has a great deal more contact with the mother than the father. In recent research on the IQs of children of interracial marriages in the United States, it was found that children with White mothers averaged approximately 9 IQ points higher than children of Black mothers,[26] a finding that fits poorly with a genetic hypothesis, but which is perfectly compatible with an environmental interpretation. Furthermore, German illegitimate children 5 to 13 years old, fathered by Black and White American servicemen, did not differ in average intelligence.[27] The child-rearing practices of their German mothers were more influential in determining IQ than the racial origins and genes of their fathers. In this, as in the other studies of racial admixture, there is no evidence to support the hereditarian hypothesis.

Common Environments. The genetic hypothesis does not preclude environmental influences from having some effect on intelligence. However, in order to assess genetic contribution per se, children of so-called different races should be reared in a single common environment. Of course, no two environments are ever identical, especially for children with different skin colors, but institutional settings such as orphanages and other residential care facilities provide a first approximation.

In one important case, 2- to 5-year-old Black, White, and mixed-race children who had lived in a high-quality residential nursery in England for at least one year were given IQ tests.[28] The IQs of the three groups of children were very similar (ranging from 103 to 108). The single significant* difference favored the Black and mixed-race children over the White children in a nonverbal test of intelligence. In a second study,[29] IQ tests were given to children of different "races" who had spent most of the first two years of their lives in a residential nursery but, subsequently, had been returned either to their generally lower-class mothers, had been adopted by upper-middle-class families, or had remained in the residential nursery. In none of these groups did the scores of White children differ from those of their non-White counterparts. On the other hand, there were clear relationships between the children's test scores and the environment: children restored to their natural mothers showed lower IQs than children in the quality institution, who in turn had lower IQs than children adopted by upper-middle-class families.

Such results are not restricted to England. In Israel, the IQ scores of children from Oriental and European Jewish families living on kibbutzim (the collective settlements where child-rearing from birth through adolescence is in the hands of trained child-care workers) were measured.[30] In earlier studies of home-reared children, Oriental Jewish children scored 16 IQ points below European Jewish children—on tests designed by Europeans, of course! However, when the IQs of Oriental Jewish children and European Jewish children raised in the same kibbutz were assessed, the two groups of children had equivalent, high IQs. That is, in groups that hereditarians would claim had genetic differences in IQ, a high-quality child-rearing environment obliterated the traditional IQ differences.

Day-care programs, in which young children spend large parts of their waking hours, also constitute at least a partially common envi-

---

* Significant in this context means "statistically significant," i.e., that there is a very small probability that the difference was a chance occurrence.

ronment for ethnically diverse groups. The more hours Black and White children spend in day care together, the more similar their environments. While, traditionally, the services of day-care centers have amounted to little more than group babysitting, recent concern for providing enriched and stimulating environments has produced a variety of innovative programs. Most careful assessments reported by day-care programs are based on exclusively Black samples or have grossly unbalanced samples with approximately 90 percent belonging to one ethnic group.[31] However, in one small-scale study, it was found that Black and White children $3\frac{1}{2}$ years of age, who had been in an especially enriched day-care program for more than one year, showed equally high IQs.[32] Among the control children who did *not* attend the day-care program, there was more than a 30-point difference between the IQ test scores of Black and White children. While attendance at the day-care center made a significant improvement for relatively advantaged White children (an average gain of 13 IQ points), its effect was massive for poor Black children, who made an average gain of 34 IQ points. We see clearly that in high-quality environments the differences in IQ between Black and White children are dramatically reduced, a result that does not fit well with the genetic position.

Transracial Adoptions. Black children adopted by White parents provide information that permits some progress to be made in untangling the biological and sociocultural contributions to IQ performance. If Black children have genetically limited intellectual potential, their IQ performance will be lower than that of White children when the Black children are reared in White, typically middle-class homes. If, on the other hand, Black children exhibit similar scores to other adoptees, it implies that IQ is highly malleable and responsive to the environment. Ideally, Black parents who have adopted White children should also be studied, but such cases are so rare that only the outcome of Black children reared in White families can be reported.

Transracial adoptions of 130 Black children into White homes were recently studied.[33] Using the most reputable individual tests (namely, the Stanford-Binet and the Wechsler tests), it was found that the Black adoptees had an average IQ of 106.3, an increase of more than 15 points over the average IQ of Blacks in the same region. A comparison between the natural children of the adoptive (White) parents and Black children adopted by White parents early in infancy showed that the two groups had the same average IQ on each of the IQ tests used.

In fact, Black children adopted into White families have the same average IQ scores as White adopted children.[34] Clearly, the IQ scores of Blacks and Whites are environmentally malleable.

The Meaning of Racial Differences in IQ. Curiously, there seems to be a negative relationship between people's knowledge of quantitative genetics and their enthusiasm for the notion that group differences in "genetic IQ" are demonstrable. Despite the evidence just reviewed showing no reasonably scientific basis for concluding that differences in IQ score between groups is due to genetics, psychologist H. J. Eysenck has written, for example, "All the evidence to date suggests the strong and indeed overwhelming importance of genetic factors in producing the great variety of intellectual differences which we observe in our culture, and *much of the difference observed between certain racial groups*"[35] (emphasis ours). And then there was Shockley's famous statement previously alluded to: "Nature has color-coded groups of individuals so that statistically reliable predictions of their adaptability to intellectually rewarding and effective lives can easily be made and profitably be used by the pragmatic man in the street."[36]

Somehow the proof that Mother Nature has assigned more genes for smartness to those with white skins than to those with dark skins has escaped the attention of most quantitative geneticists. How come? The answer is simple—quantitative geneticists are burdened with a knowledge of genetics. It is freedom from such knowledge that permitted Jensen to make the statement quoted at the end of the last chapter to the effect that high heritability within populations was *a priori* evidence that average differences between the populations had a genetic basis. *This is the most persistent and pernicious fallacy in the entire race-IQ controversy.*

Let us suppose that, contrary to existing evidence, we *knew* that the heritability of IQ was .81 in both the U.S. Black population and the U.S. White population (these populations being defined purely on the basis of measured skin color); that is, in both populations the majority of individual-to-individual variation in IQ was due to genetic differences among the individuals. Would that make it more likely that an observed average difference in IQ between those two populations was in part caused by genetic differences than if the heritability of IQ in both populations was known to be zero? The answer is an unequivocal no. The technical basis for that counterintuitive statement may be found in the literature,[37] but some simple examples can demonstrate the validity of this statement.

Suppose you were studying the skin tones of a group of White New Yorkers that included people of Irish, English, Norwegian, Italian, Spanish, and Puerto Rican ancestry. Skin color would be discovered to be a highly heritable character. Suppose you then divided the group into two subgroups at random, and in January sent subgroup A on a one-month paid vacation to Miami and kept subgroup B in New York for "further study." Immediately upon subgroup A's return, you measured the skin color of both groups and found subgroup A to be much darker than subgroup B. Now the two groups would differ in a highly heritable characteristic, but the difference you found between the groups is entirely environmentally caused![38]

Let's look at the converse case. Suppose two pairs of identical twins of the same age, one pair Black and one pair White, were adopted at birth and raised together by a liberal tan-skinned couple. Each pair of twins can be thought of as a group or a two-individual population within which the heritability of skin color is zero. You will recall from the definition of heritability that it would have to be zero since each member of a pair of identical twins has the same genotype and so there can be no genetic source of any variation within the pair. But even though the two pairs are raised in the same environment, when they are adults, one pair will still have black skin and the other pair will still have white skin. The differences *between* the groups (the pairs of twins) are *entirely* genetic, even though there is zero heritability of skin color *within* the groups.

There is no contradiction in skin color having a high heritability in the New Yorkers and zero heritability within the pairs of twins. Heritability is a property of a *given population in a given environment*. If, for instance, the New Yorkers were transported permanently to the Bahamas and spent their time in the sun, the heritability of skin color in the group would lower or disappear. If they were all toasted a dark brown, there would be little variance in skin color to analyze, and the heritability would be very low—a fact that would be confirmed by the lack of skin-color variation in offspring raised in the same "toasting" environment. By moving the New Yorkers back to the New York environment, the genetic variability could be made to reappear. It would be "unmasked," just as Waddington unmasked the genetic variability in fruit fly cross-vein structure by changing the flies' environment.

Other examples showing that knowing the degree of heritability within two populations gives *no information whatever* on the cause of differences between the populations are easily constructed. A somewhat more detailed example is given in Appendix B, which you should consult if you are still uncomfortable with the notion—for, as we indicated, it is a key one in the race-IQ controversy.

Hereditarians, people who believe the Jensen hypothesis that differences in the genes account for Blacks' scoring lower than Whites on IQ tests, frequently claim that racial differences in IQ probably reflect different selection pressures in the history of "races." Thus Eysenck speculates that American Blacks have been selected for stupidity and (by implication) that Whites have been selected for intelligence.[39] Now there is not the slightest shred of evidence that this is true, and an equally good (or bad!) case can be made for the converse of these speculations. But for the moment, let's pretend it is a historical fact. If it were true that Black-White IQ differences were the result of selection against intelligence in Blacks and for it in Whites, then one would expect a *reduction* in the heritability of IQ in each group proportional to the amount of selection that had occurred. Eysenck and his co-believers cannot have it both ways, *for the evolutionary forces that increase genetic differences between populations decrease differences within those populations—that is, those forces decrease the heritability of whatever characteristics are evolving.*[40]

To put it in a nutshell, the notion that group differences in average IQ are due to differences in genes for intelligence is not supported by any evidence, nor does it follow logically from an unwarranted assumption of high heritability of intelligence within groups. If the heritability of intelligence within Black and White populations were high, it would be less likely that Blacks and Whites would have evolved genetic differences. If the heritability were low, that result would contribute nothing to understanding the difference in average test scores between Blacks and Whites. In our opinion the emphasis on heritability in the race-IQ debate is purely a red herring promoted by those who do not understand the proper use of this statistic.

The Meaning of Group Differences: Environmental Hypotheses

There are two environmental explanations that are put forward to account for the differences in IQs between Blacks and Whites, the rich and poor, and boys and girls. One explanation is that IQ tests are biased—designed for one group and thus unfair to another that is just as bright. The other explanation is that the average environment in which the children of some groups are reared is less likely to permit the realization of intellectual potential. In that view, one group is, on the average, less bright because of its upbringing. It is not possible to choose with certainty between these explanations—for there is much about environmental influences on IQ that is not known. For the rest of this chapter, what is known will be sampled to provide some idea of the breadth and complexity of the problem of explaining group differences.

CAN TESTS COMPARE NEW YORKERS AND ESKIMOS FAIRLY?

Perhaps the best way to introduce the question of test bias is to consider not the problems of comparing Black and White Americans, but of comparing people from even more diverse cultures. While IQ tests of the same general form have been used with predictive success throughout Western culture, designing a culture-fair test to compare people from strikingly different cultures has proven impossible.

Of course, a Stanford-Binet test can be given to a group of Eskimo children and numerical scores calculated. Invariably these children will have an average score far lower than a group of White school-children of the same age from New York City. Does that prove that Eskimos are less intelligent than Whites? How would White children perform on an Eskimo test? The most casual knowledge of Eskimo culture indicates that an average New Yorker suddenly dropped into a primitive Eskimo group would flunk virtually every test of intelligence. The individual would not easily master the art of hunting seals, trapping foxes, or selecting snow for an igloo.[41]

Examples could be added without end. In such seemingly simple tasks as matching colors, different cultures and the languages that express the culture influence the outcome. Some cultures, like the Samoan, emphasize playing with words (such as in punning), and thus people from those cultures score higher on verbal ability tests than do people from cultures that do not emphasize playing with words.[42] Indeed, since language may play a sizable role in shaping an individual's world view, it is difficult to see how a verbal test could be devised in English that when translated would be fair both to an individual whose native tongue was English and to another who spoke a non-European language.[43] Furthermore, the physical surroundings of an individual can shape his or her spatial conceptions,[44] thus making cross-cultural tests emphasizing geometry equally suspect.

HOW ABOUT BLACKS AND WHITES?

But, you say, what has this got to do with American Blacks and Whites? Don't they both speak the same native language? Are they not part of the same society, striving for the same goals? Are not, then, the tests "fair" to Blacks? The answer is yes and no. Many Blacks may have adopted the striving of the dominant White culture, and the tests are then "fair" in predicting Black success within that White culture. But Blacks do form a distinct culture in the United States and, at least in ghettos, speak a distinctly different language.[44] If one takes the naive view of IQ tests—that they are supposed to measure some sort of innate ability—then the tests are very unfair. For instance, linguist William A. Steward produced the following translation of "The Night Before Christmas" into ghetto language:

> It's the night before Christmas
> and here in our house,
> It ain't nothing moving
> not even no mouse.
> There go we-all stockings,
> hanging high up off the floor,
> So Santa Claus can full them up,
> if he wak in through our dorr.[46]

He discovered by accident that a 12-year-old Black girl who had trouble "reading" was able to read his version easily. When, however, she was shown the original, she could read it only with difficulty. Similarly, we have found that colleagues and friends with no contact with ghetto language often have difficulty reading the ghetto version without stammering!

Test bias against minorities, especially Blacks, may thus result from the use of Standard English in the testing situation instead of a more familiar dialect. However, the evidence does not support this conjecture: when Black preschoolers are administered the Stanford-Binet in Negro dialect, their scores are the same as Black children who take the test in Standard English.[47]

The essence of standard testing is to give the same items administered in a standard format to different people. The results are then supposed to be due not to the conditions of the testing situation but to differences in abilities. But if one group, living in one world, is more frequently exposed to certain information than is another group, living in a different world, we should not be surprised by differences between the groups in ability to recall, define, or reason about that information. The cultures of the Blacks, the Chicanos, the rural dwellers, and the poor make salient different information than the cultures of the White middle class, urban or suburban dweller.

An examination of items on IQ tests shows clearly the advantages that a White middle-class child is likely to have over a ghetto youth. Consider an intelligence test which enjoys wide currency in public schools in many states. Imagine the position of an inner-city Black student from Oakland when faced with the following questions:

> Coal is_____; snow is white.
> R. blue   S. white   T. red   U. green   V. black
> No garden is without its_____.
> A. sun   B. rain   C. weeds   D. work   E. tools

Since many Black children in Oakland are unfamiliar with coal, snow, and gardens, it is hardly surprising that they don't do very well on this test. Or how about these items:

> drum → stick; violin → ?
> R. handle   S. music   T. stand   U. strings   V. bow
> botany → flora; zoology → ?
> L. menagerie   M. cows   N. fauna   P. farm   Q. veterinary

We know that tests can be devised that favor rural children over their city friends,[48] American Indians over Anglo-Saxons,[49] and Blacks over Whites.[50] These examples clearly indicate that IQ assessment is not simply a matter of scaling *how much* is learned from the environment, for different environments facilitate the learning of diverse information and diverse styles of attacking problems. In general, much of what the Black, the poor, and the farm dweller learn is not assessed by IQ tests and frequently is not valued by the dominant culture.

ARE ALL GROUPS SIMILARLY MOTIVATED?

The assumption of standardized tests is that the tester can obtain the full and willing cooperation of the child to do well. Then the score should reflect competence and not effort or other motivational factors. Recent work, however, suggests that motivation cannot be so easily separated from intellectual abilities. When Puerto Rican children take an IQ test, they are less concerned with the job at hand than middle-

class White children, do not follow instructions well, are easily dis-
tracted, and are described as "making irrelevant remarks."[51] The
remarks of the Puerto Rican children would be better described as
"unanticipated" by those who devised and administered the tests. They
certainly were "relevant" to the children, whose behavior reflects the
general values and orientation of their culture. Specifically, Puerto
Rican families are characterized as sociable, people-oriented, and un-
demanding of their children. While parents talk to their children a
great deal, it is mostly to communicate affection or to be sociable
rather than to encourage them in problem solving and independence.
The important point is that the Puerto Rican and the dominant Anglo
cultures have different modes of operating. It is not that one mode is
better or worse than another, for there are no absolute standards
against which to judge them. But IQ tests carry a hidden judgment—
they require a problem-solving and efficiency orientation that is not
common to all groups. If groups differ in their motivation to perform
well, the claim is undermined that intelligence tests assess underlying
mental abilities. If test-taking has different meanings for various
groups, divergence of average test scores does not necessarily indicate
differences in the underlying abilities of the groups.

The whole idea of "tests" is approached differently by different cultures and subcultures. So is the relationship of test-giver to test-taker
(such as whether the tester is perceived as being superior or equal).
Even differences in what is considered good manners can play a major
role. For instance, the distinguished anthropologist Ruth Benedict
wrote a long time ago, "Among many peoples, and especially among
American Indian tribes, a person is trained never to answer a question
or state a fact except when he is absolutely and unassailably sure of
himself. Any minor uncertainty, which an American schoolchild typically takes very lightly, will render him dumb. His great humiliation
comes, not like our children's, from being slow or backward in answering, but from having ventured at all unless he was on completely firm
ground. He will not retell the little test story at all unless he can cover
each detail; he will not interpret the picture if there is a 'Western
Union' envelope in it which he never saw before."[52]

CAN TESTS BE ADMINISTERED UNIFORMLY TO DIFFERENT GROUPS?

Most testers are White and from the middle class. How does this
affect the scores of the culturally different? Do Blacks perform less
well when given an IQ test by a White tester? Contrary to popular

speculation that the race of the tester might be important, recent findings suggest that for children of elementary school age, race of tester does not influence IQ scores derived from group tests[53] or individual tests.[54]

Thus familiarity with test content and motivation to perform in test situations certainly varies among different ethnic and cultural groups. On the other hand, factors present in the test situation (such as race of tester and dialect used) do not appear to bias the results, at least in some carefully monitored experimental situations.

CULTURE-FAIR TESTS

One approach to the problem of bias in test content is to try to design intelligence tests that minimize or eliminate content to which different groups have unequal exposure. Such tests have been called "culture-fair," a clear misnomer since it is virtually impossible to assess fairly mental abilities in cross-cultural settings. The main objective in the construction of culture-fair tests is to eliminate group biases that discriminate against the lower classes and ethnic minority groups *within* a single national culture.

What exactly is meant by a culture-fair test?[55] There are many problems in the definition of this term. For example, any definition that insists that Blacks and Whites, or the poor and the rich, score equally well rules out group differences on an *a priori* basis. Sometimes culture-fair tests try to eliminate procedural factors thought to be unrelated to intelligence. These include such factors as reading ability (in test situations where the subject must understand written instructions), speed (as in timed tests), unfamiliar content in items, writing ability.

Controlling *all* that is culturally relevant is impossible, however, for there are infinite factors that can conceivably affect performance on the IQ tests and that may differ for each ethnic group or social class.

Perhaps the soundest criterion of a culture-fair test is that prediction based on test scores should be equally effective for each person taking the test regardless of the culture from which that person comes. For example, the SAT (the Scholastic Aptitude Test for college admission) would be "fair" only if a given score predicted success in college equally well for Blacks as for Whites. On the other hand, it would be considered an unfair test if, for Whites, a given score suggested the student would have academic difficulties, while for Blacks that same score predicted success. It would be especially unfair to Blacks if college admissions did not allow people with that score to enroll.

It should be clear that defining culture fairness in terms of predictive ability sidesteps the whole issue of the nature of intelligence, and brings us once again to the pragmatic conclusion that the major focus of the testing movement is not to measure a fixed underlying ability, but to help make some difficult predictive decisions. Unfortunately, however, little is known about the predictive validity of culture-fair IQ scores for different ethnic groups. On the other hand, standard intelligence tests such as the Stanford-Binet and the Scholastic Aptitude Test predict the future performance of Blacks and Whites equally well[56] and in that regard are better than tests deliberately designed to be culture-fair, which frequently predict future performance less well for *all* groups.

Insofar as Blacks, Chicanos, and other minority group members wish to play the game of White society, and compete with White men and women on their terms, IQ tests are fair in the sense that they give a Black a reasonable measure of his or her chances for success. The function of standard intelligence tests for society is to measure operating capacity irrespective of its origin (genetic, environmental, or both), and to enable reasonably accurate prediction. Tests measure rather than account for differences. If certain groups of people score poorly on tests because of inadequate environments, it is not the test that is unfair, but the social order that permits individuals to develop under inferior conditions.

DO THE ENVIRONMENTS OF SOME GROUPS STUNT THEIR MINDS?

The major environmental camp consists of those who believe that much of the difference in IQ between Blacks and Whites or between the poor and the privileged can be accounted for in terms of different environments encountered from conception to death. While environmentalists do not agree on the extent to which intelligence has a genetic component, they do agree that the heritability of intelligence, whether high or low, is irrelevant in accounting for *group differences* on tests.

Some of the evidence that supports the environmentalist viewpoint was presented earlier:

1.   The intelligence of children, as measured by IQ, is not constant over the years. Scores change over time, and the variation for many children is 30 IQ points or more (Chapter 4).
2.   In common environments such as quality institutions or on kibbutzim,

the IQs of different "racial" or ethnic groups are equivalent (Chapter 6).
3. Adopted children often show large gains in IQ compared to their natural mother's IQ (Chapter 5).
4. Studies of selective migration—of Blacks moving from the south to the north—show increases in IQ scores (Chapter 3).

What environmental factors are implicated in intellectual development? Do the environments of Blacks and Whites, the rich and the poor, and other groups differ in these factors? An exhaustive list of the factors cannot be given because no such list exists. The search for influences on intellectual development continues. One is reminded of the agricultural scientists' search for the optimal environment for plants. Water, sunshine, and nutrients in the soil were easily identified, but the essential roles of trace elements in the soil were more difficult to discover (see Appendix B). Similarly, what is known about the psychological environment of the child probably corresponds to the most obvious factors, but it may be that the "trace elements" of the psychological environment still have not been located.

Does Nutrition Affect IQ?   Of the forty-four nutrients required by the human body, thirty-seven are essential for the normal development and functioning of the brain and the central nervous system. There is good evidence that malnutrition can impair both the structure and functioning of the brain. Controversy centers on whether the effects of malnutrition are reversible when a nutritionally adequate (or better, extra-rich) diet is supplied. Most children who suffer severe malnutrition in childhood show lasting intellectual impairment even seven or eight years later.[57] However, in most cases, after a brief period of nutritive rehabilitation, the children have been returned to their original inadequate environment, where there is chronic dietary inadequacy and where the social, economic, and familial characteristics also contribute substantially to intellectual impairment. In 11-year-olds, who as infants were malnourished, but who subsequently were adopted into homes that provided adequate nutrition and an enriched environment, intellectual functioning was found to be normal.[58] Similarly, no deficits in IQ scores were found in 19-year-old youths who were the offspring of Dutch women pregnant during a six-month famine (at the end of the Nazi occupation).[59]

If intelligence is influenced by diet, can nutritional supplements alter the IQs of children? No study has given children all of the forty-four known essential nutrients. A number of smaller-scale studies have supplemented the diets suspected to be inadequate with several nutri-

ents. For example, iron and vitamin B complex were given to pregnant
Black southern women. A control group of mothers attending the same
clinic were administered an inert placebo. At age 4, the mean IQ of
children whose mothers received supplemented diets was 101.7, while
children of the untreated mothers had a mean IQ of 93.6.[60]

Even when nutritional supplements are given to a basically well-
nourished school population, changes in IQ may be recorded. In a
careful study that tested IQ before and after a six-month administration of orange juice (which contains vitamin C), there was a rise of 3.5
IQ points for students who were initially low in ascorbic acid (vitamin
C) and no change in IQ for those students who were initially high in
ascorbic acid. At the end of the intervention, the IQs of both groups
were the same.[61]

Firm and convincing evidence exists, then, that nutrition influences
intellectual performance, although it is not known with certainty
whether the effects of nutritional deprivation are always reversible.
The next important questions are whether Blacks in our own society
commonly suffer more from undernutrition than do Whites and
whether social classes vary in the adequacy of their diets. Fortunately,
data are available to answer these questions. Both recent and older
studies concur that more American Blacks and Mexican-Americans are
seriously undernourished than are American Whites. A summary of
surveys in 1965 found that the diet of 60 percent of southern Blacks
was "obviously inadequate" as compared to 25 percent of southern
Whites.[62] The results of the *Ten-State Nutrition Survey* (TSNS)[63]
found that Blacks were significantly more malnourished than Whites,
and Spanish-Americans were intermediate between the other two
ethnic groups. There was more iron deficiency, protein deficiency, and
riboflavin deficiency among Blacks than among the other groups,
while Spanish-Americans showed high levels of vitamin A deficiency.
Among pregnant women and children under 6, the protein essential
for the brain development was deficient in significantly more Blacks
than Whites.

Can Talking to a Child Increase Its IQ? It turns out that the
amount of speech directed to and in response to a child is significantly
related to mental development at the age of 2.[64] On the other hand,
simply hearing speech, either adults talking to one another or the
television playing, does not seem to contribute to early linguistic and
intellectual competence.[65] In fact, there is evidence from careful stud-

ies that the more young children (under 3 years) watch television, the slower their language development.[66] Evidently, the direct interaction between mother (or some other adult) and child is essential in the early years for development of normal speech. For school-age children, on the other hand, TV watching may improve vocabulary until the preadolescent years.

Not all persons who talk to children are equally effective in stimulating mental development. Contemporaries and brothers and sisters do not facilitate language and intellectual competence to the same extent as mothers. Babysitters (including relatives of the child) generally do not talk to young infants as much as mothers do.[67] Primarily, it is those adults who know a child well who talk most, and who are most stimulating to the child.[68]

For infants, the sheer amount of verbal interaction correlates with mental test scores, while the quality of the mother's speech, her grammar, and the richness of her vocabulary are less important.[69] The quality, rather than the sheer quantity of language heard, influences the mental skills of children past infancy. At older ages, speech containing words of relation and comparison, such as "if," "although," "bigger," "more," forces the child to think in relational terms and fosters reasoning, and speech containing abstractions such as "justice" and "democracy" forces the child to deal with abstract concepts. On the other hand, syntactically impoverished speech oriented to description rather than analysis inhibits the child's ability to learn from the environment.[70]

In one study of Black children, it was found that by the age of 5, the best predictors of a child's verbal intelligence and scores on standardized achievement tests included the mother's vocabulary and her teaching style as assessed one year earlier.[71] Clearly, the language heard, the sheer quantity directed to the child, and its quality influence developing intellectual abilities as measured by IQ tests.

Is there a difference between the social classes in the amount or kind of language heard? Professor Higgins, the wonderful character from George Bernard Shaw's *Pygmalion*, and known more widely from Broadway's *My Fair Lady*, felt he could identify the social as well as geographic origin of people by their speech. It is known that lower-class parents talk to their infants[72] and children less, and answer their questions less often than do middle-class parents.[73] Lower-class parents use fewer specific verbal labels and attention-focusing techniques than do middle-class mothers.[74] These characteristics not only distinguish the social classes, but also correlate positively with intelligence test results within social classes.

Just as the middle classes use language differently from the lower classes, so Blacks use language differently from Whites, particularly in grammatical structure.[75] Black English is a coherent system, with richness and complexity that is obscured if one simply considers it as a deviation from the norm or as erroneous speech.[76] Nonetheless, it may be that Black English may interfere with children's school performance and test-taking skills (to say nothing of its being a handicap in a White-dominated society). Learning to read may be more difficult when the structure of the written language differs from that of the spoken word; motivation to participate in class may be diminished when a teacher either fails to understand or tries to correct every utterance a child makes.

CAN GROUP DIFFERENCES IN FAMILY STRUCTURE AND ATTITUDES CREATE GROUP DIFFERENCES IN IQ?

A child's intelligence is related, modestly but significantly, to the structure of his or her family—the number and spacing of brothers and sisters. Higher IQ is associated with smaller families, both within as well as across social classes.[77] Birth order also plays a role: firstborn children score higher on IQ tests than their brothers and sisters, with the youngest child generally scoring lowest of all.[78] Lower-class families on the average are larger than middle-class families, and median size of Black families is also larger than that of White families. So group differences in family structure may contribute to group differences in IQ.

While these structural characteristics of a family are related to the intellectual abilities of children, the interaction of parents with their children, and the attitudes toward and expectations they hold for them are suspected to be even more potent. IQs of children during the preschool and elementary school years can be predicted from parental concern for intellectual competence and ambition for their children. Unconcerned parents with few ambitions, indifferent to success or failure, giving little guidance and encouragement, are likely to have children who score low on IQ tests.[79] Even during the first few years of life, the parents' concern with intellectual mastery is associated with higher developmental quotients among toddlers.[80] Brighter toddlers tend to have mothers who play with them, especially in relatively intellectual activities (such as naming objects, counting), and who respond promptly and consistently to them. Parental emphasis on intellectual mastery during the first few years of life also is a good predictor of IQ at age 9 and 10.[81]

The emotional climate provided by the parents also influences children's IQ. Hostile mothers, those who feel irritable, angry, or upset with their children and see them as a burden, mothers who frequently ignore, or punish their children and who use fear as a means to control them have children whose IQs are depressed.[82] On the other hand, higher IQs are associated with egalitarian relationships between mothers and children, and with parents who are described as warm, accepting, and supportive of their children.

Fathers, too, influence their children's IQ. Those who spend time with their children, who listen to them, and who know how they think and feel tend to have high-IQ children who perform well at school and who care about achieving. Conversely, fathers who are critical, restrictive, and punitive tend to inhibit scholastic aptitude, but more in girls than in boys.[83]

The question remains whether Black and White families, or the poor and the privileged, provide different environments for their children. A recent review of social class and ethnic influences[84] shows that middle-class families are more accepting of their children, more democratic than authoritarian, and emphasize educational achievement more than lower-class families. Middle-class parents are more concerned about their children, help them more, program their activities more (to the point of sometimes interfering with the child's ongoing activities), and generally interact more with their children than lower-class parents. Middle-class parents are more responsive to their children's needs for affection, attention, and companionship. Middle-class families, of course, are not living under the same degree of financial stress as the poor. One wonders how many of these differences can be traced directly to anxieties over making ends meet in the lower class. Whatever the cause of the class differences, we must remember that proportionately more Black than White families are lower-class.

Most of these findings come from correlation studies that do not deal with causation. Perhaps family relationships and patterns of interaction do not affect intellectual development at all—perhaps they merely are related to other causal factors—such as the genetic endowment of the family. Persuasive evidence against this hereditarian position comes from some programs for intervention in early childhood, in

which attempts were made to change the patterns of interaction between mothers and children. The most successful of these programs
was that of Phyllis Levenstein,[85] who over a two-year period had
visitors demonstrate to lower-class mothers how to talk to toddlers and
teach them to explore books and toys. The results were clear-cut: children enrolled in this program between the ages of 2 and 4 years showed
above-average IQs at the end of the period. Even more impressive was
the retention of the advantage: three years after the program ended,
the IQs of the children in second grade was 13 points higher on the
average than the IQs of control children from the same social class
who had not been involved in the program. In addition, teachers
reported school performance was higher, and there were fewer academic and classroom problems.

The family also plays an important role in a child's intellectual
development by providing the physical and intellectual environment
in which the child grows and learns. In the course of play and explora-
tion, the child grows in understanding of his or her environment,
obtains information about the world, and also develops a sense of
mastery and competence. The quality of the home environment, ranging from the kinds of objects available to toddlers to the amount and
circumstances of TV viewing, influences the intellectual development
and motivation of children,[86] especially when the mother is actively
involved in helping the young child deal with and interpret the world
of objects.[87] In one large study, the richness of environmental stimulation correlated highest with the children's IQ on both individual and
group IQ tests at a level surpassing even parents' IQ, social class, and
parent occupation.[88]

Ethnic and social class differences in home environment are not
difficult to document. The generally larger families and smaller homes
and apartments of Blacks and the poor make crowding more common
among Blacks than Whites, and more common among the poor than
the privileged, with restrictions on the child's freedom to explore more
likely. The markedly lower incomes of Blacks, Spanish-Americans, and
lower-class Whites compared to the incomes of the White middle class
also result in dramatic differences in physical environments. In general, there are fewer educational toys, books, magazines, and so forth,
available to the poor child than to the middle-class one. Busy and
harassed mothers are less likely to have either the time or the patience
to help a child explore and understand its experiences.

CAN EDUCATIONAL DIFFERENCES CREATE DIFFERENCES IN IQ?

Certainly, the family environment has a profound influence on the development of a child's intelligence. Can the same be said of the schools? Does high-quality education influence IQ scores on a test? It is frequently claimed that the inadequate schooling received by inner-city and rural dwellers contributes to their poor performance on IQ tests. What is the evidence?

The amount of schooling received is clearly related to intelligence, but the direct effects of schooling may be small. That is, whether one attends a private school or an inner-city high school is thought to have little direct effect on IQ. While dramatic differences between schools can be found in average scores on IQ tests and on school achievement tests of their pupils, the problem lies in determining how much of this is due to the school and how much to the environment outside of school. Frequently, White middle-class children with educationally oriented parents attend superior schools. On the other hand, in the inner-city areas, poor children with few advantages in their home and whose parents have neither the skills, the energy, nor the power to monitor the quality of the educational offerings attend inferior schools. The confounding between the social class of the students and the quality of the school they attend makes it difficult to assess the schools' contribution to IQ scores. Only when students attending different types and qualities of schools are comparable in terms of social class and intellectual performance prior to entering school can the impact of schools be assessed. Furthermore, schools are almost random collections of classrooms, so while given classroom practices may influence intellectual performance on tests, schools rarely do.

Preschools. For many children, education starts with preschool. Debate rages as to whether going to nursery school increases the child's mental abilities. Early research[89] found little effect on advantaged middle-class children, who typically filled the classrooms. However, for poorer, less-advantaged children, enrollment in programs that stressed intellectual development indeed resulted in IQ gains over and above those normally accompanying increased age.

In 1965, in a determined effort to break the vicious cycle of poverty → poor preparation for school → poor school performance → early drop-out → poverty, a massively funded federal preschool program named Project Head Start was undertaken. The program was established nationwide within a period of months. Each local Head

Start program had autonomy with regard to curriculum. Some chose less-structured programs, emphasizing adjustment, self-esteem, and motivation of the child. Other programs were more structured and had clear aims concerning what the child should be taught and the sequence in which it should be presented. Although this variation was reasonable, it posed a problem for the evaluation of Head Start as a national effort.[90] To find out whether the considerable expense had been justified by significant educational advances, evaluation was undertaken by Westinghouse Learning Corporation,[91] which assessed 104 programs—75 summer programs and 29 full-year programs. The aim was to assess the impact of Head Start as a whole, averaging, over the myriad local variations, the good and the bad programs. Children in first, second, and third grade who had participated in the Head Start programs prior to starting school and a matched sample who had not had this enrichment program were compared. The results can be stated quite briefly:

1. The summer programs of Head Start did not confer significant academic benefits on the entire group of children who participated in them. There was, however, a trend for Black children to obtain some benefit.
2. Full-year Head Start programs had some positive effects on the intellectual ability of children, particularly on Blacks and on children from the southeastern region of the country. However, the magnitude of the gains was disappointingly small.

These were indeed disheartening results, and they undoubtedly influenced Arthur Jensen to declare the failure of compensatory education (and to blame that failure on the innate stupidity of Black children).[92] But it should be remembered that the national evaluation assessed the first three years of a program that was implemented with chaotic haste. Furthermore, the assessment was not as to whether a well-designed preschool program *could* have effects, but whether, nationwide, the Head Start program *did* have the desired effects. At any rate, to say that the failure of any given effort at institutionalized education is evidence that certain categories of people are inherently dumb is, to be charitable, preposterous.

   Later reviews of preschool programs have not been much more encouraging. Considering only those enrichment programs for which there were matched groups of children with and without the intervention, and where there has been a follow-up assessment of all the children for several years after the preschool program terminated, the following conclusions were reached:[93]

1. Preschool enrichment programs show strong, significant gains at the end of the intervention period.
2. The largest gains are made in the first year of the program. The second year does not confer additional benefits.
3. Two years after the programs terminated, there were significant declines in measured IQ compared to IQs right after the program was terminated. Although the largest loss in IQ occurs soon after the program of enrichment ceases, declines continue until the average IQ of the group with preschool enrichment falls back to where it was prior to the program.

Can gains in IQ be protected from such erosion? Some early enrichment strategies that permanently change the environment have been much more effective than the preschool classes. Home intervention is one such strategy,[94] for it can begin very early in the child's life, the enrichment is not limited to fixed hours, and benefits continue even when the program terminates. Assessments of several home-based interventions[95] give cause for optimism. Gains in children's IQ are large (10 or more IQ points) and are maintained after the program is terminated. Further studies are needed on this type of enrichment program to see if the encouraging results can be replicated.

Still other forms of early intervention have been successful in raising the IQs of young children. One dramatic intervention is to take very young infants and put them in extended day-care situations where they are deliberately stimulated by trained caretakers and are provided with warm, loving, and highly enriched environments. The Milwaukee Project[96] is one famous example. In this project forty newborn infants of mentally retarded mothers (IQ less than 70) of low-income, inner-city families were identified. One-third served as a control, and two-thirds were placed in a specially enriched day-care center. The aim was to prevent retardation, so the program emphasized problem-solving skills, language development, and motivation to achieve. Starting at a very early age (2 years), thirty-minute periods of exercise in language and number skills were conducted daily by teachers. Each activity was precisely structured, with twenty minutes of stimulatory exercises and ten minutes of free play with the educational materials. Classes were interspersed with free play, naps, meals, and television. Extensive assessments were made of the children, who at the last testing were nearly 4 years old.

Dramatic differences were found between the children in the intervention program and the children who served as controls and had no enrichment. At age 42 months, there was a 33-point average difference in IQ between the groups, with the day-care children scoring in the above-normal range. If these results are maintained as the children grow older, it will constitute powerful evidence of what education, in its broadest sense, can achieve.

In short, although early intervention has not been uniformly successful in raising the IQs of preschool children, there is considerable reason to believe it can bring about large intellectual gains that will not be eroded over time.

Elementary School. Since elementary school attendance is compulsory, it is not possible to get evidence of its effect on intelligence by comparing the IQs of children who do and do not have school experience. The best evidence, then, comes from school attendance, which shows that reducing the amount of schooling reduces test performance. For example, long-term interruption of schooling occurred in Holland during World War II[97] and in Prince Edward County, Virginia, where the education board abolished school in order to avoid integration.[98] When schooling was reinstituted, the IQs of the children were significantly lower than those of comparable groups with ongoing schooling.

Short-term interruptions of schooling—those lasting either weeks or months—are also associated with lowered gains and sometimes even losses in test scores, particularly on achievement tests. During summer recess, the reading scores of White students show only modest gains, while those of Black students show hardly any gains.[99] Similarly, the closing of New York City schools for several months in 1968 during a strike resulted in lowered test scores the following spring.[100]

It appears that reducing the amount of schooling lowers IQ and achievement scores. Students frequently absent from school for either legitimate or illegitimate reasons score lower on tests than classmates who attend school regularly.[101] In fact, even the length of the school day correlates significantly with test scores.[102] The longer the school day (within limits), the more students learn and the better they perform on tests.

It would be naive to assume that all schools or all classrooms have the same effect on children; there are large schools and small schools, structured and unstructured programs, crowded schools and undersubscribed schools, and so on. Several recent studies give strong testimony to the intellectual effects that different educational experiences have on children. In one study,[103] 136 first-grade and 137 third-grade classrooms were studied. The method and philosophy of teaching in each of these classrooms belonged to one of seven well-articulated and carefully specified programs of education. *Observed classroom procedures—the methods of teaching and classroom organization—were found to contribute as much to the explanation of test scores (a nonverbal IQ test, and mathematics and reading achievement tests) as did the initial ability of children.* In particular, the amount of time children spent constructively engaged at mathematics and reading was reflected in their achievement scores. Systematic (structured) instructional patterns and immediate praise or correction of work also resulted in higher reading and math scores. On the other hand, more flexible classrooms with a wide variety of materials available, and where children were given ample opportunities to explore, resulted in higher scores on perceptual problem-solving tasks.

Yet only ten years earlier, James Coleman,[104] in a famous report of a large-scale survey of schools in the United States, wrote:

Differences between schools account for only a small fraction of differences in pupil achievement. . . . The average White student's achievement seems to be less affected by the strength or weakness of his school's facilities, curriculums, and teachers than is the average minority pupil's. . . . The achievement of minority pupils depends more on the schools they attend than does the achievement of majority pupils. Thus 20 percent of the achievement of Negroes in the South is associated with the particular schools they go to, whereas only 10 percent of the achievement of Whites in the South is.

Now, 10 to 20 percent of the variability of scores is hardly trivial. The Coleman report did not investigate the instructional variables and the classroom practices that the classroom study showed to be so important. Instead, the Coleman report focused on more easily measured characteristics, such as the amount of training the teachers had, the availability of gymnasiums, libraries, etc. Coleman himself recognizes that even given the variables he measured, the impact of the schools on students is underestimated because the statistical procedures (necessary for data analyses) deal with one thing at a time, and cumulative effects tend to be lost.* In other words, upon close examination, there is no fundamental disagreement that what goes on in schools *can* importantly influence the competence of students (which is not to say that it always *does* have this effect).

High School. Since high school attendance is optional in some areas, it is possible to compare the IQs of those who continue their educations beyond the minimum required by law with the IQs of

---

* The interaction effects were also lost.

those who terminate their schooling early. There is a problem, however, in that those who continue school tend to have higher test scores
to begin with, so any advantage they manifest cannot be attributed
solely to schooling. A handful of studies have tried to separate the
effects of initial ability from the effects of schooling. While one[105]
found no effects of additional schooling on IQ scores, a pre–World
War II study[106] and several Swedish studies have shown that each
additional year of school increased the IQs of boys by 2 to 3 points.

Differences between schools at the high school level as assessed in
large-scale surveys seem to have less impact on the test scores and
abilities of students[107] than differences between schools at the elementary school level. However, these surveys did not collect the
information concerning classroom procedures that were shown to be so
important at the elementary school level.

While any given educational experience may have only modest
effects on IQ test scores, the cumulative total of all educational experiences undoubtedly plays a significant role in determining those scores.
Assuredly, the totality of educational experiences also contributes to
group differences in average IQ. It is very easy to document that the
poor, the Black, and other groups whose performances on tests are low
suffer from multiple problems concerning schooling; for example, they
spend less time in school and are exposed to an inferior quality of
school. Christopher Jencks,[108] in a provocative analysis of the importance of schools, documents the inequalities in access to and utilization
of schools. Prior to 1965, significantly more Whites than Blacks attended
private nursery schools. The advent of federally funded preschools has
reduced this disparity, although kindergarten is still more often available to White than to Black children. More Whites (84 percent) than
Blacks (66 percent) graduate from high school. Similarly, working-
class White youths are more likely to drop out of high school than
middle-class White youths.

The quality of the educational institutions available to the rich and
the poor, and to Whites and Blacks, also varies. Unfortunately, few
studies have examined intensively exactly what happens in the classroom, so we do not know how educational practices differ in schools
populated predominantly by different ethnic groups or different social
classes. The large surveys do, however, adequately document inequities in facilities, teacher training, and so on. For example, the Coleman
report[109] found that it is in the academic facilities that the schools of

minority pupils show the most consistent deficiencies; there are fewer science laboratories, fewer books in libraries, less adequate supplies of texts, and the schools themselves are less often accredited. In addition, and most important, the Coleman report (and other studies) repeatedly show that the achievement of minority pupils and students from poor homes depends more on the school they attend than does the achievement of other students. While changes in the educational environment may have only modest effects on middle-class children, it may have significantly more effect on those who need it most—ethnic minorities and the poor.

WHAT IF ENVIRONMENTS ARE GREATLY CHANGED?

Nutrition, the language environment, the family, and the schools have each been shown to be capable of influencing IQ scores. It has been found repeatedly that the IQs of Blacks and the poor are more responsive to changes in the environment than are the IQs of the advantaged.

How much increase in IQ would result if the environments of poor and minority children were dramatically changed? Most studies consider the effect of changing one factor at a time, so that cumulative, reinforcing effects probably are seriously underestimated. The students who drop out of school before graduation have often attended schools with inadequate facilities and untrained staff, schools where more time was spent in maintaining discipline than in instruction. These same children are likely to have come from homes that do not value education, that use simple language, and where nutrition has always been deficient. What is the *total* effect of such environments, when the deprivations are cumulatively compounded?

Adoption studies constitute a natural experiment in which massive environmental changes are made. Typically, adoption agencies have had stringent requirements for families seeking to adopt a child, thus ensuring that most children are placed in middle-class homes with their attendant advantages. To the extent that environments provided by a family have an impact on IQ, the IQ of adopted children should reflect the environments of the homes in which they have been reared. To assess the environmental contribution to intelligence, an optimal strategy would be to study the children of matched groups of poor parents—some of whom gave up their children to middle-class parents for adoption, others who reared their children themselves. Differences in average IQ scores of these children would reflect the contribution of the middle-class adoptive home. In fact, we have been unable to locate any studies that make this comparison.[*]

Most adoption studies of White children into White families suffer from methodological shortcomings.[110] *They do not provide valid information about the contribution of environment to intelligence because there is no satisfactory way to estimate what a child's IQ would have been if the child had not been adopted into a middle-class home.*[111] Studies of adoption of non-White children by White families do not have this problem, for the environments into which non-White children were born are usually impoverished, and the environments into which they are adopted are usually high-quality.

In one study, a group of Korean orphans (all girls), after recovering from varying degrees of malnourishment, were adopted by Americans who reared them in the United States. Years later, when the children were in elementary school, their average IQ was 107[112]—a massive 40-point increase over the IQs reported of similarly undernourished children returned to their impoverished home environments after recovering from the malnutrition. Similar results are reported for the adoption of Black children into White families. The average IQ of Black children adopted by advantaged White families in the Midwest was 107. In the same region, the average IQ of Black children is around 85 to 90.[113] We must be cautious, however, in viewing this evidence, since the problem of selective adoption has not been entirely eliminated from these studies. If only the brightest of the Korean and Black children were adopted, then the results would not rule out a hereditarian explanation. Fortunately, the degree of selective placement in the Black study was known, and could not by itself account for the observed improvement. Thus the cumulative effects of an advantaged environment could raise IQ scores from 16 to 40 points. Large-scale environmental changes, therefore, whether in extended day-care programs[114] or in adoption studies, can produce very large changes in IQ.

To reiterate the message of this chapter, "fair" comparisons of the mental capacity of two different groups are impossible unless the ability to be tested is narrowly defined as the ability to be successful in the

---

[*] Those studies evaluating a genetic hypothesis match samples according to the characteristics of the adoptive parents. Here the idea is to determine what improvement in IQ an advantaged environment provides over a disadvantaged one. It is not to determine whether equally good environments result in *equally* high IQ scores, nor to learn the magnitude of correlations between a child and his biological and adoptive parents.

milieu of one of the two groups. Tests based on such a criterion naturally tend to show group differences. And so it comes as no surprise that scores on IQ tests differ: Whites do better than Blacks, the advantaged do better than the poor, and city dwellers do better than their country cousins. Environmental factors have been shown to make important contributions to the current intellectual skills of all groups and to differentiate between groups. Minor environmental changes or changes of short duration have little or no effect. Massive improvement of the environment does increase low IQs, and this is despite psychologists' failure to identify the ingredients in the environment that are most important to mental development.

There is no scientific support whatsoever for the popular notion that group differences in intellectual abilities are inborn. We do not know the answer to the question "Is the average 'genetic IQ' of Blacks different from the average 'genetic IQ' of Whites?" for the "genetic IQ," if it exists, is unmeasurable and therefore meaningless.

7

Why Does It Matter?

> Genetic diversity is not tantamount to inequality. Human equal-
> ity or inequality are not biological phenomena but sociological
> designs; genetic diversity is a biological reality. Equality before
> the law, political equality, or equality of opportunity, stem not
> from genes but from religious, ethical, or philosophical wisdom
> or unwisdom.
> —Theodosius Dobzhansky, *Social Biology*, 1973

IN 1971, Harvard psychologist Richard Herrnstein published a
now famous (or infamous!) syllogism in the *Atlantic Monthly*:[1]

1. If differences in mental abilities are inherited and
2. If success requires those abilities, and
3. If earnings and prestige depend on success,
4. Then social standing (which reflects earnings and prestige) will be
   based to some extent on inherited differences among people.

Add to this syllogism Jensen's claim that differences in IQ between
Blacks and Whites are due largely to genetics, and you pretty much
have the hereditarian position. It is only slightly unfair to paraphrase
that position as "those people or groups on top in our society and the
world as a whole got there because they were *innately* more worthy
than the underdogs."

It should now be clear that the hereditarian position is without
scientific validity because:

1. Whatever an IQ score measures, it is certain that it does not measure
   all the important mental abilities, nor does it measure crucial social and
   emotional qualities—qualities critical to the definition of a worthy
   person.
2. There is almost no acceptable scientific evidence of heritability of IQ

in White populations and a virtual absence of evidence on heritability of IQ in Black populations.

3. There is not a shred of evidence to support Jensen's much ballyhooed estimate of a heritability of .81 for IQ.

4. There are no biological units corresponding to the socially defined "races," the quality of which so concern Jensen and Shockley and their admirers. The race-IQ controversy is really just a skin color-IQ controversy.

5. Even if both dark-skinned and light-skinned people had heritabilities of IQ of .81, that would tell us nothing about causes of Black-White differences in IQ.

6. If, as Eysenck claims, genetic differences in IQ between Blacks and Whites have evolved under natural selection, then heritability of IQ in both groups would be expected to be low and the conclusion of Herrnstein's syllogism—that social standing will be based on inherited differences in IQ—would not hold.

7. Virtually all of the observed differences in IQ within and among groups are consistent with an environmental explanation.

In spite of the utter lack of evidence for the position of the hereditarians, their ideas have been widely propounded, widely accepted, and have been used as a basis for making social policy. This is why the race-IQ controversy matters and why this book has been written. The scientific interest in the questions so solemnly posed by the Jensenists is almost nil, but the social climate in which they are posed gives them great importance.

Education and IQ

As the hereditarians would be the first to admit, it is not the intrinsic scientific interest in the IQ problem, but its social implications, that are paramount. Those implications are behind their calls for more studies of race, social class, and IQ. After all, they say, is it not crucial to determine whether nature or nurture is the cause of observed differences between Blacks and Whites or among social classes? Isn't that determination necessary so we can decide how to organize our schools? To hear the Jensenists tell it, it certainly is. Jensen's paper, which started the whole recent fuss began, after all, with the statement, "Compensatory education has been tried and it apparently has failed."[2] In describing the failure, he goes on to ask:

What has gone wrong? In other fields, when bridges do not stand, when aircraft do not fly, when machines do not work, when treatments do not cure, despite all conscientious efforts on the part of many persons to make them do so, one begins to question the basic assumptions, principles, theories, and hypotheses that guide one's efforts. Is it time to follow suit in education?[3]

The whole thrust of Jensen's argument is that the failure is due to a lack of recognition of the innate intellectual differences between Blacks and Whites. So, if his theories of racial differences should be fully substantiated, Jensen recommends:

The ideal of equality of educational opportunity should not be interpreted as uniformity of facilities, instructional techniques and educational aims for all children. Diversity rather than uniformity of approaches and aims would seem to be the key to making education rewarding for children of different patterns of ability. The reality of individual differences then need not mean educational rewards for some children and frustration and defeat for others.[4]

Jensen indicates that research is needed to substantiate his theories, followed—should they be fully supported—by an educational system that does whatever it can to help Blacks overcome the awful consequences of their intellectual inferiority. Curiously, though, Jensen has not waited (perhaps recognizing what a long wait it would be) for his theories to be substantiated. He has already appeared before congressional committees and tried to persuade them to reduce expenditures on compensatory education.[5]

It is noteworthy that the second line of Jensen's article reads, "Compensatory education has been practiced on a massive scale *for several years* in many cities across the nation."[6] The program he so roundly condemns as a failure is not only attempting a difficult task in the face of great uncertainties about *how* one might change the environment of the disadvantaged to increase their scholastic aptitude, but the effort *has barely begun!* Geneticist Richard Lewontin in 1970 demolished Jensen's conclusion in two paragraphs:

Who can help but answer [that] last rhetorical question [whether or not education should question its basic assumptions] with a resounding "Yes"? What thoughtful and intelligent person can avoid being struck by the intellectual and empirical bankruptcy of educational psychology as it is practiced in our mass educational systems? The innocent reader will immediately fall into close sympathy with Professor Jensen, who, it seems, is about to dissect educational psychology and show it up as a pre-scientific jumble without theoretic coherence or prescriptive competence. But the innocent reader will be wrong. For the rest of Jensen's article puts the blame for the failure of his science not on the scientists but on the children. According to him, it is not that his science and its practitioners have failed utterly to understand human motivation, behavior and development but simply that the damn kids are ineducable.

The unconscious irony of his metaphor of bridges, airplanes and machines has apparently been lost on him. The fact is that in the twentieth century bridges do stand, machines do work and airplanes do fly, because they are built on clearly understood mechanical and hydrodynamic principles which even moderately careful and intelligent engineers can put into practice. In the seventeenth century that was not the case, and the general opinion was that men would never succeed in their attempts to fly because flying was impossible. Jensen proposes that we take the same view of education and that, in the terms of his metaphor, fallen bridges be taken as evidence of the unbridgeability of rivers. The alternative explanation that educational psychology is still in the seventeenth century, is apparently not part of his philosophy.[7]

Unwilling to wait for society to make a sustained attempt to equalize environments (or at least dramatically improve poor ones), the hereditarians have jumped to the conclusion that equalization will make little difference. And they *know* what will work. Herrnstein in "IQ in the Meritocracy" puts it right on the line:

The false belief in human equality leads to rigid, inflexible expectations, often doomed to frustration, and thence to anger. Ever more shrilly, we call on our educational and social institutions to make everyone the same, when we should instead be trying to mold our institutions around the inescapable limitations and varieties of human ability.[8]

Once again, we see the nongeneticist's common misapprehension about genetics—the assumed immutability of the message encoded in the DNA, the "inescapable limitations" many human beings are assumed to be bound by. Furthermore, Herrnstein evinces a pathetic faith in the ability of IQ tests to reveal these "inescapable limitations" in the young so that they can be properly dealt with by newly molded institutions. He is echoing Jensen's contention that "schools and society must provide a range and diversity of educational methods, programs, and goals, and of occupational opportunities, just as wide as the range of human abilities."[9]

From reading the statements of Herrnstein and Jensen, one might think that schools today function according to some sort of Watsonian ideal—on the basis that in theory all normal human beings have equal potential and are capable of equal achievement.[10] John B. Watson, founder of the school of behaviorism in psychology, was famous for his faith in the completely environmental determination of human mental abilities. In an often quoted statement in 1930, he promised:

Give me a dozen healthy infants, well-formed, and my own specific world to bring them up in and I'll guarantee to take any one at random and train him to become any type of specialist I might select—doctor, lawyer, artist, merchant-chief and, yes, even beggarman and thief, regardless of his talents, penchants, tendencies, abilities, vocations, and race of his ancestors.[11]

But, of course, no society or school has yet to provide the world Watson would have specified. On the contrary, children from enormously diverse backgrounds are usually given IQ tests during the first few years of school, and the results of these tests are eventually used to grade children into curricula (or "lanes") that are either designed as preparatory for college or for entering low-status vocations.

This process is pernicious for a number of reasons. First of all, the students are stuck with a numerical label that, once in their files, puts them into a "slot." All too often, the tests used are group tests, and we have already seen the problems that their use can generate. Given also that individuals may score differently from one test-taking to another at about the same age and that test scores can change as a child grows up, the opportunities for abuse are numerous.

Consider, for example, the classic case of a Black San Francisco high school graduate who was washed out of the Air Force because he could barely read. In high school, he had been in a special program for the mentally retarded—a program that leads to diplomas for students who are "virtually illiterate."[12] After leaving the Air Force, he was examined by a psychologist, who found that his IQ was in the normal range, even though the school district had pegged him at 58! He was above average in some areas, below in verbal skills. The young man is alert, pleasant, and showed no signs of retardation, but this apparently did not alert the educational machinery to its mistake. The school district's one-test classification operation robbed him of a good education and a chance to fulfill his desire to serve in the Air Force.

That case is by no means unique. In the San Francisco school system in 1974, some 60 percent of the children in classes for the educable mentally retarded were Black, although only 30 percent of the students in the entire school system were Black. Suspicion that this was due to culturally biased tests led a U.S. District Court judge to enjoin California public schools from giving standardized IQ tests to Black students unless a test were developed that takes account of their different cultural background.[13]

It is no wonder that various minority groups have been campaigning against mass IQ testing. Even putting the cultural differences aside, it is difficult to see a rationale for IQ testing throughout school systems when the results will have some practical significance for only a small percentage of the students (e.g., identifying underachievers—those who score high on the tests but are not doing well in the classroom). At best, the majority of the students are given a numerical label subject to misinterpretation. At worst, low IQ scores may provide the rationalization for giving those students a diluted, unstimulating educational offering—"babysitting," rather than education. It is frightening that about 75 percent of American adults approve the use of IQ tests for assigning children to special classes,[14] but they know little about what is accomplished—or not accomplished—in them. What children in special classes should be getting, of course, are intensified efforts and new approaches to ensure that basic skills—especially reading, writing, and arithmetic—are acquired regardless of IQ score. Whatever the educational methods, a child must master the basic skills demanded by our technological society. All too often, low IQ scores, misinterpreted by teachers and parents alike as representing "inescapable limitations," allow educational systems to blame the child for the system's failures.

The dichotomy presented to us by Jensen's position is whether to revise our entire school system to deal with "inescapable limitations" or to make further attempts to build a system that provides equal opportunities for achievement to all students. There is only one choice that can be made on the basis of scientific data in hand—a choice that does not depend on whether there is a significant heritability to IQ. For whether the heritability of IQ within a given group in a given environment is .oo or .81, changing the environment can both change the IQ directly* and affect the degree of heritability itself.

Whatever the goals of the school system, there is therefore no reason to design it around the assumption that some children are walled in by "inescapable limitations." This does not mean that all children entering school will be equal in their ability to deal with a given curriculum or that all should be exposed to identical programs. *Even if the heritability of IQ in a population were zero, prenatal and preschool environments inevitably would differ and therefore so would children entering school.* Anyone who thinks that the environments of all the members

* It can also change IQ by altering gene-environment interactions.

of *any* group of human beings can be made to be identical has obviously never tried the relatively simple task of, say, making the environments of a bunch of fruit flies identical. Even identical twins raised together are never identical—physically or mentally.

We cannot here get into the complex questions of what roles schools were originally designed to play in our society, what their function now is, and what roles they might or should play in the future. These are questions on which honest people are almost certain to differ. But we disagree strongly with Herrnstein when he states that it is a "false belief in human equality" that leads to anger and to demands that our institutions "make everyone the same." We have yet to meet anyone who wants the boring situation in which everyone is "the same." What leads to anger is not a false belief in human equality but an accurate observation of systematic inequality of opportunity and treatment—an inequality based on such criteria as race and ethnic group. If this society offered real equality of opportunity and educational systems designed to maximize each individual's chances of reaching his or her goals in life (not those ordained by IQ testers who value certain intellectual abilities over all other abilities and attributes), we suspect that anger would disappear. On the other hand, if inequity becomes further institutionalized in the school systems or outside of them, society may well be torn apart.

Jobs and IQ

It is not only in the schools that minority groups find mental testing used against them. There is a widespread current practice in industry to give aptitude (ability) tests to help in the selection of suitable applicants for a position. This practice is widely recognized and widely approved of. More than half of American adults believe it is legitimate.[15] It is not clear, however, how many know that Blacks and other minority applicants frequently score lower on these tests than Whites, and hence are denied employment. In other words, mental tests are a barrier that keeps members of minorities from jobs. And disproportionately high levels of unemployment are an issue of great concern for those championing the rights of minorities.

In this area, the rights of the employer must be balanced against those of the prospective minority employed. While the employer is entitled to seek the most competent candidate, testing can also be used deliberately to exclude minorities who are entitled to equal access to jobs. The crux of the issue is the relevance of the test for predicting on-the-job performance.[16] Only where the tested abilities are truly required for on-the-job performance are aptitude tests for employment justified. The issue is further complicated by the fact that "a mental test irrelevant to *job* performance may predict success in training. To be sure, one wants to select men who will survive training. But if the training presents difficulties not inherent in the job, this barrier may be unfair. When a job is nonverbal, it is hard to defend a training program that relies heavily on reading, and that judges success by written tests."[17]

Furthermore, even if a test does predict job performance, the question has to be raised as to whether the skills required for the job could be taught to virtually all applicants in a training program, thus making the tests unnecessary.

We are not opposed to all testing related to employment. There are situations where testing is appropriate: when the test assesses a key job-related skill or ability, where a lack of skill cannot be improved by a practical training program, where the test in fact selects candidates who show very superior on-the-job performance, and where prediction of superior performance is as accurate for the minority groups (such as Puerto Ricans, Chicanos, and Blacks) as for the White majority. Not all tests on which groups show different average scores (with Blacks generally scoring lower than Whites) are unfair: if the test is locating a deficiency that is relevant to employment, exclusion of individuals on the basis of a low score on such a test is not unfair.

All too often, however, the tests are discriminatory in that the abilities assessed are not critically related to on-the-job performance. In an exaggerated and fictitious example, we might ask whether it is reasonable to give potential applicants for a janitorial job a test of abstract reasoning and set as a minimum cutoff point an IQ of 120. Many real-world situations are only marginally less outlandish. Indeed, the increase in the requirement of college educations for jobs that in no way utilize skills learned in college is already a national scandal.[18]

Dysgenics—The Social Pseudoproblem

Jensen and Herrnstein's approach to the social side of the genetics-race-IQ question is quite benign compared to the approach of some of their followers. At the extreme of these is Shockley, who, reflecting the antique views of the long-discredited eugenics movement, seems desperately concerned about "dysgenics—retrogressive evolution through disproportionate reproduction of the genetically disadvantaged."[19] He is anxious to begin research on racial genetics and has proposed as "thinking exercises" schemes for voluntary sterilization programs, such as that each person with an IQ below 100 be induced to be sterilized[20] with an offer of a cash bonus from the public treasury of $1,000 per IQ point below 100. At the moment, the effect of such a program on average IQ cannot be predicted. Should the United States remain a racist society much as it is today, the average IQ might well be raised even if there were no genetic component to variation of IQ—since the numbers of the oppressors would increase in proportion to the number of oppressed. If, miraculously, all racial discrimination were to disappear *after* Shockley's program had been in force for many generations, the average "genetic IQ" of the population could be lower, higher, or the same as at the start of the program, depending on the presently unknown relationships between genes and IQ.

Shockley tells us that "the view that the U.S. negro is inherently less intelligent than the U.S. white came from my concern for the welfare of humanity"[21]—that is, his concern over whether the "genetically dumb" were outbreeding the "genetically smart." Well, he can relax. Human geneticist Carl Bajema has shown that the notion that people with low IQs are outbreeding those with high IQs is based on a statistical error. While people with low IQs who have offspring have, on the average, more children than those with high IQs, demographers have failed to notice that relatively large numbers of people with low IQs do not have any children. As IQ test score decreases, the proportion of individuals having no children increases. So it turns out that those with high IQs are actually outbreeding those with low IQs, after all.[22] Whether this trend will have any tendency to increase the average national IQ will of course depend on whether there is a heritability of IQ in the environments of the future.

It is important that we not take lightly schemes like Shockley's because they are founded on a welter of misapprehensions about the relevant scientific issues. There are elements in our society that are always ready to forcibly sterilize "mentally incompetent persons," especially if those persons happen to have black skins. In Montgomery, Alabama, in June 1973, a federally funded family-planning center was involved in sterilizing two Black sisters, 12 and 14 years old, when neither the girls nor their mother understood what was happening.[23] That same summer in Aiken, South Carolina, a 20-year-old Black woman was involuntarily sterilized, according to the *New York Times*,

by the one doctor in town who is willing to deliver babies for women . . . who are on welfare. Dr. Clovis H. Pierce does so under one condition—that mothers of three children receiving Medicaid agree to be sterilized. He is doing so, he has said, to help reduce the welfare rolls. . . . [the young Black woman's] is not the only case in Aiken; it's not the only one in the South. . . . Aiken County Hospital records show that 18 of 34 deliveries paid for by Medicaid last year included sterilization. Sixteen of the 18 involved black women. All were performed by Dr. Pierce, the records show.[24]

The Office of Economic Opportunity (OEO) started funding sterilization operations in 1971, and drew up guidelines for use in family-planning clinics. These guidelines, which fortunately were never distributed, apparently suggested recommending sterilization where there was "the presence of physical, mental, or emotional factors that would prevent fulfillment of parental responsibility."[25] Subsequently, new guidelines were developed that would have allowed federal funds to be used for the involuntary sterilization of minors and persons judged mentally incompetent, with the approval of a local review board. This use of federal funds was later declared illegal by a federal judge.[26] It doesn't take much imagination to guess how local review boards in places like Aiken, South Carolina, might decide to employ such powers.

Eugenics plans for improving the human race—and the apparent readiness of some segments of our society to carry out such plans—are nothing new. California has had a law on the books since 1913 that permits compulsory sterilization of institutionalized persons for, among other reasons, retardation. It has performed more institutional sterilizations than any other state—more than 20,000 by the end of 1963.[27] To our knowledge, such sterilizations are no longer being carried out. These reviews simply represent a continued festering of an old and long-discredited segment of the eugenics movement. The influence of that movement at one time was so great that it reached into the Supreme Court. In a majority decision in 1927, Justice Oliver Wendell Holmes stated:

We have seen more than once that the public welfare may call upon the best citizens for their lives. It would be strange if it could not call upon those who already sap the strength of the state for these lesser sacrifices, often not felt to be such by those concerned, in order to prevent our being swamped with incompetence. It is better for all the world if instead of waiting to execute degenerate offspring for crime or to let them starve for their imbecility, society can prevent those who are manifestly unfit from continuing their kind. The principle that sustains compulsory vaccination is broad enough to cover cutting the Fallopian tubes.[28]

It would be naive to assume that such notions could not again penetrate the highest levels of government.

Science and IQ:
Do We Need More Research on Race and Intelligence?

We have already seen that taxonomic naiveté allows the hereditarians to view their concern as the relative "intelligence" of "races" rather than as what it really is, a study of the correlations between IQ test scores and degree of melanin deposition in the skin. This is a scientific issue of considerably less than cosmic importance. If indeed that study were scientifically important, the correlation of IQ with height, tooth size, various blood-group genes, or any of the other geographically varying characteristics of humans would *a priori* be equally important. But if, for example, Audrey Shuey had not written on *The Testing of Negro Intelligence*[29] but on *The Testing of the Intelligence of People with Small Teeth,* or if Shockley had written "Nature has tooth-size coded individuals," it seems unlikely that such work would have been considered to be addressed to important scientific questions—since significant correlations among phenotypic measures are expected in 5 percent of random pairings of characteristics *even if all characteristics are completely unrelated causally.*[30]

For years, Shockley bombarded the National Academy of Sciences with the request that it sponsor studies of the relative roles of heredity and environment in determining intelligence, to confirm or deny his view that the U.S. Black is inherently less intelligent than the U.S. White. The Academy decided not to, even though that nearly lily-white body did decide that the study of human racial differences was "a proper and socially relevant subject."[31] One wonders whether the Academy, with its substantial Jewish membership, would have found the study of differences in pushiness (or intelligence) between Christians and Jews "a proper and socially relevant subject."

To see the preposterousness of the Shockley-Academy position, one need only remember that for "racial" we must read "skin-color" and then engage in some thought experiments. How could one test the hypothesis that there is a genetic difference in IQ between white- and black-skinned human beings? Only by raising several generations of white- and black-skinned peoples (several generations to avoid maternal effects) in identical environments isolated from the rest of humanity. Perhaps blind people could do the rearing, since otherwise, no matter how "liberal" the background of the rearers, subtle differences in treatment related to pigmentation might occur. Matings would have to be restricted to Black with Black and White with White. After, say, three generations, standard IQ tests could then be administered, and, voilà, if the Black and White averages were significantly different, then the difference would be due to genetic factors.

But, even after carrying out this immensely difficult and long experiment, the results would still be useless. For it would only tell you about genetic IQ differences *in that one highly artificial environment.* It would still be quite possible that in the environment of the real world the genetic differences detected would give just the opposite effect! High-yielding "miracle" grain strains greatly outproduce traditional strains in an environment rich in fertilizer and water. But in an environment that is relatively dry and that lacks fertilizer, the reverse is often true. Genetic differences may cause opposite phenotypic differences in two disparate environments.[32] *We cannot emphasize too strongly that genetic determination is not immutability; that genes do not operate independent of environments; that every geneticist must be concerned with genes, environments, and the interactions of genes and environments.*

For the sake of argument, let us carry the group-difference question one step further. Let's forget the mass of information that exists on genetics and psychology and take a position more characteristic of those who are unfamiliar with much of that body of knowledge. Let's assume that each individual has an immutable "genetic intelligence" that will be largely expressed in any reasonably normal human environment. Assume further that a miraculous kind of transistorized device is invented that, when placed on the forehead of an individual, displays in light-emitting diodes the genetic intelligence of that individual—not his or her IQ score but an absolute measure of potential reasoning ability as determined by the genes. Now we can quickly determine the potential of each child in any group. Then the answer to whether big-toothed or small-toothed children, or dark-skinned or light-skinned children, have more "genes for smartness" can be obtained simply by using our transistorized device. Measurements would be made of adequate samples of children with the appropriate characteristics, the averages calculated, and then we would *know*.

To what possible use could this information be put? If, for instance, the light-skinned children had a somewhat lower genetic IQ on the average than the dark-skinned children, could we assume that Shockley would announce that the children had been color-coded for ability and recommend remedial schooling and sterilization for all the light-skinned children?

Suppose Wasserman tests showed that 15 percent of Stanford professors had syphilis but only 10 percent of Harvard's professors did. Would one then recommend penicillin for all professors at Stanford and none for the sufferers at Harvard?

The point, of course, is that to determine group differences in "genetic" intelligence with assurance would first require assaying the "genetic" intelligence of individuals. And if that were possible, the information on each individual would be far more accurate and helpful for any sane and humane use than knowledge of group averages. *The very process of gathering the required information to calculate group averages makes the whole question of group differences moot in any society that believes in judging and dealing with individuals on their own merits instead of on their membership in any "racial," ethnic, religious, sexual, or other group.*

Should Research on Race and IQ Be Banned?

With this background, we can answer the question of whether or not further research on "race and intelligence" is important. Is there any reason that science should attempt to legitimate a second round of "IQ against the Blacks"? The answer is no. It would certainly be useful to understand all that we can about human variation in what are deemed important characteristics—be they blood types or test scores—but to deal with them in a context of "races" is simply bad science and bad politics. One can, indeed, cite circumstances where knowledge of correlations of characteristics can be useful. In some circumstances, a superficial feature of a person may give a clue to some state more difficult to determine. For example, a physician, knowing a couple is Jewish, will be more alert to the possibility of Tay-Sachs disease if their child shows certain symptoms. Similarly, individuals with African ancestry should be more conscious of the possibility of sickle-cell anemia; Whites should be more concerned than Blacks with the possibility of skin cancer, and so on. But knowledge of such correlations, whatever their causation cannot substitute for careful individual diagnosis and treatment.

And, unlike the skin-color–sickle-cell correlation, correlations between scores on intelligence tests and skin color, first language, religion, social class, or other superficial characteristics would not be useful in any legitimate way. The reason is that the IQ test score is not a cryptic, life-threatening disease but a measure that was until recently made routinely in many schools. If, for instance, everyone was readily and routinely screened for Tay-Sachs, sickle-cell anemia, and skin cancer, knowledge of the associations of these maladies with other characteristics would not be useful.

But some say, What's the harm in investigating whether Blacks are genetically dumber than Whites? Isn't science the search for knowledge, and doesn't all knowledge qualify? The answer to these questions is also no. Knowing the exact number of grains of sand on Waikiki Beach would be "knowledge," as would knowing the sum of all the telephone numbers in the world. But nobody would consider the search for those facts science, and a person counting the sand grains or summing the telephone numbers would be more likely to be institutionalized than to be declared a scientist. Scientific investigations must either help us understand how the universe or some part of it works, or they must help us solve some specific practical problem. Investigating the genetics of "racial" differences in IQ would do neither.

There is also a sociopolitical reason why such research should not be done. This is that the mere announcement of research projects can serve to attack and degrade various people. Consider the following announcements of "humane" or "socially relevant" projects:

The Poles have borne the brunt of many jokes insulting their intelligence. It is high time that their IQs were thoroughly tested so we can determine on the one hand whether they are being unjustly attacked, or on the other hand whether they ought to be given special curricula in school.

Richard Nixon and numerous members of his administration clearly had criminal tendencies. We intend to investigate the honesty of other Republicans to see if there is a correlation between membership in that party and fundamental dishonesty.

Adolf Hitler, Joseph Stalin, and their henchmen were all Caucasians. We wish to test the hypothesis that there is a genetic tendency among people with white skins to commit mass murder and practice oppression.

In order to study health problems of religious establishments, we would like to examine large samples of monks and nuns for venereal disease.

All children in the school system should have the sound of their voice analyzed for decibel level so that we can correlate it with the decibel level of their parents' voices in order to determine whether Jews are innately loud.

All this in the name of science—just like giving IQ tests to Black children to determine whether or not Blacks are genetically stupid.

Should some sort of ban be established against "racial" research? We don't think so. As in the area of free speech, we feel that society must accept some harm from fallacious notions as part of the price it pays for the rewards of science. Suppose, for example, today's orthodoxy were that of Terman, Goddard, Yerkes, and Brigham of the 1920s, with the same strong political and social support. What if a ban on research on environmental determinants of racial differences had been declared then? Except in cases where the research itself can be extremely dangerous (such as certain experiments with DNA), we think scientists should investigate what they think is important and moral—no matter how wrong-headed it may seem.

Unfortunately, however, this answer is deceptively simple, since most scientists today ask for and receive support from the public coffers, and many of the results of science are utilized by society. Society thus helps decide what science does and how its products are to be employed. It is clear that in the coming decades the whole relationship of science and society will be reexamined because of issues involving race and IQ, nuclear power plants, genetic engineering, SSTs, food additives, environmental carcinogenesis, and the like. We would not even attempt to predict the outcome, but we hope it will include an increase of scientific sophistication in the general public so that more people can participate knowledgeably in making decisions about technology. But until that sophistication develops, the best cure for nonsense like Jensenism will not be constraints on what scientists can investigate. Scientists should continue to investigate what they please and to speak their minds. The cure will be forthright analysis and well-aired public discussion by other scientists. Science today needs every Leon Kamin it can get.

Genetics and IQ within Groups

It is clear that attempting to classify races according to the genetics of intellectual ability is nonscience, but what about studying differences among classes within races? Is it not important to determine, for instance, whether or not Herrnstein was correct in his assumption that those with "good genes" (for high IQ) will inevitably rise to the top in society?[33] From our previous discussion of heritability, you will see many of the problems inherent in the question itself. Not the least of them is that "good genes" in an upper-class environment may not be "good genes" in a lower-class one! The problem of the genetics of between-class heritability in many ways resembles that of between-"race" heritability and, historically, was often identified with it. The problem is the impossibility of extrapolating a within-group statistic to differences between groups.

Indeed, one cannot help concluding that the ease with which some members of the hereditarian group spin off hypotheses on "geneticity" is strongly conditioned by their limited background in genetics. In particular, there is a tendency to underrate the ease with which the genetics of quantitative characteristics can be understood. It is ironic that at the same time that Shockley at Stanford was discovering heritabilities as a tool for comparing groups of human beings from different environments, one of our research groups at Stanford was abandoning it as a tool for studying something with no social sensitivity at all— differences between butterfly populations in the size of spots on the wings! With organisms that can be raised in the laboratory and with characteristics that can easily be defined and measured, we found the heritability statistic nearly impossible to estimate with assurance and (for the same sorts of reasons already discussed) useless for generation-to-generation or group-to-group comparisons.[34] It was not until biochemical techniques were devised for studying genes one at a time (Mendelian characters) that we were able to make any statements about genetic differences among these populations.[35]

In any event, Herrnstein can rest easy. A provocative examination of the relationship of IQ to economic success shows it may be relatively unimportant when schooling (but not the intellectual abilities developed or certified in school) and family background (but not any genetic contribution from your parents) are taken into account jointly.[36] If it is not IQ *per se* that gets one to the top of the social ladder—and in most cases it is not—then Herrnstein's thesis collapses like a house of cards.

Why All the Fuss?

This brings us to what may be the key question in the whole race-IQ mess and the one area that could well stand detailed social-scientific scrutiny. Why all the fuss about IQ anyway? Many other positive human attributes in addition to wisdom have a long history of being respected and admired in Western and other cultures—love, empathy, compassion, selflessness, endurance, bravery, fairness, humility, open-mindedness, and creativity, to mention a few. As America bungles its way toward the close of the century, it does not appear that those leading the nation—men like Lyndon Johnson, Richard Nixon, Henry Kissinger, or Nelson Rockefeller—have been deficient in IQ. Why haven't we been exposed to theories of the genetics of the lust for power or of the inheritance of greed, or the chromosomal basis of staying on top?

Sociologists Samuel Bowles and Herbert Gintis make an interesting case that the renewed interest in the genetics of IQ is no accident, but is part of a process of legitimating the "overall characteristics of work in advanced United States capitalism: bureaucratic organization, hierarchical lines of authority, job fragmentation, and unequal reward."[37] An analysis of the Bowles-Gintis thesis is beyond the scope of this book; suffice it to say that we have seen the uses to which IQ testing has been put in the past. Now when many of the basic institutions of our society are being questioned, when people are dropping out of the hierarchy, when workers are turned off by the monotony of their jobs, and when minorities and women are demanding a bigger share of rewards, it may not be entirely coincidental that the hereditarian view is getting another welcoming round from the media. Did not *Time* magazine have "Second Thoughts About Man" and consider that appreciating the immutability of the genes might lead to a "new quietism, a readiness to accept things as they are rather than to work for things as they might be."[38]

That science seems again to be turning to less than ideal social goals should surprise no one in a world in which 50 percent of scientists and engineers work for the military.[39] But rarely in modern times has bad science established such currency. It could be that those of us who teach elementary genetics are in part responsible, since somehow the notion that "genetic" is synonymous with "unchangeable" or "irreversible" has become widespread in our society. Until this idea is expunged from our folk wisdom, Jensenism will probably continue to be as tenacious as the ideas that plants have emotions, that black holes are entrances to other universes, that little green men have visited us in UFOs, and that perpetual-motion machines can be built. But people who wish to continue to be prejudiced against other individuals because of their "race" must rely on pseudoscience. They cannot draw on science for support of theories of racial inferiority. Sadly, they may nevertheless receive support from the fallacious ideas promulgated by a few scientists.

APPENDIX A

Evolution

Natural selection is the creative process in evolution. Essentially, it is the differential reproduction of genetic types. In most animal and plant populations and in all human populations, individuals (with the exception of identical twins) differ from one another because each individual has a different hereditary endowment, or *genotype*. For instance, people differ from one another in such traits as skin color, eye color, height, and ABO blood type, all of which are at least partially hereditary.

Suppose people with one hereditary trait (that is, one kind of genetic information) tend to have more children than those with another. This will cause one kind of genetic information—for example, information for producing people with a certain type of hemoglobin in their blood—to become more and more common in the pool of genetic information (the gene pool) of a population. This might occur as a response to an environmental change in which mosquitoes carrying malaria become more abundant—since individuals with one kind of hemoglobin are more resistant to malaria than are those with another kind of hemoglobin. Changes in the gene pool of a population constitute the basic process of *evolution*.

The key concept to bear in mind is that natural selection is *differential reproduction* of genotypes. Natural selection often involves differential survival, which, of course, also results in reproductive differentials, since the dead don't reproduce! But differentials in reproduction may also occur even though the life expectancies of individuals with different genotypes remain identical; all may live the same length of

175

time, but some may be relatively sterile while others are highly fertile. Another key point to remember is that natural selection cannot operate unless there is genetic variability in the population. If there is no variation, all individuals will be genetically identical and there can be no differential reproduction of genotypes. Such a population would be unlikely to survive for long, since it would lack the ability to make evolutionary adjustments to changed conditions.

The factors of the environment that lead to natural selection are called *selective agents*. Changing weather can be a selective agent, leading to an accumulation of genotypes that thrive under the new climatic conditions. DDT can be a selective agent, leading to insect populations made up of genotypes that are resistant to DDT. In this case, humankind is the ultimate selective agent, but the resultant evolution was undesired.

Artificial selection occurs when human beings purposely arrange for the differential reproduction of genotypes. Artificial selection is practiced deliberately by all plant and animal breeders. Animals and plants are selectively bred on the basis of their characteristics, and the breeder controls the differential reproduction of genotypes. The purpose is to develop strains in which the characteristics most valuable to society are maximized: weight in swine, milk production in cows, egg production in chickens, shape and durability in tomatoes, height above ground for ears of corn (for ease in harvesting), beauty in flowers, and so on. These strains have undergone an evolutionary process that adapts them for a man-made environment.

Without human assistance, these strains would disappear through extinction or reversion under the countervailing pressure of natural selection. That pressure must always be reckoned with by the plant or animal breeder. Frequently, attempts to enhance a single characteristic too much will upset development and diminish fertility; thus natural selection will oppose further progress under the pressure of artificial selection. As with natural selection, artificial selection can occur only if the requisite genetic variation is present.

Evolutionary forces other than natural selection also can change the gene pools of populations. *Mutation* can change one form of a gene into another and thus can change the constitution of the gene pool. Immigrants bringing genes into the pool of a population or emigrants taking them out may have genetic constitutions different from the population as a whole, and thus *migration* can change the pool. Both mutation and migration may increase the genetic variability of a population.

Finally, chance occurrences, which are inevitable in the passage of genetic information from one generation to the next, lead to changes in the gene pool. Without going into detail, one can think of the adults of a given generation as possessing a sample of the genetic information present in those of the previous generation. Just as the frequency of heads in a sample of 100 flips of an honest coin usually will not be .50 because of *sampling error*, so the gene pool of the second generation will not be exactly the same as that of the first because of sampling error. Because sampling error causes random changes in the frequency of genes in the pool, it is referred to as *genetic drift*.

Although mutation, migration, and genetic drift are all evolutionary forces, it is important to remember that natural selection is the creative force in evolution. It is selection that shapes populations and species in response to changing environments.

APPENDIX B

Heritability and Genetic Differences Between Groups

Population geneticist Richard C. Lewontin of Harvard University has constructed an instructive example that shows why high heritability within groups does not give us information on the source of between-group differences.* He considers some hypothetical experiments with corn. Suppose seeds of two completely inbred lines of corn, lines A and B, are planted in a series of pots, one seed to a pot, in normal green-house potting soil. Then the pots are arranged randomly in a green-house, but with each pot labeled, so that we know whether it contains a seed of line A or of line B. After a few weeks of growth, the plants are measured and an average height for plants of each line calculated.

Within each of the lines, all of the observed variation would be environmental because inbreeding would have made all of the seeds genetically identical. In other words, the heritability of height in both line A and line B would be 0.00. There would be an average difference between the lines, however. This would be due largely to genetic

---

* R. C. Lewontin, "Race and Intelligence." *Bulletin of the Atomic Scientists,* March 1970, pp. 2–8.

differences between lines A and B—inbreeding having "fixed" different genes in the two lines.

For the sake of simplicity, suppose that each gene in the corn plants could exist in just two forms (that is, in genetics jargon, as two different alleles). Indicating the different alleles of the same gene by capital and lower case letters, and remembering that each individual has two alleles, one from each parent (recall the T and t factors in tomato plants), a small part of the genotypes in the two lines might be:

> Line A—All individuals ABCdeFghiJKlMnoPqR . . .
> ABCdeFghiJKlMnoPqR . . .
>
> Line B—All individuals AbCDEfghIJklMNOpqr . . .
> AbCDEfghIJklMNOpqr . . .

Each individual corn plant in line A is identical genetically with every other individual in line A, and genetically different from every individual corn plant in line B, all of which are also genetically identical. Thus, in this example, two populations differ genetically in a characteristic that has a heritability of 0.00 in each population.

Now consider another case. Suppose we select two batches of seeds at random from a bag of corn seed from an outbred, genetically variable line of corn strain C. Each individual seed will be genetically different from every other seed since it can have three different combinations of alleles of each of its many genes (e.g., AA, Aa, aa—again assuming only two alleles per gene—in reality, there may be many more alleles per gene). Parts of the genotypes of two different individuals of strain C might look like this:

> Line C—Individual X AbCDefghIjKlMnOpQr . . .
> abcDefGHIjkLMnoPQR . . .
>
> Line C—Individual Y AbCDEfGHijklmNoPqR . . .
> aBCDEFghiJklmNOPQr . . .

The two random batches, C_1 and C_2, of these genetically diverse seeds are planted in two sets of perforated plastic containers of vermiculite, a sterile, inert substance. These containers are set in two troughs in an air-conditioned laboratory under banks of special lights that are timed to give precisely the same amount of light to all the seeds. Once a day, a pump fills each trough with a special nutrient, Knop's solution, devised by plant physiologists for growth experiments. The plants of batch C_1 get complete Knop's solution, while those of C_2 get Knop's that has only half the concentration of nitrates and lacks the specified 30 parts per billion of the trace element zinc. The troughs are allowed to drain after the vermiculite is thoroughly soaked. Thus each plant in both groups exists in the same carefully controlled environment, except for one factor, the makeup of the nutrient solution.

After the plants have grown for a while, they are measured, and averages for C_1 and C_2 are calculated. It is not surprising that the C_2 plants, which received the partial Knop's, are stunted. Now the variation *within* batches C_1 and C_2 must be entirely genetic, since the environment of each plant has been carefully controlled to be identical with that of every other plant in the batch. The heritability for height in each batch will be 1.0, since differences among the diverse genotypes within batches will be the sole source of variation. The two batches, however, being random samples from the same strain, will be essentially identical genetically. Each will have contained about the same proportion of "short" and "tall" genotypes, and in identical environments we would expect the two batches to have no significant difference in average height. The differences between batches C_1 and C_2 in this case can be attributed to the differences in the Knop's solution—that is, the differences are entirely environmental. Thus, in this case, two strains, each with a heritability of 1.0 for a given characteristic (height), show an average difference in that characteristic that is entirely environmental.

Lewontin carries his example further. What, he asks, if we did not know about the difference in the nutrients and asked a plant physiologist to explain the difference in height of the two batches? The physiologist checks the solutions, detects the gross shortage of nitrates, and says that explains the stunting of batch C_2. So we repeat the experiment after replacing the missing nitrates, but to our surprise find that the second batch of plants is still stunted, growing just slightly larger than the original C_2 batch. It turns out that the key to the whole situation was the minuscule amount of zinc that was missing. Indeed, for a long time, plant physiologists did not discover the critical requirement of plants for certain trace elements because the requirements were so small that *enough would leach out of ordinary laboratory glassware to permit normal plant growth.*

This example was developed by Lewontin in response to Arthur Jensen's claim that "compensatory education has failed" (see Chapter 7). Lewontin's point was that educational psychology is in such a primitive state that it might well not be able to detect the key environmental factors causing low IQ scores in some groups—that in fact the educators were trying to "compensate" by the equivalent of adding lots of nitrate when what is required is a little zinc! As Lewontin asked, "Should educational psychologists study plant physiology?"

NOTES

1. Race and Your Future

1. W. Shockley, quoted in N. Daniels, "The Smart White Man's Burden." *Harpers*, 244:25, 1973.

2. P. R. Ehrlich and A. H. Ehrlich, *The End of Affluence* (New York: Ballantine), 1974.

3. P. R. Ehrlich, A. H. Ehrlich, and J. P. Holdren, *Ecoscience: Population, Resources, Environment* (San Francisco: W. H. Freeman), 1977.

4. Gordon W. Allport, *The Nature of Prejudice* (Garden City, N.Y.: Doubleday), 1958. In spite of its age, this book is an indispensable source on the psychology of prejudice.

5. E. Shils, "Color, the Universal Intellectual Community and the Afro-Asian Intellectual." *Daedalus*, 96:270, Spring 1967.

6. H. R. Isaacs, "Group Identity and Political Change." *Daedalus*, 96:362, Spring 1967.

7. *Ibid.*, p. 363.

8. C. E. Lincoln, "Color and Group Identity in the United States." *Daedalus*, 96:527–541, Spring 1967.

9. H. Wagatsuma, "The Social Perception of Skin Color in Japan." *Daedalus*, 96:407–443, Spring 1967.

10. *Ibid.*, p. 420.

11. K. J. Gergen, "The Significance of Skin Color in Human Relations." *Daedalus*, 96:390–406, Spring 1967.

12. Data from *Statistical Abstract of the United States* (Washington, D.C.: U.S. Government Printing Office), 1975.

13. Data from Harvard economist A. Brimmer, reported in *Palo Alto Times*, February 24, 1976.

14. See, e.g., W. H. Grier and P. M. Cobb, *Black Rage* (New York: Basic Books), 1969.

15. J. Lind, "The Color Complex in the Negro." *Psychoanalytic Review*, 1:404–414, 1914.

16. Gergen, *Significance of Skin Color.*

17. *Statistical Abstract of the United States.*

18. It is only by repeated testing and revision of hypotheses and theories that science evolves away from error. We deliberately do not say that it evolves toward the truth, which implies that there is some perfect state of knowledge lying ahead.

19. D. G. Brinton, quoted in S. J. Gould, "Racism and Recapitulation." *Natural History*, June–July, 1975, p. 18. Gould's article is well worth reading.

20. *Ibid.*

21. W. C. George, *The Biology and the Race Problem*. Reprint prepared by Commission of the Governor of Alabama, 1962. Distributed by the National Putnam Letters Committee.

22. C. S. Coon, *The Origin of Races* (New York: Knopf), 1962.

23. George, *Biology and the Race Problem*, pp. 77–78.

24. *Ibid.*, p. 11.

25. See, e.g., A. Montagu (ed.), *The Concept of Race* (New York: Free Press of Glencoe), 1964.

26. *Proceedings of the National Academy of Sciences*, 57:1771, 1967.

27. The key paper was A. Jensen, "How Much Can We Boost IQ and Scholastic Achievement?" *Harvard Educational Review*, 39:1–123, 1969.

2. What Are Races, Really?

1. The nature and definition of "species" has been the subject of long debate in the scientific literature. The classical view is well presented in E. Mayr, *Animal Species and Evolution* (Cambridge, Mass.: Harvard University Press), 1963; while a more modern position can be found in P. R. Ehrlich, "Has the Biological Species Concept Outlived Its Usefulness?" *Systematic Zoology*, 10:167–176, 1961; P. R. Ehrlich and P. H. Raven, "The Differentiation of Populations." *Science*, 165:1228–1232, 1969; and R. R. Sokal and T. J. Crovello, "The Biological Species Concept: A Critical Evaluation." *American Naturalist*, 104:122–153, 1970.

2. In the Linnaean taxonomic system, the name of a family of animals is based on the root of the name of a genus in that family combined with the ending *-idae*.

3. See, e.g., P. R. Ehrlich and R. W. Holm, "Patterns and Populations." *Science*, 137:652–657, 1962.

4. *Systema Naturae*, 1:20–22, 1758. We are indebted to D. L. Bilderback, Fresno State University, Fresno, Calif., for the translation from the original Latin.

5. C. S. Coon, *The Origin of Races* (New York: Knopf), 1962.

6. See P. R. Ehrlich, "The Distribution and Subspeciation of *Erebia epipsodea* Butler (Lepidoptera: Satyridae). *University of Kansas Science Bulletin*, 37:175–194, 1954. The subspecific division of *Erebia epipsodea* presented in this paper in no way corresponds to any biological entities. It is nice to be able to spare colleagues' feelings by selecting horrible examples from one's own work!

7. E. Mayr, *Systematics and the Origin of Species* (New York: Columbia University Press), 1942, p. 106.

8. C. S. Coon, S. M. Garn, and J. B. Birdsell, *Races, A Study of the Problems of Race Formation in Man* (Springfield, Ill.: Charles C Thomas), 1950.

9. D. F. Roberts and D. P. S. Kahlon, "Environmental Correlations of Skin Colour." *Annals of Human Biology*, 3:11–22, 1976.

10. C. L. Brace, "A Non Racial Approach Towards the Understanding of Human Diversity," in A. Montagu, (ed.), *The Concept of Race* (New York: Free Press of Glencoe), 1964, pp. 103–152. Skin cancers usually occur late in life and would tend to kill postreproductive individuals, so their prevention alone does not seem a sufficient selective factor (see Appendix A), to explain skin-color variation.

11. R. B. Cowles, "Some Ecological Factors Bearing on the Origin and Evolution of Pigment in the Human Skin." *American Naturalist*, 93:283–293, 1959.

12. Brace, "A Non Racial Approach," p. 111.

13. L. L. Cavalli-Sforza and W. F. Bodmer, *The Genetics of Human Populations* (San Francisco: W. H. Freeman), 1971, p. 747.

14. P. R. Ehrlich and P. H. Raven, "Differentiation of Populations." *Science*, 165:1228–1232, 1969.

15. See, e.g., D. F. Roberts, *Climate and Human Variability* (New York: Addison-Wesley), Module in Anthropology No. 34, 1973.

16. Brace, "A Non Racial Approach," pp. 141–142. The material in the following paragraphs on the adaptive significance of human morphological variation draws heavily on Brace's article.

17. This paragraph is, perforce, extremely simplified. For a review of genetics and

elementary population genetics, see P. R. Ehrlich, R. W. Holm, and D. R. Parnell, *The Process of Evolution*, 2nd ed. (New York: McGraw-Hill), 1974, Chapters 1–3 and 6.

18. I. M. Lerner, *Heredity, Evolution and Society* (San Francisco: W. H. Freeman), 1968, pp. 107–108.

19. See W. Bodmer and L. L. Cavalli-Sforza, *Genetics, Evolution and Man* (San Francisco: W. H. Freeman), 1976.

20. P. R. Ehrlich, R. W. Holm, and I. L. Brown, *Biology and Society* (New York: McGraw-Hill), 1976, p. 271.

21. Bodmer and Cavalli-Sforza, *Genetics, Evolution and Man*, Figures 19–1 to 19–3.

22. A thorough discussion of human genetic variation can be found in Cavalli-Sforza and Bodmer, *Genetics of Human Populations*. See also T. E. Reed, "Selection and Blood Group Polymorphisms," and F. M. Salzano, "Interpopulation Variability in Polymorphic Systems," both in F. Salzano (ed.), *The Role of Natural Selection in Human Evolution* (New York and Amsterdam: North-Holland Pub. Co.), 1975.

23. G. A. Harrison et al., *Human Biology* (New York: Oxford University Press), 1974, pp. 478–480; D. Kennedy, Personal communication.

24. H. F. Harlow, "The Evolution of Learning," in A. Roe and G. G. Simpson (eds.), *Behavior and Evolution* (New Haven: Yale University Press), 1958, pp. 269–290.

25. P. K. Benedict and I. Jacks, "Mental Illness in Primitive Societies." *Psychiatry*, 17:377–389, 1954.

26. E. O. Wilson and W. L. Brown, "The Subspecies Concept and Its Taxonomic Application." *Systematic Zoology*, 2:97, 1953.

27. P. R. Ehrlich, R. W. Holm, and D. R. Parnell, *Process of Evolution*. See also P. R. Ehrlich and R. W. Holm, "A Biological View of Race," in Montagu, *The Concept of Race*; N. W. Gilham, "Geographic Variation and the Subspecies Concept in Butterflies." *Systematic Zoology*, 5:100–120, 1965.

28. See, e.g., S. M. McKechnie, P. R. Ehrlich, and R. R. White, "Population Genetics of Euphydryas Butterflies. I. Genetic Variation and the Neutrality Hypothesis." *Genetics*, 81:571–594, 1975. See, e.g., Figure 1.

29. W. L. Brown, Jr., "Some Zoological Concepts Applied to Problems in the Evolution of the Hominid Lineage." *American Scientist*, 46:151–158, 1959.

30. This point has long been understood by some anthropologists such as Brace, "A Non Racial Approach," and F. B. Livingston, "On the Non-Existence of Human Races." *Current Anthropology*, 3:279, 1962. Many others are still stuck in the taxonomic paradigm of the 1940s.

31. For a description of the process of speciation, see Ehrlich, Holm, and Parnell, *Process of Evolution*, Chapter 10; for a more heterodox view, see P. R. Ehrlich and P. H. Raven, "Differentiation of Populations." *Science*, 165:1228–1232, 1969.

3. Races in a Social Context

1. C. N. Degler, *Neither Black Nor White* (New York: Macmillan), 1971, p. 105.

2. *Ibid.*

3. G. L. Allport, *The Nature of Prejudice* (New York: Doubleday), 1958, Chapter 2.

4. J. A. Barnett, *The Human Species* (New York: Harper & Row), 1971, pp. 143–144.

5. D. B. Davis, *The Problem of Slavery in Western Culture* (Ithaca, N.Y.: Cornell University Press), 1966, p. 453.

6. *Ibid.*, Chapter 2.

7. Pope Paul III, quoted in C. Bibby, *Race, Prejudice and Education* (New York: Praeger), 1957, p. 43.

8. The discussion of slavery owes much to discussions with historian D. L. Bilderback.

9. R. A. Goldsby, *Race and Races* (New York: Macmillan), 1971, pp. 6–7. Goldsby quotes the Nuremberg laws and similar laws dealing with Blacks in some states of the United States.

10. Resolution of the General Assembly of December 11, 1946, ratified by twenty nations in 1951. The United States did not sign it. Quoted in R. Daniels and H. H. L. Kitano, *American Racism* (Englewood Cliffs, N.J.: Prentice-Hall), 1970, p. 28. Note that the UN resolution speaks against the killing of certain groups, but not of others (such as social classes). Presumably this is because once an individual is labeled as a member of a race to be suppressed, there is nothing he or she can do to be cleared of the crime of membership in the proscribed group. Thus, if you label someone a Black or a Jew and then kill him because of it, you are committing genocide; if you label him "kulak" or "deviationist" and kill him because of it, you are presumably not subject to the sanction of the United Nations. In theory, of course, it is possible for a person to stop being a kulak or deviationist, but not to stop being a Jew or a Black. It seems a fine line to draw.

11. See, e.g., A. M. Josephy, Jr., *The Patriot Chiefs* (New York: Viking Press), 1961.

12. V. Deloria, *Custer Died for Your Sins* (New York: Avon Books), 1969, p. 42.

13. C. Sardi, quoted in *New Internationalist*, October 1973. See also J. Hillaby, "Genocide in Paraguay." *New Scientist*, January 16, 1975, p. 153.

14. M. Munzel, quoted in *New Internationalist*, October 1973.

15. M. Howe, "Slaughter in Burundi: How Thousands Died in Ethnic Conflict." *New York Times*, June 1, 1972. See also *Time*, June 26, 1972.

16. "Elite Presses War Against Unborn Babies." *Muhammad Speaks*, March 13, 1970; R. Chrisman, "Ecology Is a Racist Shuck." *Scanlons*, August 15, 1970, pp. 46–50.

17. The history of these attitudes is dealt with in detail by R. G. Weisbord in his excellent "Birth Control and the Black American: A Matter of Genocide?" *Demography*, 10:571–590, 1973.

18. The material on birth rates and family planning among poor and minorities is from P. R. Ehrlich, A. H. Ehrlich, and J. P. Holdren, *Ecoscience: Population, Resources, Environment* (San Francisco: W. H. Freeman), 1977.

19. "Family Size and the Black American." *Population Bulletin*, 30(4), 1975, Population Reference Bureau, Washington, D.C.

20. F. S. Jaffe, "Low Income Families: Fertility Changes in the 1960s." *Family Planning Perspectives*, 4(1):43–47, January 1972; F. S. Jaffe, "Family Size and the Black American." *Population Bulletin*, 30(4), 1975.

21. W. E. B. DuBois, "Birth." *Crisis*, 24:248–250, 1922.

22. W. E. B. DuBois, "Black Folk and Birth Control." *Birth Control Review*, 16:166–167, 1932.

23. M. L. King, Jr., "Family Planning—A Special Urgent Concern." Planned Parenthood-World Population, New York (speech given in 1966).

24. C. Jones, "Abortion and Black Women." *Black America*, 1:48–49.

25. S. Chisholm, quoted in Weisbord, "Birth Control and the Black American," p. 584.

26. See D. C. Pirages and P. R. Ehrlich, *Ark II: Social Response to Environmental Imperatives* (San Francisco: W. H. Freeman), 1974, especially Chapter 7; Ehrlich, Ehrlich, and Holdren, *Ecoscience*, especially Chapter 15.

27. See Ehrlich, Ehrlich, and Holdren, *Ecoscience*, Chapter 10.

28. Lord Raglan, quoted in C. Stern, *Principles of Human Genetics*, 3rd ed. (San Francisco: W. H. Freeman), 1973, p. 840.

29. Reprinted in T. H. Huxley, *Lectures and Lay Sermons* (New York: E. P. Dutton), 1910, p. 115.

30. *Ibid.*, p. 116.

31. T. Bilbo, quoted in Degler, *Neither Black Nor White*, pp. 120–121.

32. C. D. Darlington, *The Facts of Life* (London: Allen and Unwin), 1953. See also Darlington, *Genetics and Man* (London: Allen and Unwin), 1964, in which the language is more tempered but the extreme genetic determinism remains.

33. C. S. Coon, *The Origin of Races* (New York: Knopf), 1962, p. 657.

34. Coon's book was subjected to detailed criticism in A. Montagu (ed.), *The Concept of Race* (New York: Free Press of Glencoe), 1964, and in numerous reviews in scientific journals.

35. Coon, *Origin of Races*, p. 105.

36. *Ibid.*, p. 110.

37. N. Weyl and S. Possany, *The Geography of Intellect* (Chicago: Regnery), 1963.

38. J. J. Sherwood and M. Nataupsky, "Predicting the Conclusions of Negro-White Intelligence Research from Biographical Characteristics of the Investigator." *Journal of Personality and Social Psychology*, 8:53–58, 1968.

39. F. Galton, *Hereditary Genius* (New York: Macmillan), 1869.

40. A. Jensen, "Race and the Genetics of Intelligence: A Reply to Lewontin." *Bulletin of the Atomic Scientists*, May 1970, p. 17.

41. E. L. Thorndike, quoted in *ibid.*, p. 21.

42. R. C. Lewontin, "Further Remarks on Race and the Genetics of Intelligence." *Bulletin of the Atomic Scientists*, May 1970, p. 23.

43. A. Binet and T. Simon, *The Development of Intelligence in Children*, trans. by E. W. Kits (Baltimore: Williams and Wilkins), 1916.

44. H. Goddard, "Mental Tests and the Immigrant." *Journal of Delinquency*, 2:252, 1917, Table II. See also comments on p. 244. For even more horrifying reading about how Goddard and his colleagues could tell mental defectives by simply looking at them, see "The Binet Tests in Relation to Immigration," *Journal of Psycho-Asthenics*, 18:105–107, 1913.

45. L. J. Kamin, *The Science and Politics of IQ* (New York: Wiley), 1974, p. 16. Chapter 2 details the way IQ tests were used against immigrants.

46. *Ibid.*, p. 30.

47. R. Pinter, *Intelligence Testing: Methods and Results* (New York: Holt), 1923.

48. L. Terman, *The Measurement of Intelligence* (Boston: Houghton Mifflin), 1916.

49. *Ibid.*, pp. 91–92.

50. W. Shockley, "Dysgenics, Geneticity, Raceology: A Challenge to the Intellectual Responsibility of Educators," *Phi Delta Kappan*, January, 1972, p. 307.

51. *Ibid.*

52. H. J. Eysenck, *The IQ Argument* (Freeport, N.Y.: Library Press), 1971, p. 12, emphasis ours.

53. For a history of eugenics in the United States, see K. Ludmerer, *Genetics and American Society* (Baltimore: Johns Hopkins Press), 1972, Chapter 2.

54. See, e.g., M. H. Haller, *Eugenics* (New Brunswick, N.J.: Rutgers University Press), 1963, pp. 70 ff.

55. See, e.g., Ludmerer, *Genetics*, Chapter 2.

56. M. Grant, *The Passing of the Great Race* (New York: Scribner's), 1916.

57. Ludmerer, *Genetics*, p. 73.

58. L. L. Cavalli-Sforza and W. Bodmer, *The Genetics of Human Population* (San Francisco: W. H. Freeman), 1971, p. 753. Chapter 12 contains an excellent survey of the technical side of eugenics.

59. See, e.g., E. H. Beardsley, "The American Scientist as Social Activist: Franz Boas, Burt G. Wilder, and the Cause of Racial Justice, 1900–1915." *Isis*, 64:50–66, 1973. See also Ludmerer, *Genetics*, pp. 82–83.

60. Material in these paragraphs on Wilder and Boas is documented in Beardsley, *The American Scientist*.

61. *Ibid.*, pp. 59–60.

62. R. Benedict, *Race: Science and Politics* (New York: Viking), 1943.

63. C. C. Brigham, *A Study of American Intelligence* (Princeton, N.J.: Princeton University Press), 1923.

64. *Ibid.*, p. 207.

65. *Ibid.*, p. 210.

66. Kamin, *Science and Politics of IQ*, p. 22.

67. R. Yerkes, in Brigham, *Study of American Intelligence*, pp. vii–viii.

68. Ranking data from A. Montagu, "Intelligence in Northern Negroes and Southern Whites in the First World War." *American Journal of Psychology*, 58:161–188, 1945.

69. Data in this paragraph from Benedict, *Race: Science and Politics*, pp. 75–76; and T. R. Garth, *Race Psychology, A Study of Racial Mental Differences* (New York: McGraw-Hill), 1931, p. 219.

70. O. Klineberg, *Negro Intelligence and Selective Migration* (New York: Columbia University Press), 1935. See especially Chapter 9 and the closing statement on p. 62.

71. O. Klineberg, *Race Differences* (New York: Harper and Bros.), 1935, p. 189.

72. C. C. Brigham, "Intelligence Tests of Immigrant Groups." *Psychological Review*, 37:165, 1930.

73. R. Benedict, *Race: Science and Politics* (New York: Viking Press), Compass Books Edition with a foreword by Margaret Mead published in 1959.

74. A. Jensen, "How Much Can We Boost IQ and Scholastic Achievement?" *Harvard Educational Review*, 39:95, Winter 1969, second emphasis ours.

75. W. F. Brazziel, "A Letter from the South." *Harvard Educational Review* (HER), 39:348–356; material on p. 200 of HER reprint on the Jensen controversy, *Environment, Heredity and Intelligence*, 1969.

76. *Ibid.*, p. 201 of reprint.

77. J. Alsop, *Washington Post*, March 11, 1969, quoted by Brazziel, reprint p. 203.

78. Jensen, "How Much Can We Boost IQ?" pp. 81–82, 108.

79. M. E. Goodman, *Race Awareness in Young Children* (Cambridge, Mass.: Addison-Wesley), 1952.

80. H. M. Proshansky, "The Development of Intergroup Attitudes." In L. W. Hoffman and M. L. Hoffman (eds.), *Review of Child Development Research*, Vol. II (New York: Russell Sage Foundation), 1966.

81. E. L. Horowitz, "The Development of Attitudes Toward the Negro." *Archives of Psychology*, No. 194, 1936.

82. T. Aderno, E. Frenkel-Brunswick, D. J. Levinson, and R. N. Sanford, *The Authoritarian Personality* (New York: Harper & Row), 1950.

83. B. Bettleheim and M. Janowitz, *Social Changes and Prejudice: Including Dynamics of Prejudice* (New York: Free Press), 1964.

84. L. L. Knowles and K. Prewitt (eds.), *Institutional Racism in America* (Englewood Cliffs, N.J.: Prentice-Hall), 1969, pp. 15–16. Data in Knowles and Prewitt are for 1968, based on an ownership of 50,000 firms by Blacks. *The Statistical Abstract of the U.S., 1976*, indicates that in 1972 (latest year) there were 195,000 Black-owned businesses, or only one-fifth of "proportional" representation. We do not know the source of the discrepancy, but it is noteworthy that the *Abstract* gives the receipts of Black businesses as only 0.3 percent of all business receipts, while Blacks make up 11.3 percent of the population. In receipts, the Blacks therefore account for only about 2.7 percent of their "share."

85. According to A. Brimmer, "The Negro in the National Economy," in J. P. David (ed.), *The American Negro Reference Book* (Englewood Cliffs, N.J.: Prentice-Hall), 1966, p. 297, in 1963 Black-controlled financial institutions had only 0.12 per cent of the combined assets of such institutions. In 1972, according to the *Statistical Abstracts*, Black-owned financial institutions and real-estate ventures (the categories are lumped together) had only 0.2 percent of the receipts of such business.

86. A. Roos and H. Hill, *Employment, Race and Poverty* (New York: Harcourt, Brace and World), 1967, pp. 409–410.

87. H. M. Baron, "The Web of Urban Racism." In Knowles and Prewitt, p. 146.

88. Genealogy is still a brisk trade. There is one legendary firm in England that for £150 will prove that one of your ancestors came from Normandy with William the Conqueror. For £200, they will prove that one of your ancestors *was* William the Conqueror.

89. This entire section, "Why Does Racism Persist?" is based on lively discussion with historian D. L. Bilderback.

4. Intelligence and Intelligence Tests

1. F. S. Freeman, *Theory and Practice of Psychological Testing*, 3rd ed. (New York: Holt, Rinehart and Winston), 1962.

2. L. M. Terman and M. A. Merrill, *Stanford Binet Intelligence Scale* (Boston: Houghton Mifflin), 1973.

3. M. E. Shimberg, "An Investigation into the Validity of Norms with Special Reference to Urban and Rural Groups." *Archives of Psychology*, No. 104, 1929.

4. A. Dove, "Chitling Test of Intelligence," Mimeo, 1969.

5. L. J. Cronbach, *Essentials of Psychological Testing*, 3rd ed. (New York: Harper & Row), 1970.

6. L. M. Terman, *Genetic Studies of Genius* (Stanford, Calif.: Stanford University Press), Vol. I, 1925; Vol. II, 1926; Vol. III, 1930; with Melita Oden, Vol. IV, 1947; with Melita Oden, Vol. V, 1959.

7. Information from D. L. Bilderback.

8. The square of the correlation coefficient is often used instead of the correlation coefficient. For a thorough discussion of correlation, see the excellent text *Biometry* by R. R. Sokal and F. James Rohlf (San Francisco: W. H. Freeman), 1969, Chapter 15, especially Figure 15.3.

9. E. A. Bond, *Tenth Grade Abilities and Achievements* (New York: Teachers College, Columbia University), 1940.

10. B. R. McCandless, A. Roberts, and T. Starnes, "Teachers' Marks, Achievement Test Scores and Aptitude Relations by Social Class, Race and Sex." *Journal of Educational Psychology*, 63:153–159, 1972.

11. L. B. Ames and R. N. Walker, "Prediction of Later Reading Ability from Kindergarten Rorschach and IQ Scores." *Journal of Educational Psychology*, 55:309–313, 1964.

12. We must also note that testing is a big business, and the sales ability of the vendors of the tests cannot be ignored.

13. L. M. Terman, "The Discovery and Encouragement of Exceptional Talent." *American Psychologist*, 9:221–230, 1954.

14. W. K. Baller, D. C. Charles, and E. Miller, "Mid-Life Attainment of the Mentally Retarded. A Longitudinal Study." *Genetic Psychology Monograph*, 75:235–329, 1967.

15. L. Longstreth, *Psychological Development of the Child*, 2nd ed. (New York: Ronald Press), 1974.

16. O. D. Duncan, D. L. Featherman, and B. Duncan, *Socioeconomic Background and Occupational Achievement: Extensions of a Basic Model*. Final Report. Project No. 5-0074, EO-191 (Washington, D.C.: U.S. Department of Health, Education and Welfare), May 1968. Reported to Jensen, 1969.

17. J. Cronbach, *Essentials of Psychological Testing*, 3rd ed. (New York: Harper & Row), 1970.

18. R. B. McCall, M. I. Appelbaum, and P. W. Hogarty, "Developmental Changes in Mental Performance." *Monographs of the Society for Research in Child Development*, 38(150), 1973.

19. E. S. Lee, "Negro Intelligence and Selective Immigration." *American Sociological Review*, 16:227–233, 1951.

20. M. M. Skeels, "Adult Status of Children with Contrasting Early Life Experiences." *Monographs of the Society for Research in Child Development*, 31(3), 1965.

21. P. Levenstein, "VIP Children Reach School: Latest Chapter. Progress Report 1973–1974," Follow Up Study of the Mother-Child Home Program, Freeport, New York.

22. L. W. Sontag, C. T. Baker, and V. L. Nelson, "Mental Growth and Personality Development: A Longitudinal Study." *Monographs of the Society for Research in Child Development*, 23(68), 1958.

23. K. T. Hill and S. B. Sarason, "The Relation of Test Anxiety and Defensiveness to Test and School Performance over the Elementary School Years." *Monographs of the Society for Research in Child Development*, 31(Whole No. 104), 1966.

24. N. Bayley, "On the Growth of Intelligence." *American Psychologist*, 10:805–818, 1955.

25. N. Bayley, "Consistency and Variability in the Growth of Intelligence from Birth to 18 Years." *Journal of Genetic Psychology*, 75:165–196, 1949.

26. J. Piaget, *The Psychology of Intelligence* (London: Routledge and Kegan Paul), 1950; J. Piaget, *The Origins of Intelligence in Children* (New York: International Universities Press), 1952.

27. N. Bayley, "Research in Child Development: A Longitudinal Perspective." *Merrill-Palmer Quarterly*, 11, 1965.

28. K. P. Bradway and C. W. Thompson, "Intelligence at Adulthood: A Twenty-Five Year Follow-up." *Journal of Educational Psychology*, 53:1–14, 1962; J. Kangas and K. Bradway, "Intelligence at Middle Age: A Thirty-Eight Year Follow-up." *Developmental Psychology*, 5:333–337, 1971; W. A. Owens, "Age and Mental Abilities: A Second Adult Follow-up." *Journal of Educational Psychology*, 57:311–325, 1966.

29. R. Flaste, "I.Q. Tests: Parents Are Eager to Learn Meaning of Scores." *New York Times*, March 28, 1975.

30. *Ibid.*

5. Is IQ Inherited?

1. See, e.g., F. Galton, *Natural Inheritance* (New York: Macmillan), 1889.

2. For further information on basic genetics at a relatively simple level, see P. R. Ehrlich, R. W. Holm, and I. L. Brown, *Biology and Society* (New York: McGraw-Hill), 1976, Chapter 9. A more condensed and technical treatment is in P. R. Ehrlich, R. W. Holm, and D. R. Parnell, *The Process of Evolution*, 2nd ed. (New York: McGraw-Hill), 1974, Chapter 3. A good, comprehensive human genetics text is C. Stern, *Principles of Human Genetics*, 3rd ed. (San Francisco: W. H. Freeman), 1973. L. L. Cavalli-Sforza and W. F. Bodmer, *The Genetics of Human Populations* (San Francisco: W. H. Freeman), 1971, is *the* comprehensive reference book on statistical behavior of genes in populations of *Homo sapiens*. A less technical treatment by the same authors is *Genetics, Evolution and Man* (San Francisco: W. H. Freeman), 1976.

3. W. Johannsen, *Uber Erblichkeit in Populationen und in reinen Linien*, Jena,

1903. Technically, Johannsen's experiment showed that there was no *additive* genetic variance for bean size.

4. C. H. Waddington, "Genetic Assimilation of an Acquired Character." *Evolution*, 7:118–126, 1953.

5. For a detailed discussion of heritability, see D. S. Falconer, *Quantitative Genetics* (Edinburgh: Oliver and Boyd), 1960.

6. Technically, heritability (H) is the ratio of the variability of a characteristic in a population assignable to genetic differences among individuals (V_G) to the total variability (V_T), in that character. Furthermore, V_T is the sum of V_G and the environmental variability (V_E). Thus,

$$H = \frac{V_G}{V_T} = \frac{V_G}{V_G + V_E}$$

H ranges from $0(V_G = 0)$ to $1(V_E = 0)$. In the technical literature, heritability is usually designated h^2; variability is called "variance," and H is calculated in a special way.

7. Those familiar with quantitative genetics will realize that this test measures heritability in the narrow sense—that is, the ratio of the *additive* genetic variance to the total variance—and does not include variation due, for example, to gene-environment interactions.

8. This statement is not precisely correct, but the inaccuracy is trivial in terms of this discussion.

9. In the technical literature, identical twins are often called monozygotic (MZ) and fraternal twins, dizygotic (DZ).

10. This result would apply only for the population studied and for the environment in which it was studied. Technically, the population for which this would hold is the population of twins, since there is evidence that they live in a different set of environments from the general population because the very presence of twins in a family has a dramatic effect on the family environment. Furthermore, identical and fraternal twins produce different effects on each other and the family as a whole. See, e.g., B. Snider, *A Comparative Study of Achievement Test Scores of Fraternal and Identical Twins and Siblings.* Unpublished doctoral dissertation, State University of Iowa, 1955.

11. These studies have been analyzed in great detail by L. J. Kamin in *The Science and Politics of IQ* (New York: Wiley), 1974, Chapter 3.

12. C. Burt, "The Genetic Determination of Differences in Intelligence: A Study of Monozygotic Twins Reared Together and Apart." *British Journal of Psychology*, 57:137–153, 1966.

13. *Ibid.*

14. A. Jensen, "How Much Can We Boost IQ and Scholastic Achievement?" *Harvard Educational Review*, 39:51, 1969.

15. Kamin, *Science and Politics of IQ.*

16. *Ibid.*

17. *Ibid.*

18. C. Burt, "The Evidence for the Concept of Intelligence." *British Journal Educational Psychology*, 25:167–168, 1955; Burt, "Genetic Determination of Differences," p. 146.

19. C. Burt and M. Howard, "The Relative Influence of Heredity and Environment on Assessments of Intelligence." *British Journal of Statistical Psychology*, 10:39, 1957.

20. N. Wade, "IQ and Heredity: Suspicion of Fraud Beclouds Classic Experiment," *Science*, 194:916–919, 26 November 1976. *Newsweek*, 20 December 1976, p. 45.

21. Jensen, "How Much Can We Boost IQ," p. 52. He described Burt's work as "the most interesting" of the twin studies because of the size of the sample, the representativeness of the twins (in IQ and variance) of the general population, the earliness of separation, and the range of socioeconomic levels represented.

22. A. Jensen, "Kinship Correlations Reported by Sir Cyril Burt." *Behavioral Genetics*, 4:24, 1974.

23. J. Shields, *Monozygotic Twins, Brought Up Apart and Brought Up Together* (London: Oxford University Press), 1962.

24. Kamin, *Science and Politics of IQ*, pp. 49–52.

25. Descriptions in this paragraph and the next are from Shields, *Monozygotic Twins*, Part II, Case Histories.

26. H. H. Newman, F. N. Freeman, and K. J. Holzinger, *Twins: A Study of Heredity and Environment* (Chicago: University of Chicago Press), 1937.

27. N. Juel-Nielsen, "Individual and Environment: A Psychiatric-Psychological Investigation of Monozygotic Twins Reared Apart." *Acta Psychiatrica et Neurologica Scandinavica*, Monograph Supplement 183, 1965.

28. For technical discussion of this and related points see M. W. Feldman and R. C. Lewontin, "The Heritability Hang-Up." *Science*, 190:1163–1168, 1975; and D. Layzer, "Heritability Analyses of IQ Scores: Science or Numerology?" *Science*, 183:1259–1266, 1974.

29. D. Layzer, *Heritability Analyses of IQ Scores*, p. 1265.

30. The last paper, in which references to the others may be found, is M. Skodak and H. M. Skeels, "A Final Follow-Up Study of One Hundred Adopted Children." *Journal of Genetic Psychology*, 75:85–125, 1949.

31. Kamin, *Science and Politics of IQ*, pp. 124–131.

32. M. Skodak and H. M. Skeels, "A Follow-Up Study of Children in Adoptive Homes." *Journal of Genetic Psychology*, 66:21–58, 1945.

33. See, e.g., L. M. Terman and M. A. Merrill, *Measuring Intelligence* (Boston: Houghton Mifflin), 1937, Table 12, p. 48.

34. In a correlation study, making the sample of one variable more homogeneous reduces the correlation coefficient. Income, for example, is highly correlated with number of years of school attended if the sample of people is drawn at random from the population. The correlation will be much weaker, or nonexistent, if the sample of people is drawn from those who have completed at least two years of college. Similarly, the relative homogeneity of the sample of adoptive mothers' educational achievements in the second study could account for the drop in the correlation of that achievement with the IQs of the foster children.

35. Kamin, *Science and Politics of IQ*, p. 126.

36. *Ibid.*, Chapter 5; A. S. Goldberger, *Professor Jensen, Meet Miss Burks*. Mimeographed Research Report, University of Wisconsin Institute for Research on Poverty, December 1974.

37. Kamin, *Science and Politics of IQ*, pp. 130–131.

38. *Ibid.*, p. 124. Natural-child correlation was slightly higher than adopted-child correlation in one study and the pooled data of three studies, "adopted child" was slightly higher in one study, and in one study there were no data on natural children.

39. *Ibid.*

40. The same can be said of studies of inbreeding effects on IQ, such as W. J. Schull and J. V. Neel's study, *The Effects of Inbreeding on Japanese Children* (New York: Harper & Row), 1956. If the IQs of children of marriages between relatives were lower than those of nonrelated parents, everything else being equal, this would indicate a genetic component to variation in IQ. But in the Schull and Neel study, everything else wasn't equal, because the related couples tended to have a lower social and economic status than the nonrelatives.

41. See, e.g., Kamin, *Science and Politics of IQ*, Chapter 6; J. Hirsh, "Jensenism: The Bankruptcy of 'Science' Without Scholarship." *Educational Theory*, in press; A. S. Goldberger, *Professor Jensen*. See also Jensen's own statement, "Kinship Correlations" (p. 5), on Burt's use of "assessments" instead of raw scores: "But one may question whether the subjective element in this procedure is one that can be wholeheartedly recommended in scientific research on the genetics of mental abilities. Since it is not completely explicit, it cannot be completely objective, and therefore not entirely repeatable by other investigators." Jensen should, of course, have said, "The

subjective element in this thus unrepeatable procedure means it *must* be whole-heartedly condemned in scientific research on the genetics of mental abilities."

42. See, e.g., even the somewhat "unfriendly" review by D. M. Jackson, *Science*, 189:1078–1080, 1975; and a curious review of a paper by Kamin containing the essence of his book, published as Appendix H in J. C. Loehlin, G. Lindzey, and J. H. Spuhler, *Race Differences in Intelligence* (San Francisco: W. H. Freeman), 1975, in which the authors seem incapable of accepting the conclusion any scientist must draw about Burt's work once Kamin's statements about it are confirmed.

43. A. Jensen, "The Differences Are Real." *Psychology Today*, December 1973, p. 81. This confusion also pervades the recent book by Loehlin, Lindzey, and Spuhler, *Race Differences in Intelligence*.

6. Group Differences in Intelligence

1. L. J. Kamin, *The Science and Politics of IQ* (New York: Wiley), 1974.

2. R. K. Davenport, "Implication of Military Selection and Classification in Relation to Universal Military Training." *Journal of Negro Education*, 15:585–594, 1969; B. D. Darpinos, "The Mental Test Qualification of American Youths for Military Service and Its Relationship to Educational Attainment." *Proceedings of the 126th Annual Meeting of American Statistical Association*, 1966.

3. W. A. Kennedy, "A Follow Up Normative Study of Negro Intelligence and Achievement." *Monographs of the Society for Research in Child Development*, 34(126), 1969; W. A. Kennedy, V. Van de Riet, and J. C. White, "A Normative Sample of Intelligence and Achievement of Negro Elementary School Children in Southeastern United States." *Monographs of the Society for Research in Child Development*, 28(90), 1963; A. Shuey, *The Testing of Negro Intelligence*, 2nd ed. (New York: Social Science Press), 1966.

4. P. L. Nichols and V. E. Anderson, "Intellectual Performance, Race, and Socioeconomic Status." *Social Biology*, 20:367–374, 1973.

5. Kennedy, Van de Riet, and White, "Normative Sample of Intelligence."

6. The estimates from recent studies is not exact. Seven studies reported in Loehlin, Lindzey and Spuhler were averaged. However, each study defined lower class and middle class somewhat differently, although, of course, comparably for each group. The findings from the studies have been averaged despite different ages of the children, different tests used, and different sample sizes.

7. J. C. Loehlin, G. Lindzey, and J. N. Spuhler, *Race Difference in Intelligence* (San Francisco: W. H. Freeman), 1975.

8. For example, in data from Project Talent, where six mental abilities in twelfth-grade Blacks, Jews, Oriental Americans and non-Jewish Whites were studied, the most marked differences in the profile of scores were not due to ethnic group membership or social class, but to sex, which accounted for fully 69 percent of the total variability. See M. E. Backman, "Patterns of Mental Abilities: Ethnic, Socioeconomic and Sex Differences." *American Educational Research Journal*, 9:1–12, 1972.

9. E. E. Maccoby and C. N. Jacklin, *The Psychology of Sex Differences* (Stanford, Calif.: Stanford University Press), 1974.

10. In less-developed countries, IQ-class correlations disappear entirely, according to the work of S. Heynemann of George Washington University.

11. E. M. Johnson, "Applications of the Standard Score IQ to Social Statistics." *Journal of Social Psychology*, 27:217–227, 1948.

12. A. Anastasi, *Differential Psychology*, 3rd ed. (New York: Macmillan), 1958; L. Tyler, *The Psychology of Human Differences*, 3rd ed. (New York: Appleton-Century-Crofts), 1965.

13. G. Lesser, G. Fifer, and D. H. Clark, "Mental Abilities of Children from Different Social-Class and Cultural Groups." *Monograph of the Society of Research in Child Development*, 30, 1965.

14. O. D. Duncan, "Ability and Achievement." *Eugenics Quarterly*, 15:1–11, 1968; G. W. Mayeske et al., *A Study of Our Nation's Schools*. Department of Health, Education and Welfare No. (OE) 72-162. (Washington, D.C.: U.S. Government Printing Office), 1972; P. L. Nichols, *The Effects of Heredity and Environment on Intelligence Test Performance in 4 and 7 year old White and Negro sibling pairs*. Ann Arbor, Mich., University Microfilms, No. 71-18, 874, 1970.

15. Anastasi, *Differential Psychology*.

16. M. Young and J. B. Gibson, "Social Mobility and Fertility," in J. E. Meade and A. S. Parkes (eds.), *Biological Aspects of Social Problems* (Edinburgh: Oliver and Boyd), 1965.

17. J. H. Waller, "Achievement and Social Mobility: Relationships Among IQ Score, Education, and Occupation in Two Generations." *Social Biology*, 18:252–259, 1971.

18. Anastasi, *Differential Psychology*.

19. O. Klineberg, "The Intelligence of Migrants." *American Sociological Review*, 3:218–224, 1938; Anastasi, *Differential Psychology*.

20. R. C. Lewontin, "The Apportionment of Human Diversity." *Evolutionary Biology*, 4:381–398, 1967.

21. A. M. Shuey, *The Testing of Negro Intelligence*, 2nd ed. (New York: Social Science Press), 1966. It must be noted that since Blacks with lighter skins may be treated differently from those with darker skins, even a substantial difference in IQ scores would not be valid evidence for the genetic hypothesis.

22. M. A. Tanser, cited in Loehlin, Lindzey and Spuhler, *Race Differences in Intelligence*, p. 121.

23. J. C. Loehlin, S. G. Vandenberg, and R. T. Osborne, "Blood Group Genes and Negro-White Ability Differences." *Behavior Genetics*, 3:263–270, 1973.

24. P. A. Witty and M. D. Jenkins, cited in Anastasi, *Differential Psychology*, p. 580.

25. W. B. Shockley, Letter to *Proceedings of the National Academy of Sciences*, 1968 (1390A), 1971. A problem of considerable technical difficulty is the estimation of the degree of "Caucasian ancestry," even when an arbitrary blood-group definition of "Caucasian" is accepted. T. E. Reed, "Caucasian Genes in American Negroes." *Science*, 165:762–768, 1969; and J. Adams and R. H. Ward, "Admixture Studies and the Detection of Selection," *Science*, 180:1137–1143, 1973, have stressed this point. In the face of this, Shockley persists in believing that he can estimate the proportion accurately enough to validate his claim.

26. L. Willerman, A. F. Naylor, and N. C. Myrianthopoulos, "Intellectual Development of Children from Interracial Marriages." *Science*, 170:1329–1331, 1970.

27. K. Eyferth, "Leistungen verschiedener Gruppen von Besatzungskinder in Hamburg-Wechsler Intelligenztest fur Kinder (HAWIK)," *Archiv fur die Gesamte Psychologie*, 113:222–241, 1961.

28. B. Tizard, "IQ and Race." *Nature*, 247:277, 1974.

29. B. Tizard and J. A. Rees, "A Comparison of the Effects of Adoption Restoration to Natural Mothers and Continued Institutionalization on the Cognitive Development of Four-Year-Old Children." *Child Development*, 45:92–99, 1974.

30. M. Smilansky, cited in S. Scarr-Salapatek, "Genetics and the Development of Intelligence," in F. O. Horowitz, *Review of Child Development Research*, Vol. 4 (Chicago: University of Chicago Press), 1974.

31. U. Bronfenbrenner, *A Report on Longitudinal Evaluations of Preschool Programs*. Vol. II: *Is Early Intervention Effective?* Department of Health, Education and Welfare Publication No. (OHD) 74–25 (Washington, D.C.: U.S. Government Printing Office), 1974.

32. H. B. Robinson and N. M. Robinson, "Longitudinal Development of Very

Young Children in Comprehensive Daycare Program: The First Two Years." *Child Development*, 42:1673–1683, 1971.

33. S. Scarr-Salapatek and R. A. Weinberg, "IQ Test Performance of Black Children Adopted by White Families." Paper presented at Society for Research in Child Development, Denver, Col., 1975; S. Scarr-Salapatek and R. A. Weinberg, "Intellectual Similarities Within Families of Both Adopted and Biological Children." *Intelligence*, in press.

34. B. S. Burks, "The Relative Influence of Nature and Nurture upon Mental Development. A Comparative Study of Foster Parent–Foster Child Resemblance and True Parent–True Child Resemblance." *27th Yearbook of the National Society for the Study of Education*, 1928, Pt. 1, 219–316; J. M. Horn, J. C. Loehlin, and L. Willerman, "The Texas Adoption Project," in L. Carter-Sattzman, *Adoption Studies: Similarities of Children to Adoptive and Natural Parents.* Symposium at meeting of Behavior Genetics Association, Texas, 1975; A. M. Leahy, "A Study of Certain Selective Factors Influencing Prediction of the Mental Status of Adopted Children." *Journal of Genetic Psychology*, 41:294–329, 1932.

35. H. J. Eysenck, *The IQ Argument* (New York: Library Press), 1971.

36. W. Shockley, quoted in N. Daniels, "The Smart White Man's Burden." *Harpers*, 247:25, 1973.

37. See, e.g., R. C. Lewontin, "Genetic Aspects of Intelligence." *Annual Review of Genetics*, 9:387–405, 1975.

38. This example is based on M. W. Feldman and R. C. Lewontin, "The Heritability Hang-Up." *Science*, 190:1166, 1975.

39. Eysenck, *IQ Argument*, pp. 39–40.

40. Lewontin, "Apportionment of Human Diversity," p. 399. Note that selection reduces only heritability in the narrow sense (the additive component of the variance) and that other evolutionary forces, population structure, and environmental changes affect heritabilities. Furthermore, observed differences between two populations that have been under selection for a trait are not necessarily genetic differences. Therefore the material in this paragraph does not contradict the statement above that knowing the degree of heritability in two populations gives no information on the cause of interpopulation differences.

41. This paragraph is based on P. R. Ehrlich's experience with the Aivilikmiut in 1952.

42. R. Benedict, *Race: Science and Politics* (New York: Compass Books), 1943.

43. See, e.g., B. L. Whorf, *Language, Thought and Reality* (New York: Wiley), 1956.

44. M. H. Segal, D. T. Campbell, and M. J. Herskovits, *The Influence of Culture on Visual Perception* (New York: Bobbs-Merrill), 1966.

45. The Black ghetto dialect exhibits some of the following characteristics:
    1. Lack of agreement of subject and verbs in third person singular; e.g., He *say* he finished; One dog *have* a bone.
    2. Lack of agreement of subject and verbs in using the verb *to be*; e.g., I *is* going out.
    3. Omission of the verb *to be*; e.g., You crazy, that my dog.
    4. Nonstandard use of verb form, e.g., He *don't* like it; She *bes* my friend; *Do* he know it?
    5. Nonstandard use of pronouns; e.g., *Her* went shopping.
    6. Nonstandard use of noun forms; e.g., I see two *mans*.
    7. Double negatives; e.g., We *don't* have *no* time.

W. D. Loban, *Problems in Oral English* (Champaign, Ill.: National Council of Teachers), 1966.

46. W. A. Stewart, *Time*, May 9, 1969.

47. L. C. Quay, "Language Dialect, Re-inforcement and the Intelligence-Test Performance of Negro Children." *Child Development*, 42:5–15, 1971.

48. M. E. Shimberg, "An Investigation into the Validity of Norms with Special Reference to Urban and Rural Groups." *Archives of Psychology*, 1929, no. 104.

49. P. H. Dubois, "A Test Standardized on Pueblo Indian Children." *Psychological Bulletin*, 36:523, 1939.

50. A. Dove, *The Chitling Test of Intelligence*. Mimeo.

51. M. E. Herzig, H. G. Birch, A. Thomas, and O. A. Mendez, "Class and Ethnic Differences in the Responsiveness of Preschool Children to Cognitive Demand." *Monographs of the Society for Research in Child Development*, 33, 1968.

52. Benedict, *Race: Science and Politics*, p. 73.

53. A. R. Jensen, "The Effect of Race of Examiner on the Mental Test Scores of White and Black Pupils." *Journal of Educational Measurement*, 2:1–4, 1974.

54. N. Solkoff, "Race of Experimenter as a Variable in Research with Children." *Developmental Psychology*, 7:70–75, 1972.

55. Over the years, a variety of supposedly culture-fair tests have been devised. Raven's Progressive Matrices consists of a series of abstract geometrical designs in which a part of each has been removed. The child (or adult) is required to choose the missing part from a set of alternatives. The easier items require mainly accuracy of visual perceptions, the more difficult ones involve analogies and other logical relationships. However, this test was not successful in eliminating class differences or ethnic group differences. Blacks typically score nearly one standard deviation below Whites, and a smaller but still significant difference is found between lower-class and middle-class scores. We were unable to locate any studies comparing the predictive validity of Blacks' and Whites' scores on this test, even though it is one of the most popular of the so-called culture-fair tests of intelligence.

Another, the Goodenough Draw-A-Man Test (now called the Goodenough-Harris Drawing Test) requires children 3 to 15 years old to draw the best man and the best woman they can. Scoring takes into account the basic structure of the drawing (e.g., whether the limbs are attached to the trunk as the test designers think they should be) and details of features, clothing, etc. The test is not free of cultural influence, although social class differences are smaller in this test than in most others. Comparative studies of children's drawings in different cultures both within the United States and between countries suggest that both the subject matter and technique of the drawing reflect cultural factors. (See Anastasi, *Differential Psychology*.)

Other culture-fair tests, including the Davis-Eells Games, the Cattell Culture Fair Intelligence Test, and the Leiter International Performance Scale, have been developed. They all share the same kinds of problems just described.

56. J. C. Stanley, "Predicting College Success of the Educationally Disadvantaged." *Science*, 171, February 1971; A. T. Cleary, "Test Bias—Prediction of Grades in Negro and White Students in Integrated Colleges." *Journal of Educational Measurement*, 5, 1968.

57. Loehlin, Lindzey, and Spuhler, *Race Difference in Intelligence*.

58. M. Winick, K. K. Meyer, and R. C. Harris, "Malnutrition and Environmental Enrichment by Early Adoption." *Science*, 190:1173–1175, 1975.

59. Z. Stein, M. Susser, G. Saenger, and F. Marolla, "Nutrition and Mental Performance." *Science*, 178:708–713, 1972.

60. R. F. Harrell, E. R. Woodyard, E. R. Gates, and I. A. Gates, "The Influence of Vitamin Supplementation in the Diets of Pregnant and Lactating Women on the Intelligence of their Offspring." *Metabolism*, 5:555–562, 1956.

61. A. L. Kabala and M. M. Katz, "Nutritional Factors in Psychological Test Behaviors." *Journal of Genetic Psychology*, 96:343–352, 1960.

62. J. Mayer, "Food Habits and Nutrition Status of American Negroes." *Postgraduate Medicine*, 37A:110–115, 1965.

63. *Ten State Nutrition Survey* 1968–70. U.S. Department of Health, Education and Welfare, 1972, Vols. I–V, DHEW Publication No. HSM, 72-8130-34 (Washington, D.C.: U.S. Government Printing Office), 1972. This large-scale survey was carried out in California, Washington, Michigan, Massachusetts, New York, Kentucky, West Virginia, South Carolina, Louisiana, and Texas, and yielded a representative sample of low-income families, and some nonrepresentative samples of middle-income families. The TSNS studied only a dozen or so of the forty-four

nutrients judged essential for good health. They interviewed more than 24,000 people and clinically evaluated more than 10,000 of them. Detailed biochemical evaluations were made of special groups, such as infants, young children, adolescents, pregnant and lactating women, and elderly people.

64. A. Clarke-Stewart, "Interactions Between Mothers and Their Young Children: Characteristics and Consequences." *Monographs of the Society for Research in Child Development*, 38:153, 1973; M. Engel and W. M. Keane, "Black Mothers and Their Infant Sons. Antecedents, Correlates and Predictors of Cognitive Development in the Second and Sixth Year of Life." Paper given at Society for Research in Child Development, Denver, Col., 1975.

65. Clarke-Stewart, "Interactions Between Mothers and Their Young Children."

66. K. Nelson, "Structure and Strategy in Learning to Talk." *Monographs of the Society for Research in Child Development*, 38(Whole No. 149), 1973.

67. J. Rubenstein and F. Pederson, "A Comparison of Maternal and Surrogate Caretaking Behavior in Five-Month-Old Infants." Paper given at Society for Research in Child Development, Philadelphia, 1973.

68. B. Tizard, O. Cooperman, A. Joseph, and J. Tizard, "Environmental Effects on Language Development: A Study of Young Children in Long-Stay Residential Nurseries." *Child Development*, 43:337–355, 1972.

69. Engel and Keane, "Black Mothers and Their Infant Sons."

70. B. Bernstein, "Social Class and Linguistic Development: A Theory of Social Learning," in A. H. Halsey, J. Floud, and C. A. Anderson (eds.), *Education, Economics and Society* (New York: Free Press), 1961.

71. R. Hess and V. Shipman, "Cognitive Elements in Maternal Behavior," in J. P. Hill (ed.), *Minnesota Symposium on Child Psychology* (Minneapolis: University of Minnesota Press), 1967, pp. 57–81.

72. D. Tulkin and J. Kagan, "Mother Child Interaction in the First Year of Life." *Child Development*, 43:31–41, 1972.

73. B. Bernstein and D. Young, "Some Aspects of Relationships Between Communication and Performance in Tests," in J. E. Meade and A. S. Parkes (eds.), *Genetic and Environmental Factors in Human Ability* (Edinburgh: Oliver and Boyd), 1966.

74. J. Brophy, "Mothers as Teachers of Their Own Preschool Children: The Influence of SES and Task Structure." *Child Development*, 41:79–94, 1970; K. L. Bee et al., "Social Class Differences in Maternal Teaching Strategies and Speech Patterns." *Developmental Psychology*, 1:729–734, 1969.

75. See note 44.

76. W. Labov, P. Cohen, C. Robins, and J. Lewis, *A Study of the Non-Standard English of Negro and Puerto Rican Speakers in New York City*. Final Report, U.S. Office of Education, Co-operative Research Project No. 3255 (New York: Columbia University), 1965.

77. L. Belmont and F. A. Marolla, "Birth Order, Family Size, and Intelligence." *Science*, 182:1096–1101, 1973.

78. *Ibid.*

79. V. J. Crandall, "Achievement," in H. Stevenson (ed.), *Child Psychology NSSE Yearbook* (Chicago: University of Chicago Press), 1963; N. Freeberg and D. Payne, "Parental Influence on Cognitive Development During Childhood. A Review." *Child Development*, 35:65–87, 1967; N. Kent and D. Davis, "Discipline in the Home, and Intellectual Development." *British Journal of Medical Psychology*, 30:27–34, 1957.

80. B. White and J. C. Watts, *Experience and Environment* (Englewood Cliffs, N.J.: Prentice Hall), 1973.

81. M. Honzik, "Environmental Correlates of Mental Growth. Prediction from the Family Setting at Age 21 Months." *Child Development*, 38:337–364, 1967; J. Kagan and M. Freeman, "Relation of Childhood Intelligence, Maternal Behaviors and Social Class to Behaviors During Adolescence." *Child Development*, 34:899–911, 1963.

82. N. Bayley and E. S. Schaefer, "Correlations of Maternal and Child Behaviors with the Development of Mental Abilities: Data from Berkeley Growth Study." *Monographs of the Society for Research in Child Development* 29, 1964.

83. D. Lynn, *The Father: His Role in Child Development* (Monterey, Calif.: Brooks/Cole), 1974.

84. R. D. Hess, "Social Class and Ethnic Influences upon Socialization," in P. Mussen (ed.), *Carmichael's Manual of Child Psychology*, Vol. 2 (New York: Wiley), 1970.

85. J. Madden, P. Levenstein, and S. Levenstein, "Longitudinal IQ Outcomes of Mother-Child Home Programs." *Child Development*, pp. 1015–1025, 1976.

86. The literature at this point is vast. The interested reader can refer to L. Yarrow, J. Rubinstein, F. Pederson, *Infant and Environment: Early Cognitive and Motivational Development* (New York: Wiley), 1975; Clarke-Stewart, "Interactions Between Mothers and Their Young Children"; R. R. Collard, "Exploratory and Play Behaviors of Infants Reared in an Institution and in Lower and Middle Class Homes." *Child Development*, 42:1003–1016, 1971; J. Rubenstein, "Maternal Attentiveness and Subsequent Exploratory Behavior in the Infant." *Child Development*, 38:1089–1100, 1967; L. Yarrow, "Research Dimensions of Early Maternal Care." *Merrill-Palmer Quarterly*, 9:101–114, 1963; White and Watts, *Experience and Environment*; R. Elardo, R. Bradley, and B. Caldwell, "The Relations of Infants' Home Environments to Mental Test Performance from 6–36 Months: A Longitudinal Analysis." *Child Development*, 46:71–76, 1975.

87. G. A. Bogatz and S. Ball, *A Summary of the Major Findings in "The Second Year of Sesame Street: A Continuing Evaluation"* (Princeton, N.J.: Educational Testing Service), 1971.

88. E. Werner, "Sex Differences in Correlations Between Children's IQs and Measures of Parental Ability and Environmental Ratings." *Developmental Psychology*, 1:280–285, 1969.

89. J. Swift, "Effects of Early Group Experiences: The Nursery School and Day Nursery," in M. L. Hoffman and L. W. Hoffman (eds.), *Review of Child Development Research*, Vol. 1 (New York: Russell Sage Foundation), 1964.

90. S. H. White, "The National-Impact Study of Head Start," in J. Hellmuth (ed.), *Disadvantaged Child*, Vol. 3 (New York: Brunner/Mazel), 1970, p. 168.

91. Westinghouse Learning Corporation/Ohio University, *The Impact of Head Start: An Evaluation of the Effects of Head Start on Children's Cognitive and Affective Development*, Vols. I and II, 1969.

92. A. Jensen, "How Much Can We Boost IQ and Scholastic Achievement?" *Harvard Educational Review*, 39:2, 1964.

93. Bronfenbrenner, *Report on Longitudinal Evaluations of Preschool Programs*.

94. S. White, *Federal Programs for Young Children: Review and Recommendations*, Vol. II. *Review of Evaluation Data for Federally Sponsored Projects for Children*. Department of Health, Education and Welfare Pub. No. 74-102, 1973.

95. *Ibid.* See also Chapter 4 of this book for a discussion of P. Levenstein's successful home-intervention program.

96. R. Heber, H. Garber, S. Harrington, and C. Hoffman, *Rehabilitation of Families at Risk for Mental Retardation* (Madison, Wis.: Research and Training Center in Mental Retardation, University of Wisconsin), 1972.

97. A. D. De Groot, "The Effects of War upon the Intelligence of Youth." *Journal of Abnormal and Social Psychology*, 43:311–317, 1948.

98. Cited in C. Jencks, *Inequality: A Reassessment of the Effect of Family and Schooling in America* (New York: Basic Books), 1972.

99. D. F. Hayes and J. Grether, *The School Year and Vacations: When Do the Students Learn?* (Washington, D.C.: The Urban Institute), 1969.

100. Jencks, *op cit.*

101. M. L. Harris, *Student Effort in High School as a Product of the Perceived Links Between Work and School*. Unpublished doctoral dissertation, Stanford University, Stanford, Calif., 1976.

102. J. Stallings, "Implementation and Child Effects of Teaching Practices in

Follow Through Classrooms." *Monographs of the Society for Research in Child Development*, 40(Whole No. 163), 1975.

103. *Ibid.*

104. J. Coleman et al., *Equality of Educational Opportunity* (Washington, D. C.: U.S. Government Printing Office), 1966, p. 22.

105. K. Bradway and C. W. Thompson, "Intelligence at Adulthood. A Twenty-Five Year Follow Up." *Journal of Educational Psychology*, 53:1–14, 1962.

106. I. Lorge, "Schooling Makes a Difference." *Teachers College Record*, 46:483–492, 1945.

107. Jencks, *op. cit.*

108. *Ibid.*

109. Coleman, et al., *Equality of Educational Opportunity.*

110. H. Munsinger, "The Adopted Child's IQ: A Critical Review." *Psychological Bulletin*, 82:623–659, 1975. This article gives a committed hereditarian's view of the problems for environmentalists in adoption studies. Kamin, *Science and Politics of IQ*, gives the view of a committed environmentalist in showing that adoptive studies give no support for the hereditarian position.

111. See Chapter 5 for evidence as to why expected IQ of child could not be calculated from the biological mother's IQ. Kamin, *Science and Politics of IQ*, documents that there is no evidence that supports a genetic hypothesis.

112. M. Winick, K. K. Meyer, and R. C. Harris, "Malnutrition and Environmental Enrichment."

113. R. Heber, H. Garber, S. Harrington, and C. Hoffman, *Rehabilitation of Families at Risk for Mental Retardation.*

114. Scarr-Salapatek, "Genetics and the Development of Intelligence."

7. Why Does It Matter?

1. R. Herrnstein, "IQ in the Meritocracy." *Atlantic Monthly*, September, 1971, pp. 58–59.

2. A. Jensen, "How Much Can We Boost IQ and Scholastic Achievement?" *Harvard Educational Review*, 39:2, 1969.

3. *Ibid.*, p. 3.

4. *Ibid.*, p. 117.

5. N. Daniels, "The Smart White Man's Burden." *Harpers*, 247:25, October 1973.

6. Jensen, "How Much Can We Boost IQ," p. 7, emphasis ours.

7. R. Lewontin, "Race and Intelligence." *Bulletin of the Atomic Scientists*, March 1970, pp. 2–3.

8. Herrnstein, "IQ in the Meritocracy," p. 59.

9. Jensen, "How Much Can We Boost IQ," p. 117.

10. Herrnstein, "IQ in the Meritocracy," p. 7.

11. J. B. Watson, *Behaviorism*, rev. ed. (Chicago: University of Chicago Press), 1930, p. 104.

12. Material on the young man from *San Francisco Chronicle*, December 24, 1974.

13. *Ibid.*

14. O. G. Brim, Jr., J. Neulinger, and D. C. Glass, *Experiences and Attitudes of American Adults Concerning Standardized Intelligence Tests*. Technical Report No. 1 on the Social Consequences of Testing (New York: Russell Sage Foundation), 1965.

15. *Ibid.*

16. J. Cronbach, *Essentials of Psychological Testing*, 3rd ed. (New York: Harper & Row), 1970.

17. *Ibid.*, p. 299.

18. C. Bird, *The Case Against College* (New York: Bantam), 1975.

19. W. Shockley, "Dysgenics, Geneticity, Raceology: A Challenge to the Intellectual Responsibility of Educators." *Phi Delta Kappan*, January 1972, p. 297.

20. W. Shockley, "Case for the Plaintiff." *New Scientist*, 22 February 1973, p. 435.

21. *Ibid.*

22. C. J. Bajema, "Estimation of the Direction and Intensity of Natural Selection in Relation to Human Intelligence by Means of the Intrinsic Rate of Natural Increase." *Eugenics Quarterly*, 10:175–187, 1963; R. C. Lewontin, "Further Remarks on Race and the Genetics of Intelligence." *Bulletin of the Atomic Scientists*, May 1970, p. 24.

23. *Time*, July 23, 1973.

24. *New York Times*, August 1, 1973.

25. H. A. Katchadourian and D. T. Lunde, *Fundamentals of Human Sexuality*, 2nd ed. (New York: Holt, Rinehart and Winston), 1975, p. 505, emphasis ours. This superb book is a goldmine of information—the quote is from Chapter 16, "Sex and the Law."

26. *Ibid.*, p. 505.

27. S. S. Beserra, N. M. Jewel, and M. W. Matthews, *Sex Code of California* (Los Altos, Calif.: Wm. Kaufmann), 1973.

28. *Buck* v. *Bell*, 274 U.S. 200 (1927).

29. A. Shuey, *The Testing of Negro Intelligence*, 2nd ed. (New York: Social Science Press), 1966.

30. This problem of nonsense correlation and "type I error" is well known to students of elementary statistics—see e.g., R. R. Sokal and F. J. Rohlf, *Biometry* (San Francisco: Freeman and Co.), 1969, pp. 523–526.

31. *Newsweek*, May 10, 1971.

32. See, e.g., M. W. Feldman and R. C. Lewontin, "The Heritability Hang-Up." *Science*, 190:1166, December 1975.

33. Herrnstein, "IQ in the Meritocracy."

34. P. R. Ehrlich and L. G. Mason, "The Population Biology of the Butterfly *Euphydryas editha*, III. Selection and the Phenetics of the Jasper Ridge Colony." *Evolution*, 20:165–173, 1966.

35. P. R. Ehrlich, R. R. White, S. W. McKechnie, and L. G. Gilbert, "Checkerspot Butterflies: A Historical Perspective." *Science*, 188:221–228, April 1975; S. W. McKechnie, P. R. Ehrlich, and R. R. White, "Population Genetics of *Euphydryas* butterflies. I. Genetic Variation and the Neutrality Hypothesis." *Genetics*, 81:571–594, 1975.

36. S. Bowles and H. Gintis, "IQ in the United States Class Structure." *Social Policy*, 3(4 and 5), November–December 1972 and January–February 1973. Reprinted in Alan Gartner, Colin Green, and Frank Riessman (eds.), *The New Assault on Equality* (New York: Harper & Row), 1974, pp. 7–84. Subsequent page number references are to this reprint. The bibliography contains entry to the literature on the sociology of "success." See also Jencks, *Inequality: A Reassessment of the Effect of Family and Schooling in America* (New York: Basic Books), 1972.

37. Bowles and Gintis, "IQ in the United States Class Structure," p. 37.

38. Quoted in Daniels, "The Smart White Man's Burden." *Harpers*, 247:24 October 1973.

39. Stockholm International Peace Research Institute (SIPRI), "Why Arms Control Fails." *Atlas World Press Review*, February 1976, pp. 11–13.

FURTHER READING

Anastasi, A., 1976. *Psychological Testing*, 4th ed. New York: Macmillan. A scholarly account of the state of testing by one who is committed to the testing enterprise.

Butcher, J., 1968. *Human Intelligence: Its Nature and Assessment*. New York: Harper Torchbooks. A competent account by a British scholar with something of a hereditarian bias.

Davis, David B., 1966. *The Problem of Slavery in Western Culture*. Ithaca, N.Y.: Cornell University Press. A Pulitzer Prize winning examination of the problem.

Degler, Carl N., 1971. *Neither Black Nor White: Slavery and Race Relations in Brazil and the United States*. New York: Macmillan. A classic comparative history which deals extensively with the social definition of race. Won the Pulitzer Prize for History in 1972.

Gartner, Alan, Colin Greer and Frank Riesman, eds., 1974. *The New Assault on Equality: I.Q. and Social Stratification*. New York: Harper and Row. See especially the article by Bowles and Gintis "I.Q. in the United States Class Structure."

Gravbard, Stephen R., ed., 1967. *Color and Race*. Cambridge, Mass.: *Daedalus*, vol. 96, no. 2, Spring. A fascinating compendium dealing with the sociology of race in various nations.

Harvard Educational Review, 1969. *Environment, Heredity and Intelligence*. Reprint Series no. 2. Cambridge, Mass.: Harvard University Press. This volume reprints Jensen's controversial "How much can we boost I.Q. and scholastic achievement and various reactions to it."

Kamin, L., 1974. *The Science and Politics of I.Q.* New York: Halstead Press. A detailed dissection of the literature on the inheritance of I.Q., with much startling historical material.

Loehlin, J. C., Lindzey, G., & Spuhler, J. N., 1975. *Race Differences in Intelligence*. San Francisco: Freeman. A careful, up-to-date account that leans toward a hereditarian viewpoint.

Montagu, Ashley, ed. *The Concept of Race*. New York: Free Press. Several articles on non-racial approaches to human variation and critiques of Coon's *The Origin of Races*.

Tyler, L., 1965. *The Psychology of Human Differences*. New York: Appleton Century Crofts. A fundamental text.

INDEX